695

HERBAL DELIGHTS

HERBAL DELIGHTS

*Botanical information and recipes for
cosmetics, remedies and medicines,
condiments and spices, and sweet and
savory treats for the table*

by MRS. C.F. LEYEL

With drawings by
M.E. RIVERS-MOORE

GRAMERCY PUBLISHING COMPANY
New York

This 1986 edition is published by Gramercy Publishing Company,
distributed by Crown Publishers, Inc., 225 Park Avenue South,
New York, New York 10003.

Publisher's Note: This work, containing suggested herbal
recipes and folk remedies, was originally published in 1938.
Some of these remedies and recipes are now considered by
modern medicine inadequate or potentially harmful, and are
not intended as a substitute to professional medical advice.

Printed and Bound in the United States of America

LIBRARY OF CONGRESS CATALOGING IN PUBLICATION DATA

Leyel, C. F., Mrs., 1890-1957.
    Herbal delights.

    Reprint. Originally published: Boston: Houghton
Mifflin, 1938.
    Includes indexes.
    1. Cookery (Herbs)   2. Herbs.   3. Canning and
preserving.   I. Title.
TX819.H4L49   1986   641.6'57   86-18945
ISBN 0-517-62515-6
h g f e d c b a

NOTE

The herbs that are traditionally used medicinally fall more or less into two groups; those that are pleasant to the taste and are used either for culinary purposes or for brewing, distilling, flavouring or for making tisanes, and those that are used for their more definitely medicinal properties.

I have included only those herbs that belong to the first class. I shall not include any of the poisonous herbs, as that knowledge is too dangerous to be disseminated in a book intended for the general public.

H. L.

CONTENTS

8

9

FOREWORD

Herbs. Medicinal and mystical, savory and bitter, dried and fresh, herbs have been a mainstay of man from his earliest existence on earth. Strictly defined, the term "herbs" refers to plants that die down after flowering and do not have persistent aboveground woody parts. In an even more restricted sense, "herbs" is applied to plants used for their aromatic, savory, or medicinal properties. In this sense the term covers pot herbs, culinary herbs, condiment herbs, and medicinal herbs.

It was with this latter definition that Mrs. C.F. Leyel was most concerned in 1938 when she produced *Herbal Delights,* concentrating on herbs used for their soothing rather than medicinal properties. Thus, she provides us with recipes for tisanes — herbs used to relieve a condition not serious enough to require a doctor; cordials — herbs used in drinks for their calming and fragrant qualities; cooling herbs — literally said to "cool the blood"; refreshments to relieve thirst, whether induced by fever or by a hot day; pot herbs, whose name comes from their use in the pot that was hung over the fire and filled with the day's meal; spices and condiments — considered the most precious of all herbs; natural perfumes such as roses, used for deliciously scented potpourris; and cosmetic herbs — the purest and safest, even to this day.

Where did herbs come from, and how was man able to discover their myriad uses? In the earliest days of civilization the rituals of harvesting crops and herbs were tied to the changing forces of the sun, the moon, and the seasons. These rituals became part of the myths and legends that were handed down through the generations. Herbal medicine played an integral part in these legends, as it developed from simply eating herbs as part of the diet to elaborate ceremonies directed by the spiritual leader or leaders of the group.

During these early times, two ideas for herbal treatment developed that were later expanded and called the "doctrine of similars" and the "doctrine of contraries." The first considered the appearance or character of a plant a clue to its use as a medicinal treatment. For example, plants from which a red juice could be extracted were thought to be of great value in treating wounds. The doctrine of contraries maintained that herbs whose properties were opposite to the symptoms of the illness were best used in treating that illness.

The first known herbal, or book of herbs, is said to have been written by the Chinese emperor Shen Nung, approximately 5,000 years ago. There is a Sumerian herbal written about 2200 B.C., and an Egyptian one from around 2800 B.C. Spices identified in herbals were traded to the Egyptians from southern Arabia and the East from about 2000 B.C. Brought into ports on the Mediterranean, the spices were shipped overland to Egypt. The Phoenicians in the port cities also traded for a share, then sailed with them to Spain, and continued north up the Atlantic coast. The Phoenicians were also responsible for introducing the spice trade to the great civilizations of ancient Greece and Rome.

In the Dark Ages, after the fall of the Roman empire, the herb trade continued in southern Europe, but the northern European routes were plagued by pirates and robbers and disrupted by war. In Britain, the only organized communities at this point were monasteries. The monks recorded the herbal remedies, incorporating them into their chants and incantations. Trade once again picked up in the late eighth century as the Muslim empire rose to rule in the Middle East and Mediterranean.

During the Crusades, Salerno, Italy, home of a famous medical school, became a stopping off point for the wounded Crusaders. Those who were treated there carried home to Britain and elsewhere tales of cleaner living, healthier habits, and tastier cooking. Soon the foods of the Norman countries were enhanced by the flavors, colors, and textures supplied by herbs and spices. As time passed the spice routes from the East were disrupted by war, and Christopher Columbus searched unsuccessfully for a new sea route to the Spice Islands. In 1498, however, the Portuguese explorer Vasco da Gama sailed around the Cape of Good Hope to Calcutta harbor and Portuguese domination of the spice trade began and continued for the next hundred years.

During the early years of the Renaissance, the science of medicine was developing in the northern countries, influenced by the Arab physicians and the Salerno medical school. A belief grew that pestilence — prior to this, thought to be divine punishment which affected priests and laymen alike — might be due to "fowle contageous ayre," so fumigants of spices and herbs were burned in private homes and public meeting places. At this time even greater attention was being paid to diet, hygiene, and living conditions, and, with the advent of the printing press, herbals were published and distributed, reaching a large portion of the public.

Herb women, root gatherers, and apothecaries began to appear in the cities and towns. Herb gardens also became popular at this time, with new species being added as sailors and seafarers returned from the Americas and other ports. Herbs were also arriving in the American colonies, as the early settlers came from England. Many of the colonists carried with them the most popular herbals of the day, including Nicholas Culpeper's *The English Physitian,* published in 1652. In *Herbal Delights,* Mrs. Leyel frequently refers her readers to Culpeper's work, which, despite its questionable astrological observations, remains worthwhile.

During the seventeenth century there were changes in European eating habits. Herbs and spices were more readily and less expensively available, and the common pot was replaced by single dishes of lightly seasoned meats, fruits, and vegetables. Late in the century, herbalism and botany began to take separate paths, and the next two centuries saw the development of chemistry and biology and the beginnings of modern pharmacology.

Today, with a combination of modern medical advances and a renewed interest in how our ancestors lived, we enjoy the best of both worlds. As Mrs. Leyel states in her introduction, "Herbs are the oldest form of medicine and have, therefore, been tested longer than anything else." What more encouragement do we need?

D.J. DeChristopher

New York
1986

INTRODUCTION

Vegetation is the primary source of food for every form of life.

If the earth were not covered with its green growth it would be uninhabitable because the violence of the elements would reduce its surface to powder. Without the shade of trees, shrubs and herbs, the earth would be a desert. The moisture absorbed by plant life is given out again and keeps the surface of the earth from getting parched.

Plants bind the soil together and prevent tempests and floods from washing it away, as grasses bind the sand dunes on the seashore.

All living things from the highest to the lowest can be entirely maintained by this vegetation which appeared on the earth just before the creation of man. Vegetable life before that was strange and flowerless.

The vegetable world is man's natural food and man's natural medicine. It is the link between the animal and mineral kingdoms, as it absorbs mineral products and makes them easy for man to assimilate.

Even more important is the peculiar property of green plants to absorb carbon dioxide from the air by means of their green colouring matter, chlorophyll; in the light of the sun they not only breathe in carbon dioxide and give out oxygen, which is the precise opposite to the process of respiration by animals, but they combine carbon with oxygen and hydrogen and build them into carbohydrates, *i.e.* the various forms of sugars and starches that make food.

In fact it is the production of organic material from the air by green plants that makes animal life in this world possible, for animals possess no such powers.

All the tissue salts and all the component parts of the blood are contained in a higher and lesser degree in vegetables—in the vegetable life of the earth and the sea.

Every vegetable that grows in the sea contains iodine, every plant that grows on the earth contains potassium, and the pulses contain phosphorus. Roots and seeds are storehouses of energy for new life.

In the case of annuals the most virtue resides in the seeds, in perennial plants, in the roots. With knowledge of the constituents of herbs it is possible to correct and supply the surpluses and deficiencies which cause illness in mankind.

Chemical analysis has proved the truth of a great deal of the traditional knowledge which was based in some cases on deductions from the appearance and growth of plants. Homoeopathy has also confirmed some of the traditions about herbs, especially the sphere of their action on the human body. It is almost incredible that one plant should, for instance, benefit the left upper lung, and another the left lower lung; and that other plants should act specifically on the *right* upper and *right* lower lung, and yet this is actually so.

The blue forget-me-not, which is known to everyone, acts on the left lower lung; the common daisy on the muscular fibres of the heart; the red Virginia Creeper on the elbow joints; the wild strawberry on the mesenteric glands; yellow mullein on the inferior maxillary branch of the fifth pair of the cranial nerves; oats on the brain; cactus on the circular muscular fibres; lime on the muscles of the eye, and so on.

Green plants contain chlorophyll or they would not be green. Iron is in all probability a constituent of red plants. The Horsetails and Marestails are stiff and harsh to the touch because they contain silica.

Herbs are the oldest form of medicine and have, therefore, been tested longer than anything else. The word drug is derived from an Anglo-Saxon word 'Dregen' meaning 'to dry', in reference to dried herbs—the first drugs. Centuries later the Arabians made medicinal herbs more palatable by concocting them into various forms of syrups. These juleps and robs and electuaries—a relic of Mohammedan invasion—are still a vital part of all European

15

Pharmacopoeias, though few know how to prepare them, and their differentiating features have disappeared. Some were made by infusion, others by decoction, and some were made by the extraction of the juices of the plant. Juleps were prepared for immediate use and did not keep. Electuaries were a composition of powdered herbs blended with honey. Proper syrups were a more elaborate affair altogether, and were expected to keep. A lohoch was thicker in consistency than a syrup and yet not as thick as an electuary. It was eaten off the end of a stick of liquorice.

Nicholas Culpeper gives minute instructions as to how they should be made.

The Eastern taste for sweet things, such as Turkish Delight, is the natural taste before it has been vitiated by strong food and drink, and no medicine recommends itself so well to children as these sugared confections and syrups.

A rob of Elderberries will prevent a chill after bathing. Coltsfoot syrup cures a simple cold, and confection of wild roses a sore throat, and who indeed could refuse such herbal delights as a nightcap of syrup of Cowslips, or a conserve of lilies for a tired heart?

HILDA LEYEL

Shripney Manor,
  Shripney,
    Sussex

Chapter I

AROMATIC TISANES

AROMATIC HERBS

Chapter I

AROMATIC TISANES

Tisanes come to us from France. Other countries have adopted them, and other countries have introduced them into their official pharmacopoeias, but in France tisanes are a national habit. A tisane of herbs is the Frenchman's way of relieving a condition that is not serious enough to see a doctor about. A bad sleeper takes a tisane of tilleul before going to bed; poor digestion is improved by a cup of camomile tea; a chill is cured with peppermint and elderflower tea, or a tisane of anise and menthe. The Frenchman is too much of a gourmet to choose any herbs that are not pleasant to the taste; and, as the carminative herbs are usually the aromatic ones, his needs do not, as a rule, go beyond these. Melilot, Hyssop, Lovage, Golden Rod and Costmary are some of them, and all the other herbs found in this chapter make fragrant tisanes if they are not infused long enough to become bitter. They cover a wide range of minor illnesses which can be dealt with successfully in this simple and pleasant way.

The Camellia, from which the tea we usually drink is gathered, is also included, for it is a herb like any other, and is sometimes mixed with Bergamot, Speedwell, Wood Betony or other herbs. Bergamot is better known by its old name of Oswego tea, and Speedwell was at one time so universally used as an adulterant of ordinary tea, or as a substitute for it, that it was called 'Thé de l'Europe'. Ground-Ivy was called Gill tea. Willow Herb went by the name of Kaporie tea in Russia, and Ceanothus was the well-known Jersey tea of America.

Dittany tea is another old-fashioned tisane, a pleasant and effective remedy for indigestion. The plant grows in the island of Candy in Dalmatia and is a species of Marjoram.

19

Last, and pleasantest of all, are Rosemary, Lavender and Queen of the Meadow—so sweetly scented and so English that for centuries they have figured in royal household accounts as a necessary expenditure for strewing floors, making pot-pourri and for scenting linen. Amongst those who work in the Lavender and Rosemary fields a tea made from either of these flowers is a quick cure for a nervous headache. Rosemary has become the symbol for remembrance because it is actually used in herbal medicine to cure forgetfulness.

ANGELICA

Angelica, the happy counter bane
Sent down from heaven by some celestial scout
As well its name and nature both avow't.

Joshua Sylvester

Botanical name	Angelica archangelica (Linn.)
Natural order	Umbelliferae
Country name	The Root of the Holy Ghost
French name	Angélique
German names	Engelwurz, Brustwurz
Italian name	Angelica
Spanish name	Angélica
Dutch name	Engelwortel
Under the dominion of	Sun in the sign of Leo
Symbolises	Inspiration
Parts used	Stems, leaves, seeds, root
Natural habitat	Scotland, East Prussia, Iceland, Lapland, Syria

The great reputation of Angelica in ancient medicine is shown by its botanical name. Today, it is little used medicinally, except as a flavouring, and combined with other herbs to produce perspiration in feverish colds. Its decorativeness and its pleasant aroma make it a very popular plant in the kitchen garden, and these two factors may have contributed to the high esteem in which it was held.

Another reason may have been its time of flowering, which coincides with the Archangel Michael's own day, 8th May. The Letts endowed Angelica with magical powers, and the songs which are chanted by them when the herb is carried to market are very ancient. The Laplanders believe that it prolongs life, and they chew it and smoke it in the same way as tobacco.

The plant is cultivated on a large scale in France—near Clermont Ferrand—and is sold for making liqueurs and sweets. It is said to be an ingredient of Chartreuse, anisette, and of French vermouths. The musk-like scent pervades the whole plant and makes it extremely pleasant when candied. It has cordial properties and helps digestion.

The seeds are generally used in medicine though some prefer the root, but it is the root and stems that are sold for confectionery. The Norwegians and Laplanders use the root for bread. The plant has the reputation of causing a distaste for alcohol in those who drink too much.

A tisane of Angelica can be freely used in feverish colds and makes a very pleasant drink if lemons and honey are added.

TO CANDY ANGELICA

Cut the young stalks into lengths about five inches. Arrange them in a pan and pour over them enough boiling syrup to cover them. Cover with vine leaves and leave it to stand till the next day, then drain the stems, throw away the vine leaves and return the syrup to the boil, strain it and again pour it over the Angelica stems which have been placed for a second time in the pan. Leave it to stand again till the next day, adding fresh vine leaves.

This process must be repeated once more till the Angelica is quite green. Then it must be bottled, care being taken not to break the stems.

ANGELICA WATER

Take eight handfuls of the leaves, wash them and cut them and lay them on a table to dry; when they are dry put them into an earthen pot and put to them four quarts of strong wine; let it stay for twenty-four hours, but stir it twice in the time; then put it into a warm still or an alembic and draw it off.

Cover your bottles with a paper and prick holes in it; so let it stand two or three days. Then mingle it all together and sweeten it, and when it is settled bottle it up and stop it close.

ARBOR-VITAE

The true and only friend is he
Who like the arbor vitae tree
Will bear one image on his heart.

Sir W. Jones

Botanical name	Thuja occidentalis
Natural order	Coniferae
Country names	Tree of Life, Yellow Cedar, False White Cedar
French names	Thuja de Canada, Arbre de vie, Arbre de paradis
German name	Lebensbaum
Italian names	Tuja, Albero della vita
Turkish name	Ŏ mur aḡ
Under the dominion of	Saturn
Symbolises	Unchanging friendship
Part used	The recently dried leafy twigs
Natural habitat	North America

The Arbor-Vitae was introduced into England in 1566. This species of Conifer makes one of our best garden hedges; once established it grows superbly and never gets thin and shabby at the bottom as some hedges do.

Single specimens grow to as much as forty or fifty feet in height and become conical in form.

The botanical name of Thuja is derived from a Greek word meaning to fumigate, because the tree was used in ancient times in sacrifices, and, at a later date, to strew floors and fumigate dwellings.

It has an aromatic scent and flavour, and is used to cure warts.

23

ARENARIA

Among the loose and arid sands
The humble arenaria creeps!
Slowly the purple star expands
But soon with shut up calyx sleeps.

Charlotte Smith

Botanical name	Arenaria rubra (Linn.)
Natural order	Caryophillaceae
Country names	Common Sandspurry, Spergularia, Bird's Rubra, Red Sandwort
French names	Sabline rouge, Spergulaire rouge
German names	Tissa rubra, Roter Spärkling, Sandkraut
Italian names	Lupinaia, Spergola
Part used	Herb
Natural habitat	Europe, including Great Britain, North America, Australia, Russia, Asia

This plant is often found in waste places and on heaths, especially in the proximity of the sea.

It has a salty, aromatic flavour and the resinous substance that it contains is a cure for calculus.

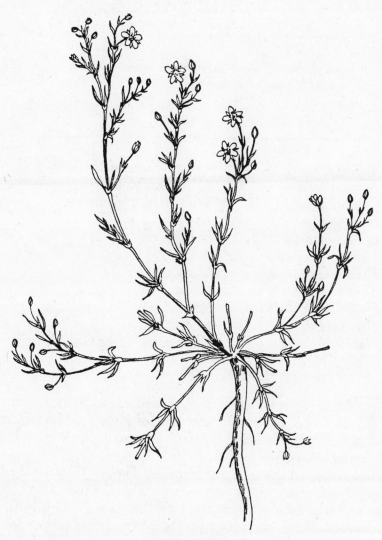

ARENARIA

Arenaria rubra

ASARABACCA

Botanical name	Asarum Europaeum (Linn.)
Natural order	Aristolochiaceae
Country names	Wild Nard, Hazelwort
French name	Asaret
German name	Haselwurz
Italian name	Asaro
Dutch name	Mansoor
Turkish name	Asarun
Under the dominion of	Mars
Part used	Root
Natural habitat	Europe, including Great Britain

This is the only one of the Aristolochias which is indigenous to Great Britain; another species known as Birthwort is sometimes found in the south-eastern counties but it is not its natural habitat.

The Aristolochias are a rather curious family. They are used in their own country to stupefy snakes and render them innocuous. The serpents become intoxicated by the juice of the plants. In medicine they are prescribed for their stimulating properties, in cases of rheumatism. The Birthwort is an aromatic herb and it removes obstructions that interfere with the circulation of the blood.

There are several varieties, such as the long-rooted birthwort, the climbing birthwort and the round birthwort, but the last, according to (Sir) John Hill, was considered the most useful in medicine.

Take of leaves of Asarabacca three parts and of Marjoram and Lavender flowers of each one part.

Reduce all to powder and keep it well stoppered for use.

LADY'S BEDSTRAW

. . . August, September, October—our uplands faint out in semi-tones, grey scabious, grey harebell, pale bedstraw, white meadow-sweet like the lace of an old lady's cap.

Maurice Hewlett

Botanical name	Galium verum (Linn.)
Natural order	Rubiaceae
Country names	Pretty Mugget, Cheese Rennet, Our Lady's Bedstraw, Maid's Hair
French names	Gaillet, Petit Muguet
German name	Labkraut
Italian name	Gaglio
Spanish name	Cuaja Leche
Dutch name	Walstroo
Under the dominion of	Venus
Part used	Herb
Natural habitat	Great Britain

This pretty golden flower is closely allied to the Common Clivers and the sweet-smelling Woodruff, though the Lady's Bedstraw itself has little scent. Its country names refer either to its use as a substitute for ordinary rennet, or to its use as a dye for the hair. The name Lady's Bedstraw is an abbreviation for Our Lady's Bedstraw. It has been suggested that this herb, which was constantly used for stuffing mattresses, was the actual bedding of the manger at Bethlehem.

In agricultural districts the Lady's Bedstraw is commonly used to curd cheeses, to which it gives a good yellow colour. This yellow dye belongs to all the madder family, and the Lady's Bedstraw boiled with alum produces the golden colour so much in request as a hair dye.

The plant has been used in medicine to cure epilepsy and also calculous complaints.

28

A decoction of the whole herb makes a most soothing foot bath after too much walking, and the white Bedstraw has a specific sphere of action on the arteries, the sinews and the joints.

Culpeper, in speaking of the white Bedstraw, says that its stems are so weak that it always lies down unless it is supported, which means that the plant contains little or no silica. Both the white and the yellow Bedstraw are ruled by the planet Venus.

DISTILLED WATER OF BEDSTRAW AS A SUMMER DRINK

Gather the Bedstraw before it seeds. Cut into short lengths and put into your still and cover with water. Make a good fire under it and when it is near boiling and the still begins to drop, if you find your fire too hot, draw a little away that the liquor may not boil over. The slower your still drops the cleaner and stronger will be the water. All simple waters must stand several days before they are bottled.

DIRECTIONS FOR USING A STILL

In order to distil properly with an alembic the top must be filled with cold water when it is set on, and close the bottom with a little stiff paste made of flour and water. If you use a hot still, when you put on the top, dip a cloth in white lead and oil and lay it close over the edges, and a coarse cloth well soaked in water on the top, and when it becomes dry from the heat of the fire, wet it and lay it on again. It will require little time, but that as hot as possible.

The Housekeepers' Instructor

BERGAMOT

Botanical name	Monarda didyma
Natural order	Rustaceae
Country names	Oswego Tea, Scarlet Monarda, Bee Balm
French name	Bergamote
German name	Bergamottenbaum
Italian name	Bergamotta
Spanish name	Bergamota
Symbolises	Your whims are quite unbearable
Part used	Leaves
Natural habitat	America

Bergamot is of rather recent cultivation in Great Britain, but its bright colour and its orange scent make it a very useful acquisition to the aromatic herb garden.

It is an ornamental plant with scarlet flowers which grow in whorls at the top of grooved, square stems. It grows best in moist soil and is particularly suitable for a bog garden at the end of a pond or stream. It does not like much sun.

The plant is very familiar to Americans, who have long used the leaves as a substitute for ordinary tea, under the name of Oswego tea.

A tisane of the leaves makes a fragrant and delicious drink.

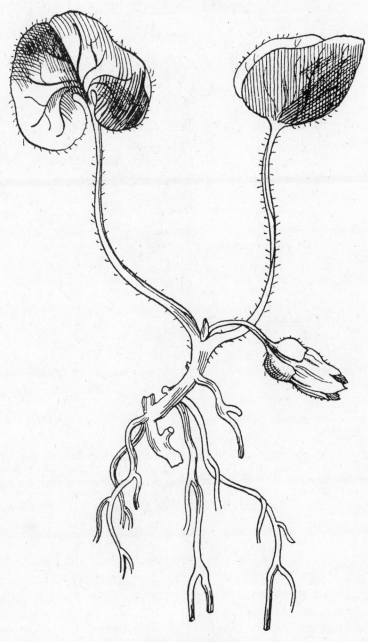

ASARABACCA

Asarum Europaeum

BIRCH

Where weeps the birch with silver bark and long dishevelled hair.

Botanical name	Betula alba (Linn.)
Natural order	Betulaceae
Ancient names	Berke, Birchen Tree, Bere
Country name	White Birch
French name	Bouleau
German name	Birke
Italian name	Betula
Spanish name	Abedul
Swedish name	Biork
Danish name	Birk
Russian name	Beresa
Under the dominion of	Venus
Symbolises	Meekness
Parts used	Leaves, bark
Natural habitat	Europe from Sicily to Iceland, Northern Asia.

From an economic point of view the Birch is one of the most useful of trees. The bark is of unusual whiteness and it is not affected by weather. These two points in its favour have made it particularly suitable for furniture, though it is not a very durable wood. Beds, chairs, tables, carts and waggons are all made from it.

Some of the ancient books were inscribed on the bark of this tree and the name is derived from a Sanscrit word meaning 'to write upon'. Pliny and other writers have commented on the peculiar whiteness of the wood.

The Russians believe that this tree is never struck by lightning, and the Indians believe the same thing of the Beech.

The Birch grows in the coldest countries, and thrives in the Highlands of Scotland as well as in Sweden and Russia, but as it gets nearer the Arctic region it becomes less tall, until it finally grows in the form of a dwarf bush.

The fragrant odour that emanates from the Birch is very noticeable after a shower of rain. The bark makes an aromatic tisane which is used in Germany for skin diseases. In the same country the leaves are considered better for women and the bark for men. The oil that exudes from the tree is also applied externally in skin complaints, and in Russia a regular trade is carried on in the tar obtained from the Birch tree. The oil contains methyl salicylate and it is a good substitute for wintergreen oil as a rheumatic liniment. The sap from the tree makes a delicious cordial wine when mixed with lemon peel, honey and spices, and fermented with yeast; and Birch wine made from the bark itself is an old country drink.

BIRCH WINE

In March bore a hole in a Birch tree, and put in a faucet, and it will run two or three days together without hurting the tree; then put in a pin to stop it and the next year you may draw as much from the same hole: put to every gallon of the liquor a quart of good honey, and stir well together; boil for an hour. Skim it well, and put in a few cloves and a piece of lemon peel; when it is about cold put in so much ale yeast as will make it work like a new ale; and when the yeast begins to settle, put it in a roundlet that will just hold it—so let it stand for six weeks, or longer if you please, then bottle it, and in a month you may drink it. It will keep a year or two.

BUCHU

The good physician Melampus, loving them all,
Among them walked, as a scholar who reads a book.

George Meredith

Botanical names	Barosma betulina, Diosma betulina
Natural order	Rutaceae
Country names	Bucku
French names	Diosme, Buchu
German name	Götterduft, Bukkostrauch
Italian name	Diosma
Turkish name	Diozma
Part used	Leaf
Natural habitat	South Africa

This is such a useful plant in the treatment of catarrhal inflammations, that in the vicinity of Cape Town, where it is collected commercially, casual pedestrians are forbidden to pick it.

It has a very fragrant, aromatic scent and taste, and a tisane of the leaves is a quick and very successful diuretic; the leaves are antiseptic as well as emollient. They are sometimes infused in brandy instead of in water and this drink acts as a tonic.

The plant has been introduced into England but either the climate or the soil does not suit it. Buchu belongs to the same family as the Angostura, the Indian Bael tree, and the Burning Bush.

CAMELLIA

The chaste Camellia's pure and spotless bloom,
That boasts no fragrance and conceals no thorn.

Roscoe

Botanical name	Camellia thea (Linn.)
Natural order	Camelliaceae
Other names	Thea sinensis, Thea viridis, Thea bohea, Thea stricta, Jassamica
French names	Camelia, Rose du Japon, Théier
German names	Kamelie, Teestrauch
Italian names	Camelia, Té
Spanish name	Camelia
Symbolises	Unpretending excellence
Part used	Leaf
Natural habitat	Assam. Cultivated in China, Japan, Java, Ceylon.

Camellias are evergreen shrubs with long, very glossy leaves and lovely flowers of various colours ranging from deep red to pale pink and white. The exotic appearance of the flowers make it almost incredible that they can live out of doors through an English winter and come into bloom soon after Christmas, but they flourish in most English gardens, especially in the South, if they are protected from piercing winds. They don't like heat when they are in flower and they don't like too much water, on the other hand if they are allowed to get too dry the buds drop off.

The Camellia Thea, however, will only grow in a tropical climate. The lovely flowers of the species used for tea are of a more drooping appearance than those we are familiar with in English gardens. The Thea viridis is kept for green tea and the Thea bohea for black. The leaves of the viridis are a brighter green than the other and more pointed and wrinkled.

Green tea is sometimes known as Ding, after the man who first

35

introduced it, or Hyson tea after the first European merchant who sold it. Hyson tea is almost a blue-green in colour with very curled leaves. The Chinese have many varieties of bohea tea, one of them is called Soo-cheun or Souchong. This is a superior kind of Cong-fou tea. The tea they call Padre-Souchong is drunk by their priests. It has a very fine taste and smell, the leaves are not rolled and it gets spoilt by a sea journey, so is conveyed by caravan. Russia used to consume large quantities of it before the war.

Oamho or Soum-La is a tea called after the place where it grows; it has a scent of violets; and jasmin tea, which is dried with the heavily scented jasmin flowers of China, is kept by the Chinese for their own use.

In China it is very usual to mix sweetly scented flowers of different kinds with tea—rose petals are sometimes used.

The Chinese of all classes drink tea all day long. It is made so weak that we should hardly recognise it as tea, and it is so carefully prepared that all its narcotic and dangerous properties are dried out. It is left there for years before it is ever used. The caffeine in tea acts as a mild stimulant to the nervous system, and though it causes sleeplessness in overdoses, it induces sleep if taken in the right way.

In Japan, an oil is expressed from the seeds of the Camellia Japonica and is used by the Japanese in cooking food; and another species, the Camellia Susanquo, is sometimes added to ordinary tea to give it a better scent. The Japanese women use the leaves of this Camellia to wash and scent their hair. It smells very sweet.

TEA SHERBET

Melt half a cupful of sugar in half a cupful of water and when it begins to boil take it off the fire and add the juice of a lemon and an orange. Stir well—add two cupfuls of tea and freeze, adding more sugar if necessary.

TEA FRAPPÉ

Pour a pint and a half of boiling water over two teaspoonfuls of tea and strain if off after five minutes.

Let it cool, add four teaspoonfuls of sugar and two tablespoonfuls of lemon juice and freeze to a mush.

Serve in sherbet glasses with a mint leaf in each glass.

CHASTE TREE

Agnus-castus

CAMOMILE

Whilst some still busied are in decking of the bride,
Some others were again as seriously employed
In strewing of those herbs at bridals used that be
Which everywhere they throw, with bounteous hands and free
The healthful balm and mint from their full laps do fly
The scentful camomile, the verdrous Costmary.

Michael Drayton

Botanical name	(Common) Anthemis nobilis (Linn.)
	(German) Matricaria Chamomilla (Linn.)
Natural order	Compositae
Country name	Maythen
French name	Camomille
German name	Kamille
Italian name	Camomilla
Spanish name	Manzanilla
Under the dominion of	The Sun
Symbolises	Energy in adversity
Part used	Flower
Natural habitat	Europe, including Great Britain; North Africa and temperate Asia

The word Camomile is derived from a Greek word meaning apple, in allusion to the scent of the flowers, which the Greeks thought resembled the smell of apples. They called the plant 'Ground apple'.

There are two well-known species of Camomile. The common one which is usually known as Belgian Chamomile and the much smaller flower of the Matricaria which goes under the name of German Camomile, or Common Camomile.

Both plants are of low growth and both have white single or double composite flowers with a yellow centre. The Common

Camomile has a scale between each two florets which is the distinguishing feature of the anthemis varieties.

The leaves are silver grey and the plant prefers a sandy soil.

The Camomiles have strong antiseptic properties and the oil they contain gives them their peculiar aromatic scent. When the plant is growing, the more it is trodden on the stronger it smells.

A plant of Camomile keeps a whole border of other plants healthy.

The essential oil is bright blue when it is first extracted but it becomes yellow after exposure to the air.

In medicine the yellow centre of the Camomile flower is the most important part, and this is where the oil in all probability is found. At one time consumptive people used to be made to sit near a bed of Camomile to breathe the perfume, which was said to have a purifying effect on the lungs.

The plant is more used today as a digestive tonic, and a tisane of Camomile is excellent for those with a weak digestion, to be taken after a heavy meal. It also beautifies the complexion.

Externally, the flowers mixed with poppy heads make a good poultice to relieve pain.

The flowers make a lovely golden dye for the hair and the oil is much used in hair lotions of all kinds. It has a comforting effect on the head and on the brain.

The Spanish Camomile is used to flavour the particular Sherry which they call after the flower, Manzanilla. It is usually drunk in Spain with olives.

The German Camomile has a most soothing effect on babies, especially while teething. The flowers are aromatic but much more bitter than the Common Camomile.

Both kinds can be used in the form of a tisane for ague, for nightmare, and as a sedative to the nerves and the digestion, but Camomile tea must not be drunk to excess.

In England we have four varieties of this Camomile, *Anthemis nobilis* or Common Camomile, the stinking mayweed, *Anthemis cotula*, the Corn Camomile, *Anthemis arvensis*, and the Yellow Camomile in which the rays are yellow instead of white.

The Camomiles have a very ancient reputation in domestic medicine, and put into a bath remove fatigue.

CEANOTHUS

Bathed in blue transparency of Heaven.

Botanical name	Ceanothus Americanus (Linn.)
Natural order	Rhamnaceae, Red Root
Country names	New Jersey Tea, Wild Snowball, Blue Tea Bush
French name	Céanothe
German name	Säckelblume
Italian name	Ceanoto
Turkish name	Zeres Cayt
Parts used	Root, bark, leaf
Natural habitat	North America

This species of Ceanothus, which goes in medicine by the name of Red Root, must not be confused with another plant also called Red Root—the *Lachnanthes tinctoria*, which yields a useful red dye.

The leaves of the American Ceanothus are used as a substitute for tea in America under the name of New Jersey tea.

The plant is semi-hardy and grows as a shrub. It has downy leaves and decorative white flowers, but other varieties have flowers of a lovely powder blue.

In domestic medicine it is used in chest complaints and to make gargles and mouth washes.

In Canada the plant is used to dye wool a cinnamon colour.

CHASTE TREE

A bunch of Agnus Castus in her hand
She bore aloft, her symbol of command.
Chaucer

Botanical name	Agnus-castus
Natural order	Verbenaceae
Country names	Monk's Pepper, Hemp Tree, Abraham's Balm
French names	Agneau chaste, Gottillier, Arbre au poivre
German names	Keuschbaummüllen, Abrahamsbaum
Italian names	Agno casto, Peperello
Turkish name	Yemen safront
Symbolises	Indifference
Parts used	Ripe berries, seeds
Natural habitat	Sicily and the shores of the Mediterranean

This small shrub with aromatic flowers and berries is a native of Sicily, where two varieties grow—the broad-leaved and the narrow-leaved Chaste Trees.

The branches grow from the bottom and sides of the stalk, are very pliable, and have long joints; the leaves are so cut and divided as to give the appearance of an open hand, and the flowers grow in whorled spikes of a bluish purple, and sometimes white, at the end of the branches, and do not make their appearance until it is almost autumn. The part of the tree used in medicine is the ripe berries, which, as they are seen on the tree, are half concealed by the green calyces which surround them. The berries themselves are not unlike peppercorns. They have an acrid, pungent taste and though strongly aromatic are not pleasant. The flowers, on the other hand, are extremely fragrant.

This is a tree with a very ancient reputation for preserving chastity. Athenian women used it as a symbol of chastity in religious rites, and Dioscorides recommended it to be used as medicine. It is taken sometimes for premature old age and also to restore life to paralysed limbs.

The tree is a great acquisition in any garden because of its late bloom, but in England it won't ripen its berries.

COSTMARY
Tanacetum balsamita

COSTMARY

Fresh Costmary and breathful Camomile
Dull poppy and drink quickening Setewale.
Vein heating Verven and head purging Dill
Sound savory and basil harty-hale.

Michael Drayton

Botanical name	Tanacetum balsamita (Linn.)
Natural order	Compositae
Country names	Alecost, Balsam Herb, Maudlin, Balsamita
French names	Herbe Sainte-Marie, Baume de coq, Tanaisie balsamite
German names	Alecost, Rainfarn, Wurmkraut
Italian names	Tanaceto balsamico, Bonerba, Costa
Under the dominion of	Jupiter
Symbolises	Impatience
Parts used	Leaves, flowers
Natural habitat	Orient, introduced into Southern Europe

Costmary is not unlike Tansy, but its leaves are not feathery and it has a pleasanter scent. Its yellow flowers grow in loose clusters. The plant was introduced into England in the sixteenth century and from that time was used to perfume linen, to strew floors and to flavour dishes.

It ranks with lavender as a herb to put amongst fine linen.

Culpeper recommended it to be used for all kinds of dry agues and for pains in the head arising from catarrhal affections and especially for a condition called Cachexia.

A tisane of Costmary helps catarrh in the head.

A teaspoonful of the leaves should be infused in a small teapot for fifteen minutes and a cupful can be drunk once or twice a day.

Pick the flowers when they are dry, only use the petals, weigh them and to every pound of petals take two pounds and a half of loaf sugar. Beat the two together in a stone mortar, adding the sugar by degrees. When well incorporated press into gallipots without first boiling. Tie over paper and leather on the top of the paper and it will keep seven years.

Mrs. Glasse

COUCH-GRASS

Better to hunt in fields for health unbought
Than fee the doctor for a nauseous draught.

Dryden

Botanical names	Triticum repens (Linn.)
	Agropyron repens (Beauv.)
Natural order	Graminaceae
Country names	Dog's Grass, Quick Grass, Twitch Grass
French names	Chiendent, Pied de poule
German names	Echte Quecke, Grasquecken
Italian names	Gramigna, Caprinella, Granaccino
Under the dominion of	Jupiter
Part used	Root
Natural habitat	Europe, including Great Britain, Northern Asia, Australia, North and South America

The old name for Couch-grass is Dog's grass. The Hindus call it drib grass and darble, and its reputation as a medicine in India dates from the time of the Vedas in which it is mentioned.

In France another species is more used, the *Cynodon dactylon* (Pers.), and this is really the Couch-grass that they call Chiendent; but both that and our *Triticum repens* have the same properties and are very similar.

Though Couch-grass is a tiresome weed which farmers deplore because of its underground creeping stems, it is helpful on sandy seashores because it binds the sand and prevents the dunes from shifting. In England it is found near Penzance on the sea shore, on the east coast, and in parts of Devonshire. It is plentiful in deserts like the Sahara, where it is extremely useful.

The stalks of the grass are jointed and it has purplish green spiked heads with a husk in them containing hard seeds.

As a medicine it has a very soothing effect on the kidneys, for which it has been used by herbalists for centuries. The root is so nutritious that it has been made into bread when corn was scarce.

GOLDEN GORSE

The commons over grown with ferns and rough,
With prickly gorse, that shapeless and deformed,
And dangerous to the touch, has yet its bloom,
And decks itself with ornaments of gold.

Cowper

Botanical name	Ulex europaeus (Linn.)
Natural order	Leguminosae
Country names	Ruffet, Fray, Goss, Furze, Whin, Prickly Broom
French names	Agone, Joue marin, Landier
German names	Europäische Stechgenister, Echte Heckensame
Spanish name	Hiniesta espinosa
Italian name	Ginestra, Ginestrone
Dutch name	Heybrem
Under the dominion of	Mars
Symbolises	Love for all seasons, Anger, Enduring affections

This lovely yellow flower with its prickly stem grows in great profusion on moors and commons throughout England and in the vicinity of the sea. Its flowers yield a beautiful yellow dye.

It is mentioned by Theophrastus under the name of Scorpius, and Pliny refers to it as Ulex. It grows abundantly in deserted towns like Santa Margere in Tesono and in France.

It was a very old custom in the past to put a sprig of Gorse in a bride's bouquet and it was this that gave rise to the rhyme:

When Gorse is out of bloom
Kissing's out of season.

The leafy buds are sometimes used as a substitute for tea, and cattle will eat the young shoots when other fodder is scarce.

Golden Gorse is a remedy for scarlet fever in children. It also cures jaundice.

COUCH-GRASS

Triticum repens

GOLDEN ROD

True love lies bleeding, with the Hearts-at-ease;
And Golden Rods, and tansy running high
That o'er the pale top smiled on passer by.

John Clare

Botanical name	Solidago Virgaurea (Linn.)
Natural order	Compositae
Country names	Aaron's Rod, Golden Wings, Woundwort
French names	Verge d'òr, Herbe des juifs
German names	Echte Goldrute, Goldruthe
Italian names	Verga d'oro, Verga aurea, Erba giudaica
Under the dominion of	Venus
Symbolises	Precaution, encouragement
Part used	Leaf
Natural habitat	Europe, including Great Britain; North America, Central Asia

---

Golden Rod is too familiar to need a description. Its tall sheaves of leaves and long feathery golden heads have had a place at the back of herbaceous borders ever since there were gardens in England.

A very superior Golden Rod has lately taken the place of the old variety, but it remains the same in character, only the flowers are fatter and more luxurious and they are sweet scented.

Golden Rod is one of the old wound herbs. Its name Solidago is taken from *solidare*, to unite, and its old country name of Woundwort commemorates its virtues.

This plant is the only one of its family that is a native of Great Britain.

An infusion of the leaves of Golden Rod makes a pleasant aromatic tisane with stimulating, carminative and astringent properties.

Golden Rod is an ingredient in the Swiss vulnerary known as faltrank.

At one time the American sweet-scented Golden Rod which has become popular in gardens lately, was imported to England at great expense, and sold at Bucklesbury in Cheapside at a very high price.

It has the same properties as the old-fashioned variety and used to grow, at a later date, in the Hampstead woods.

The plant was originally introduced into England by the Crusaders, who gave it the name of *Solidago Saracenia*. The latter part of the name was changed later but it has always borne the reference to its healing power. The order under which the plant has been placed gives no indication of its appearance.

GROUND-IVY

And there upon the sod below,
Ground ivy's purple blossoms show,
Like helmet of the Crusade Knight,
Its anthers crossed like form of white.

Bishop Mant

Botanical name	Glechoma hederacea (Linn.)
Natural order	Labiatae
Country names	Red-hofe, Alehoof, Tunhoof, Cats-foot, Hedgemaids, Gill-go-by-the-hedge, Gill-creep-by-ground, Lizzy-run-up-the-hedge, Robin-run-in-the-hedge
French names	Lierre terrestre, Lierre de terre
German name	Echter Gundermann
Italian names	Edera terrestre, Erba di San Giovanni
Spanish name	Hiedra terrestre
Under the dominion of	Venus
Part used	Herb
Natural habitat	Great Britain

Ground-Ivy was so popular at one time as a blood tonic that it was one of the London street cries. It gave its flavour to English beer and clarified it and made it keep well at the same time.

As a cooling tea it was known as Gill tea, and mixed with sugar candy it was a famous old wives' remedy for coughs and colds.

From the time of the Anglo-Saxons, who called it Read-hofe, this plant has figured conspicuously in domestic medicine. The juice was a cure for singing noises in the ear if administered locally, and the plant had such a reputation as a cure-all that it was even given to the insane. It is still used in hysterical complaints, and so is its closely related plant, Catmint.

52

It also has pectoral properties in common with the Catmint.

Painters use infusions of Ground-Ivy to cure and prevent lead colic.

Ground-Ivy has the usual labiate flowers in the axils of the upper leaves—they are blue in colour. It has a spicy aroma and taste which makes it a pleasant tisane when infused in hot water. The plant grows in hedges and waste places throughout England, and creeps along the ground, sending forth roots at the corners of its jointed stalks.

The leaves remain green well into the winter and will live through the whole of a mild winter.

The plant infused in wine is an old cure for sciatica. It clarifies wine and makes wine that has got thick and cloudy, clear again.

HOLLY

PARAGUAY MATTÉ TEA

I in the wisdom of the holly-tree can emblems see.

Southey

Botanical names	Ilex aquifolium (Linn.)
	Ilex Paraguayensis
Natural order	Aquifoliaceae
Country names	Hulver Bush, Holy Tree, Christ's Thorn, Holm, Hulm
French names	Houx, Thé du Paraguay, Maté
German names	Stechpalme, Matéstrauch
Italian names	Aquifoglio, Aquifoglio Paragua
Spanish name	Acebo
Under the dominion of	Saturn
Symbolises	Foresight
Parts used	Leaves, berries, bark
Natural habitat	Central and Southern Europe

The leaves of several species of Holly are used in different countries as a substitute for ordinary tea—the best known being the *Ilex Paraguayensis*, which has been popularised under the name of Yerba Maté tea. In Brazil and South America, where it grows by the side of streams, it is cultivated on a large scale and universally drunk instead of other tea. This small shrub has white flowers, which are succeeded by small red fruit. The leaves are collected and dried and made into tea with the addition of burnt sugar and lemon juice, and the word maté is taken from the vessel in which the leaves are infused.

Maté tea contains a large percentage of caffeine and is a powerful stimulant which enables the natives to work hard on little food.

The ordinary Holly tree, *Ilex aquifolium*, also furnishes us with a useful medicine, and both the bark and berries are used as well as

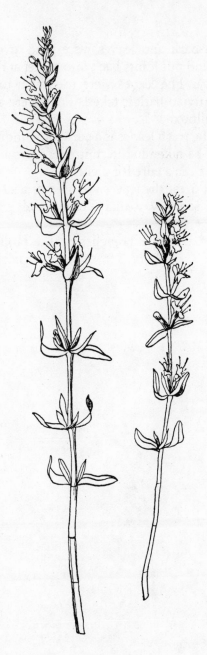

HYSSOP
Hyssopus officinalis

the leaves. The bark and leaves were used at one time to knit bones together and put joints back into place, and the berries were taken for dropsy. The leaves were used as a tonic much in the same way as Peruvian bark is taken. They were also prescribed as a remedy in smallpox.

The juice of the fresh leaves is a cure for jaundice.

Holly tea can be taken in intermittent fevers and for a catarrhal condition and is even a cure for pleurisy.

In the Black Forest the leaves are used as a substitute for ordinary tea in the same way that Yerba maté is drunk in South America.

Pliny believed that the branches of the Holly defended men from the Evil One, and houses from being struck by lightning.

HYSSOP

Hyssop with spikenard, sacred and precious,
Bergamot, Orris root, Costmary too.

Botanical name	Hyssopus officinalis (Linn.)
Natural order	Labiatae
French name	Hysope
German names	Echter Ysop, Isop
Italian names	Isopo, Issopo celestino
Spanish name	Hinojo
Under the dominion of	Jupiter, and under the sign of Cancer
Symbolises	Cleanliness
Part used	Flowering tops
Natural habitat	Southern Europe

Hyssop has a sweet scent and a most decorative appearance. The flowers are blue, white or red, and can be used in salads or in broths, to flavour liqueurs, or to make refreshing aromatic baths. It was one of the strewing herbs and was used in the bouquets that were carried during plagues and pestilences as a prophylactic against infectious diseases.

Hyssop honey is delicious in flavour and has all the properties of the herb, which is pectoral and carminative.

HYSSOP FLIP

Sweeten three ounces of Hyssop water with sugar candy to taste and beat into the yolk of an egg.

This is excellent for hoarseness or a cold.

QUEEN ELIZABETH'S CORDIAL ELECTUARY OF HYSSOP

Boil a pint of the best honey; and having carefully taken off all the scum, put into this clarified liquid a bundle of Hyssop which has been well bruised before being tied up. Let them boil together till the honey tastes strongly of the Hyssop—then strain the honey very well and add a quarter of an ounce of pulverised liquorice root and the same of aniseed with half the quantity of pulverised elecampana root and angelica root and a pennyweight each of pepper and ginger.

Let all boil together for a short time and stir well—then pour into gallipots and stir till cold. Keep covered for use and whenever troubled with straightness at the stomach, or shortness of breath, take some of the electuary, which will very soon give relief.

The New London Family Cook

LAVENDER

Pure Lavender, to lay in bridal gown.

Leigh Hunt

Botanical name	Lavandula vera (Linn.)
Natural order	Labiatae
French name	Lavande
German name	Lavendel
Italian names	Lavanda, Spigo, Nardo
Spanish name	Espliego
Under the dominion of	Mercury
Symbolises	Distrust
Parts used	Herb, oil
Natural habitat	England, France and Spain

Lavender is essentially an English plant. It was one of the old London cries

> *Lavender, sweet blooming Lavender,*
> *Six bunches a penny today.*
> *Lavender, sweet blooming Lavender,*
> *Ladies buy it while you may.*

It likes our soil and climate and nowhere else does it produce such good oil. The perfume of Lavender is in keeping with the best English traditions. Englishmen who never use other scents like to use what has come to be known as Mitcham Lavender.

Mitcham and the surrounding district was the soil in which it was said to grow best, but it is now cultivated much more widely in parts of Hertfordshire, Cambridgeshire, Suffolk, Lincolnshire and Kent, though it still bears the name of Mitcham Lavender in commerce.

At Long Melford and Market Deeping fields of Lavender can be seen growing luxuriantly, the beauty of its scent and the immense purple patches of colour make a great appeal to the senses—especially if seen just before it is harvested.

The clean, spicy smell of English Lavender made it a very appropriate scent to put amongst fine linen and freshly laundered linen. At one time it was used in every laundry, especially when frills and ruffles were in fashion. Court ruffles were scented with it in the seventeenth century, and it was put into baths—this was the origin of the name. It was derived from 'lavare', to wash.

Even Puritans didn't disapprove of the scent of Lavender, which in earlier days was distilled from the flowers themselves. No Lavender water, made as it is today with oil and spirit, can compare with the old method which is too costly for the modern purse and too laborious; and private stills are not encouraged.

The late Sir Joseph Swan made it in his own home, but he was a scientist and, so long as it was the most perfect expression of the plant, the cost was immaterial to him.

Queen Henrietta Maria grew Lavender in her gardens at Wimbledon and she introduced a white variety which we never see today.

In France it was first introduced by Charlemagne, but French Lavender, though much better than that grown in Spain, bears no comparison with English. We are told that Charles VI of France had white satin cushions stuffed with it; and in England it is sometimes used to stuff cushions hanging over the backs of chairs. In Wales, Lavender is called Llafant. Its virtues were well known to the mysterious physician of Myddrai—the founder of Welsh herb lore. In the Great School of Medicine at Salerno it was also used in medicine as a cure for palsy.

Its effect on the brain is very pronounced. A tisane of Lavender, or even a spray of Lavender worn under a hat, as the harvesters themselves apply it, will generally get rid of a nervous headache. It also is a soothing nerve tonic, and tincture of red Lavender, which was at one time a combination of white roses and other exotic flowers mixed with Lavender, is a very famous old nerve soother.

There are other varieties of Lavender besides the *Lavandula vera*, and it has become the fashion lately to grow a French variety with darker flowers and practically no scent.

The spike Lavender is cultivated for its oil and used in lotions to keep away mosquitoes, but it is crude and almost unpleasant.

LOVAGE

Levisticum officinale

The *Lavandula vera* must always hold its own against all fashions. Its scent alone is so healing and its effect so soothing on 'the tremblings and passions of the heart'.

TO DISTIL LAVENDER

Method:

A pound of flowers stripped of their stems is packed into a quart retort. Pour over 8 ounces of spirit. Heat the retort in a saucepan of water and keep it boiling till the essence has come over; it will make about $7\frac{1}{2}$ ounces but it will be better than anything you can buy.

COMPOUND SPIRIT OF LAVENDER

Take of the spirit of Lavender	3 pounds
Spirit of Rosemary	1 pound
Cinnamon	$\frac{1}{2}$ ounce
Nutmeg	$\frac{1}{2}$ ounce
Red Saunders	3 drachms

Digest for ten days and then strain off. This is often taken upon sugar and is a salutary cordial, far preferable to drams, which are too often had recourse to by persons feeling a great sinking or depression of the spirits.

LOVAGE

Weeds of glorious feature.

Botanical name	Levisticum officinale (Linn.)
Natural order	Umbelliferae
Country names	Italian Lovage, Scotch Lovage, Court Lovage, Mountain Hemlock
French names	L'Angélique à feuilles d'ache, Livèche, Séséli
German name	Echte Liebstöckel
Italian names	Ligustico, Levistico, Seseli
Spanish name	Ligustico
Under the dominion of	The Sun
Parts used	Seeds, root, leaf, stem
Natural habitat	Countries of Mediterranean, Greece, Balkans, mountains of south of France

Lovage is not indigenous to England though it is sometimes found wild in parts of England. It is a perennial plant not unlike angelica in appearance, with ribbed leaves resembling celery, and an aromatic scent which pervades the whole plant.

The flowers grow in yellow umbels and are rather like the flower of the parsnip. The foliage is exceedingly ornamental and the whole plant is very decorative, though less so than angelica. The young stems are used, like angelica, as a flavouring and are candied to make a sweetmeat; the leaf stalks can be eaten as a substitute for celery.

Lovage cordial is made by steeping the fresh seeds in brandy and adding sugar. This is an excellent medicine to comfort and warm the stomach. At one time public houses sold a drink called Lovage which contained the plant in some form.

Scotch Lovage is a different species from the *Levisticum officinale*. It is used in the Hebrides as a vegetable and is eaten raw as a salad and called 'Shunis'. If taken fasting it is said to act as a prophylactic against infectious complaints. The distilled water of ordinary Lovage, or the juice of the plant, removes freckles.

The plant is ruled by the sun and comes under the sign Taurus, so Culpeper recommended it for the throat troubles to which people born under this sign are prone.

CANDIED LOVAGE

Cut the young stems in April and boil in water till tender, then drain very carefully. Scrape slightly and dry carefully in a cloth, and lay in a syrup previously prepared. Leave three days with the vessel well covered, then heat but do not let the syrup boil. When it is thoroughly heated lay the pieces on a dish to dry—near the fire.

LOVAGE CORDIAL

Lovage cordial is made by steeping the fresh seeds in brandy and sugar. It has properties rather like Angelica and the plant is useful in feverish colds.

WOOD BETONY

Betonica officinalis

MEADOWSWEET

The almond scented meadowsweet, whose plumes of powerful odour incense all the air.

Botanical name	Spiraea ulmaria (Linn.)
Natural order	Rosaceae
Ancient name	Dolloff
Country names	Queen of the Meadow, Bridewort, Meadowsweet
French names	Reine des prés, Spirée ulmaire
German names	Wiesenkönigin, Echtes Mädesüss
Italian names	Ulmaria, Regina dei prati, Piè di becco
Spanish name	Barbe de Cabra
Under the dominion of	Venus
Symbolises	Uselessness
Part used	Herb
Natural habitat	Europe, including Great Britain

Of all plants this is the most fitting to be described as 'Queen of the Meadow'. It is almost a part of the English landscape with its sweet hawthorn-like smell and its lovely cream coloured flowers.

The scent pervades the whole air when it grows by the sides of rivers and brooks and in damp meadows intersected with streams. The dancing feathery heads of the flowers are a lovely sight in the summer meadows. It grows in great profusion along the banks of streams and in the adjoining meadows.

Chaucer, our earliest and most English poet, was familiar with it. Even as early as his day it was added to English beers and drinks for its scent and its wholesome qualities; it was strewn in churches at weddings and made into garlands for brides, as its old country names still testify; a cordial water was distilled from its flowers and it was gathered on St. John's Day to reveal a thief.

In Iceland, where it also grows, it is believed that it can not only discover a thief but detect the sex of the robber by sinking for a man and floating for a woman.

The leaves of the Meadowsweet are scented as well as the flower, but differently, and both are used in herbal medicine.

Its great value is as an anti-acid remedy. It has a soothing effect on the sympathetic nerves, it restores elasticity to the muscles, and is so safe that it can be used daily with excellent results and the root can even be made into bread. It makes, as Culpeper says, 'a merry heart'.

MEADOWSWEET BEER

Take 2 ounces of Meadowsweet, Betony, Raspberry leaves and Agrimony and boil in 2 gallons of water for 15 minutes. Strain and add 2 pounds of white sugar. Bottle when nearly cool.

Does not require yeast.

ROSEMARY

Rosemary only grows well when the mistress is master.

Botanical name	Rosmarinus officinalis (Linn.)
Natural order	Labiatae
Country names	Polar Plant, Compass Plant
French names	(Old French) Incensier, (Modern) Romarin
German name	Echter Rosmarin
Italian names	Rosmarino, Ramerino
Spanish name	Romero
Under the dominion of	Sun
Symbolises	Remembrance
Parts used	Herb, root
Natural habitat	Europe

Rosemary, in common with Lavender and Peppermint, grows better and smells sweeter in England than anywhere else. The damp climate has something to do with this. It was grown at Hampton Court in Queen Henrietta Maria's time and Sir Thomas More allowed it to spread all over his garden because his bees liked it, and because it symbolised friendship. The plant was actually introduced into England in the fourteenth century by Queen Philippa of Hainault, though it is mentioned in an Anglo-Saxon herbal of the eleventh century.

There is an old tradition that Rosemary grew to the height of Our Lord while He was on earth and after His death remained the same height and only grew in breadth. There are many legends about the plant and it was commonly believed that Rosemary only flourished in the gardens of the righteous.

'Lavender and Rosemary is as a woman to man, and white rose to red. It is an holy tree and with folke that has been just and right-fulle it groweth and thryveth.'

It has also been said that Rosemary will only grow well where the house is ruled by a woman.

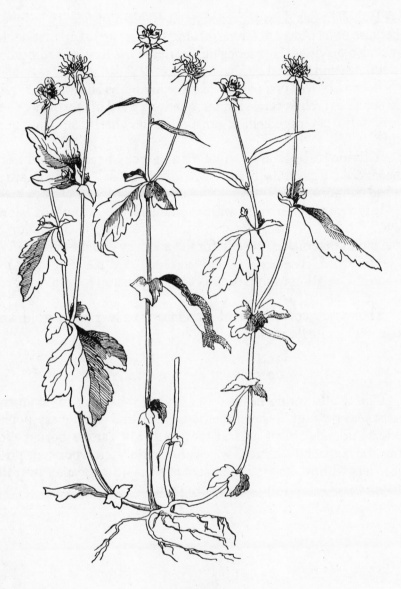

AVENS

Geum urbanum

The plant has been regarded as an emblem of fidelity in lovers because of its power of strengthening the memory, and that is why it is also a symbol of friendship. In this sense it was used both at weddings and funerals.

Rosemary was one of the old strewing herbs and was burnt for its scent, as well as carried in bouquets, to ward off pestilences and fevers. It is an ingredient of pot-pourris and herbal smoking mixtures.

A tisane of Rosemary will cure a nervous headache and has a beneficial effect on the brain. Its constant use will greatly improve a bad memory.

It is a cordial herb and was recommended by Pliny for failing eyesight. It is probably its stimulating effect on the circulation of the blood that makes it useful for the memory and the eyes.

The word 'rosemary' is derived from 'ros' meaning dew and 'marinus' relating to the sea, probably in allusion to its filmy, grey colour.

There are two varieties of Rosemary, a silver and a gold, and one with white flowers as well as blue.

CONSERVE OF ROSEMARY

Pick the flowering heads when dry, rub them off the stem and sift them through a sieve, then weigh them and to every pound add 2½ pounds of loaf sugar. Beat together in a stone mortar, adding the sugar by degrees. When thoroughly incorporated, press into jars without first boiling. Cover well, putting leather over the paper covers and it will keep seven years.

SPEEDWELL

*Unhealed we wait my speedwell whom they name
Veronica, namesake of the woman blest with love's
True image.*

Newman Howard

Botanical name	Veronica officinalis
Natural order	Scrophulariaceae
Country names	Paul's Betony, Cat's Eye
French names	Thé d'Europe, Véronique
German names	Ehrenpreis, speedwell tee
Italian name	Veronica
Spanish name	Veronica
Under the dominion of	Mercury
Symbolises	Female fidelity
Part used	Herb
Natural habitat	Europe, including Great Britain

Veronica holds a special place in Christian minds because it is called after the Saint who wiped away the blood from Our Lord's face and was rewarded by having His image stamped for ever on her handkerchief. The plant therefore is associated with miracles and special powers are attributed to it.

As a strengthening medicine it was so much valued that it became at one time in Europe a universal substitute for ordinary tea, and was known as Thé de l'Europe.

There are several other varieties, of which the Germander Speedwell, *Veronica chamaedrys*; the Thyme-leaved Speedwell, *Veronica serpyllifolia*; and the Water Speedwell, *Veronica anagallis*, are perhaps the best known and the most common in England.

The Spiked Speedwell, *Veronica spicata*, is rarely found wild, but is very common in gardens. Another species, *Veronica beccabunga*, is better known as Brooklime; it is often found in marshes and by rivers and goes by the name of Water Purpie in Scotland.

71

It is taken as a spring drink to purify the blood, and in Germany is called Bach-bunge.

Other varieties are the Alpine Speedwell, *Veronica alpina*, sometimes found in the Highlands; the Blue Rock Speedwell, *Veronica saxatilis*, the flesh coloured Speedwell, *Veronica incarnata*, both rare; the Ivy-leaved Speedwell, the Wall Speedwell, the Vernal Speedwell, and the Blunt-fingered Speedwell.

The Germander Speedwell is the most popular substitute for the Common Speedwell, and it has much more attractive flowers and, as some people think, a better flavour, it is often preferred in herbal medicine to the other. It is good for all affections of the brain, headaches and drowsiness.

BUTTERBUR

Petasites vulgaris

SWEET VERNAL GRASS

A blade of silver hair grass nodding slowly
In the soft wind, the thistle's purple crown,
The ferns, the rushes tall and mosses lowly.

Botanical name	Anthoxanthum odoratum (Linn.)
Natural order	Graminaceae
Country name	Spring grass
French names	Flouve odorante, Anthoxanthe
German names	Echtes Ruchgras, Wilder Lavendel
Italian names	Antossanto, Paleino odoroso
Turkish name	Kokulu Yonca
Symbolises	Poor but happy
Part used	Flower

Sweet Vernal Grass is different from other grasses because it has not three stamens. It is an annual, and its flowers are arranged on short spike heads which are broader at the bottom than at the top. When dried it exhales a coumarin type of perfume, very like Woodruff.

It is used to cure hay fever, but the medicine is not effective unless the grass is first dried.

TANSY

At stoolball, Lucia, let us play,
For sugar cakes or wine;
Or for a tansy let us pay,
The loss be thine or mine.

Robert Herrick

Botanical name	Tanacetum vulgare (Linn.)
Natural order	Compositae
Country name	Buttons
French name	Tanaisie
German name	Reinfahren
Italian names	Tanaceto, Tanasia
Spanish names	Tanaceto, Balsamita menor
Under the dominion of	Venus
Symbolises	I declare against you
Natural habitat	Europe, including Great Britain

Tansy grows wild in most parts of England in any soil. It is found in hedges, by seas and rivers, and in waste places. It has a smell not unlike Camphor, and its flat yellow heads make it recognisable at once.

It is in flower for a very long period and its Greek name of Athanasie, which means everlasting, is probably a reference to its power of duration. The plant was used by the ancients to preserve dead bodies from pollution, and in mythology it was given to Ganymede to make him immortal.

It keeps away moths and insects and, as one of the strewing herbs, disinfected churches, courts of law, and other public buildings in the days of plagues.

The antiseptic property of Tansy made it useful in the kitchen, and meat was rubbed with the leaves to keep flies away. As a flavouring it was used in Tansy cakes, which were eaten at Easter, and a 'Tansy' was a kind of custard flavoured with this plant. The roots cooked in honey were sometimes used for gout. The roots give a good green dye.

A tisane of the leaves or the whole herb is an excellent cordial tonic. It aids digestion, dispels rheumatism and soothes the nerves.

This herb, because of its good effect on the sinews, was one of the six remedies which, in the ancient School of Medicine at Salerno, were recommended for palsy. It is considered an excellent tonic to take after exhaustion, diseases and fevers. An infusion produces quiet sleep in restless people. It is mildly narcotic.

A TANSY

Blanch and pound $\frac{1}{4}$ pound of Jordan almonds; put them into a stewpan; add a gill of syrup of roses, the crumbs of a French roll, some grated nutmeg, half a glass of brandy, two tablespoonfuls of tansy juice, three ounces of fresh butter, and some slices of citron; pour over it $1\frac{1}{2}$ pints of boiling cream or milk; sweeten, and when cold, mix it. Add the juice of a lemon, and 8 eggs beaten. It may be either boiled or baked.

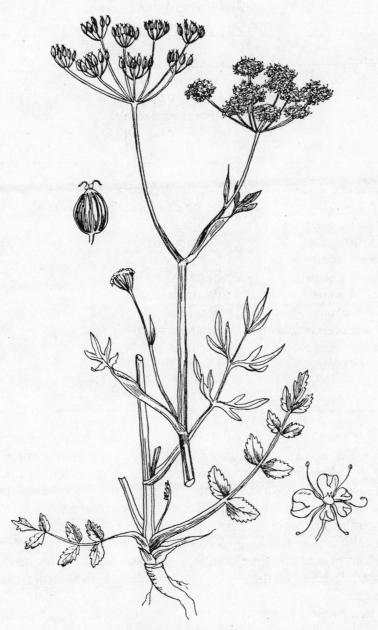

BURNET SAXIFRAGE

Pimpinella saxifraga

WOOD BETONY

Next these here Egremony is,
That helps the serpent's biting;
The blessed betony by this
Whose cures deserving writing.

Michael Drayton

Botanical name	Stachys Betonica
	Betonica officinalis (Linn.)
Natural order	Labiatae
Country name	Bishopswort
French name	Bétoine
German name	Betonie
Italian name	Betonica
Spanish name	Betonica
Under the dominion of	Jupiter and the sign Aries
Symbolises	Surprise
Part used	Herb
Natural habitat	Europe, including Great Britain

'Sell your coat and buy Betony' is an old Italian proverb which records the high esteem in which the herb was held in earlier days. So important was it in medicine in the time of the Roman emperors that Antonius Musa, the physician of the Emperor Augustus, wrote a whole treatise on its virtues.

Nicholas Culpeper referring to this fact says, 'It was not the practice of Octavius Caesar to keep fools about him.'

Betony was at one time used as a substitute for ordinary tea. It has a tonic effect on the brain and often takes away a nervous headache.

It is sometimes used as an ingredient in herbal smoking mixtures. The fresh leaves are said to be intoxicating.

Betony was much used in magical rites. It was worn round the neck as a charm, and planted in churchyards to keep away the devil. In Wales it is called the Criban St. Fraid.

The plant is not unlike the Deadnettle in appearance. It has bright, purplish-red flowers and an aromatic smell. Unlike other plants of the same species, the whorls of the flowers are arranged closely together and the stalk below the flower is bare.

Francis Bacon, referring to the nature of the ground which Betony prefers, says, 'Betony and strawberries showeth ground fit for wood—Camomile showeth mallow ground fit for wheat.'

Wood Betony grows in woods and on heaths and moors. It likes lime in the soil.

CONSERVE OF BETONY

Cut the flowering stems when they are dry and before they begin to seed. Free the flowers from the stems and pass through a sieve, then weigh the flowers and for every pound take $2\frac{1}{2}$ pounds of loaf sugar. Beat together in a stone mortar, adding the sugar by degrees. Do not cook and when thoroughly incorporated press into pots and cover well.

Chapter II

CORDIAL HERBS

CORDIAL HERBS

Chapter II

CORDIAL HERBS

Cordial herbs are the herbs that are used in wine cups and cooling drinks to give them an aroma.

They actually do more than impart their fragrance to the beverages they decorate, they also endow them with their own particular virtues. Some of these herbs have a beneficial action on the heart and others on the liver or smaller glands; so they cheer, refresh and give courage as tradition says they do. 'I, Borage, give courage!' is not a meaningless boast. Borage strengthens the adrenal glands—the organ that is most pronounced in courageous people. Viper's Bugloss, another flower belonging to the Borage family, has the same reputation for driving away melancholy, and Herb Bennet (one of the Geums) removes obstructions from the liver and is under the dominion of Jupiter, which is said to have power over the liver. Clove Carnations are also under jovial Jupiterian influence, and Carnation soup is an old remedy for depression.

Other cordial herbs are governed by Venus or the Sun. Culpeper gives red roses to Jupiter and damask roses to Venus.

The Romans used Roses of all kinds in their drinks and they crowned themselves with roses to avoid intoxication. The presence of Roses in the wine was believed to have the same effect.

In the time of the Stuarts, Melicot baths were used to drive away melancholy; and Marigolds have ever had the reputation of cheering, and have been used in Holland and other countries in broths as well as in cups.

Woodruff is put into drinks in Germany to produce a cheerful spirit and is dedicated more particularly to May Day. In England we generally depend on lemon Verbena, Balm or some of the

Mints; but Wood Sorrel with its heart shaped leaf, Burnet, Saxifrage, Butterbur, Motherwort, and Calamint all cheer, refresh and cool and give their perfumes.

The four special cordial flowers of the eighteenth century were Borage, Anchusa, Roses and Violets.

AVENS

GEUM

Nature, exerting an unwearied power,
Forms, opes and gives scent to every flower.
                                    William Cowper

Botanical name	Geum urbanum (Linn.)
Natural order	Rosaceae
Country names	Herb Bennet, Way Bennet, Blessed Herb, Clove Root, Golden Star, Colewort, Wild Rye, Harefoot, Cowwort
Ancient names	Sanamunda, Minarta, Pesleporis
French name	Benoite commune
German name	Nelkenwurz
Italian names	Erba benedetta, Ambretta
Spanish name	Ganiofilia
Under the dominion of	Jupiter
Parts used	Herb and root
Natural habitat	Europe, including Great Britain

The Avens that we know is probably the Geum of Pliny. The botanical name Geum is derived from a Greek word meaning 'giving perfume', in allusion to the pleasant scent of the root. This clove-like odour gave a distinctive note to the Augsburg ale to which it was added to flavour it, and to prevent it turning sour. The root was, and is still, used to scent linen; and it imparts its fragrance to water, so as a tisane it makes a very pleasant drink.

The plant is quite common in England and throughout Great Britain, growing almost anywhere, but preferring shade. It grows to over a foot in height; the firm, slender stalk is divided into branches with leaves at every joint, the leaves are large, rough and hairy as is also the stalk; and the leaves that grow from the root are winged and indented. The flowers grow at the tops of the branches, are small, yellow, consisting of five petals, and are not unlike the Cinquefoil. The flower is succeeded by a rough head of greenish-purple seeds which adhere to anything they come in contact with. The trefoiled leaf and flowers of the Avens is a common design in thirteenth-century architecture. The root consists of brownish fibres; it must be dried with very great care to prevent the loss of its aroma. It should not be cut up until it is actually needed. The old date for taking up the root was 25th March and it was attended by a regular ceremony. Curiously enough, though the plant prefers shade, it was considered better if it was gathered in a sunny place.

The virtue of the Avens is imparted to alcohol or water. A tisane can be made from the herb itself or the sliced root; the root can be chewed or it can be made into a decoction. There are various ways in which it can be administered. The plant is such a useful tonic and has so many good properties, and is so safe, that it can be used instead of ordinary tea, or to help digestion. It contains a good deal of tannin. It is a good substitute for Peruvian bark and relieves pain and brings down a temperature.

In feverish colds it combines very well with Angelica root. The herb is also a cordial and can be used in wine cups and refreshing summer drinks. It cheers the heart and raises the spirits.

As a protection against witches it has a very ancient reputation. One of the oldest of all herbals says, 'When the root is in the house Satan can do nothing and flies from it, wherefore it is blessed before all other herbs, and if a man carries the root about with him no venomous beast can harm him.'

Furthermore, the plant is a good cosmetic and an infusion of it will take away spots and freckles if it is used to bathe the face.

Finally, it strengthens the joints, cures a tertian fever, removes obstructions from the liver, and is so generally useful that its daily use either in wine or water is to be strongly recommended, especially in those who are debilitated after a long illness.

It can be infused in red wine or white.

AVENS CORDIAL

Take of Avens root bruised, 1½ ounces; Angelica root bruised, 1 ounce; Tormentil root bruised, 1 ounce; Jar raisins stoned, 2 ounces; French brandy, 2 pints.

Macerate for a month in a warm place, then filter through paper. Dose: ½ ounce.

CALAMINT

Calamintha officinalis

BALM

The several chairs of order look you scour
With juice of Balm and every precious flower.

Shakespeare

Botanical name	Melissa officinalis (Linn.)
Natural order	Labiatae
Country names	Lemon Balm, Sweet Balm
French name	Mélisse
German names	Melisse, Zitronenmelisse
Italian names	Cedronella, Melissa
Spanish name	Balsamita major
Under the dominion of	Jupiter and the sign of Cancer
Symbolises	Pleasantry
Part used	Herb
Natural habitat	Southern Europe, in mountainous districts

The sweet-scented lemon Balm which is now such a favourite plant in English flower gardens was introduced by the Romans and has become naturalised in the South of England. The whole plant is scented and it imparts its lemon flavour to wines and cups. In earlier days it was infused in canary wine and was drunk as a cordial and for its balsamic effect on the heart. John Evelyn recommends it for this.

The plant is a perennial with whitish-yellow flowers which grow in small bunches and bloom all through the summer. Its botanical name refers to its use as a plant for bees and Balm describes it as a balsam.

The leaves are often dried and used in pot-pourri, and an infusion of the fresh leaves makes an excellent drink in feverish complaints. The leaves can also be mixed with the leaves of blackcurrant trees and taken in the same way for feverish colds or fevers generally.

Balm is one of the plants that were so much used for strewing, and its juice disinfected and perfumed furniture as well as floors.

Balm is under the dominion of Jupiter and so it helps the spleen. The juice was at one time made into a tansy with eggs, rosewater and sugar and taken medicinally.

COMPOUND SPIRIT OF BALM

Take of the fresh leaves of balm, 8 ounces; lemon peel bruised, 4 ounces; nutmegs and caraway seeds, of each, 2 ounces; cloves, cinnamon and angelica root, of each, 1 ounce. Distil all together with a quart of brandy. It must be well preserved in bottles with ground glass stoppers.

BORAGE

Here is sweet water and borage for blending,
Comfort and courage to drink at your will.

N. Hopper

Botanical name	Borago officinalis (Linn.)
Natural order	Boraginaceae
French name	Bourrache
German names	Borretsch, Gurken Boretsch
Italian names	Borraggine, Borrana
Spanish name	Boraga
Under the dominion of	Jupiter
Symbolises	Bluntness, courage
Parts used	Leaves, flowers
Natural habitat	Aleppo, naturalised in Europe

The name of the plant is derived from a Celtic word meaning a man of courage. The reputation of Borage as a bringer of courage is a very old one. The herb was used by the ancient Greeks and Romans in their wine cups and has been put into drinks ever since. It has now been identified with the Euphrosinum of Pliny, and it is referred to in the fourteenth century by Nicholas Mysepius as Pourakion.

With the present knowledge of glands, there is little doubt that it has a specific sphere of action on the adrenal gland—the organ of courage—and by strengthening the gland it actually does increase courage in those who are lacking in the secretion of the adrenal gland.

Borage contains potassium and calcium, but in its fresh state has more nitrate of potash than it has after it is dried. It has demulcent and emollient properties and reduces temperature in fevers. The plant is allied to Comfrey and is very like it in appearance, having the same roughness, but the flowers are bright blue with black anthers like the garden Anchusa.

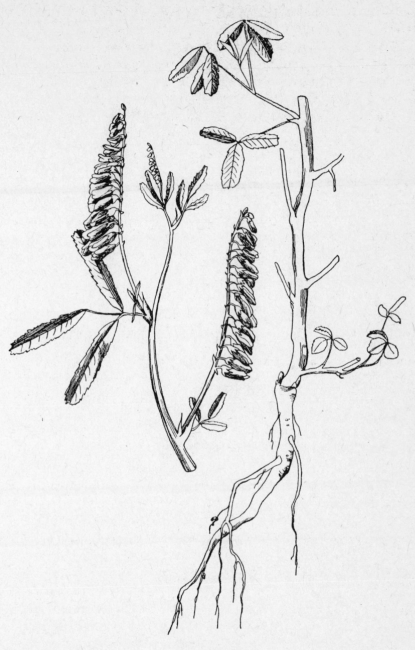

MELILOT
Melilotus officinalis

It grows in waste places, has a scent of cucumber, and imparts its fragrance and coolness to any liquid in which it is infused.

Borage is one of the four cardinal flowers of the ancients.

The Herbal of Renodaeus says: 'Its flowers put into broth give a special taste, and taken in wine they cause great joy and fearlessness according to that old saying "Ego Borrago gaudia semper ego". Its flowers in condiments recreate the eyes and jaws and in medicaments augment their cordial facultie.'

CANDIED BORAGE FLOWER

Take the best white loaf sugar and dip it piece by piece in water, put them into a vessel of silver and melt them over the fire; when they just boil, strain and set on the fire again and allow it to boil till it draws in, then put in the flowers and after having well dipped them in the sugar put them in glasses.

SYRUP OF BORAGE FLOWERS

Infuse 3 pounds of the flowers freed from their stems in a gallon of water in a well-glazed earthen jar with a narrow mouth for 8 hours, and cover well so that none of the virtue can escape; then heat the water again and after squeezing out the flowers to get all their goodness put in another 3 pounds and leave them for another 8 hours, then press out by hand and to every quart of the infusion add 4 pounds of loaf sugar and boil it to a syrup.

BURNET SAXIFRAGE

It gives a Grace in the drynkynge.

Botanical name	Pimpinella saxifraga (Linn.)
Natural order	Umbelliferae
Country names	Salad Burnet, Pimpinella, Lesser Burnet, Greater Burnet
French names	Boucage, Pied de bouc
German name	Kleine Bibernelle
Italian names	Pimpinella, Piè di becco
Spanish name	Sanguisorba
Under the dominion of	Moon
Symbolises	Affection
Parts used	Root, herb
Natural habitat	Great Britain

The Burnet Saxifrages, the greater and the lesser, grow in damp meadows throughout Great Britain and also in chalky districts.

The leaves, which rise immediately from the root, are winged and are set opposite to each other. They are slightly pointed, indented and, as Culpeper says, 'of a sad green colour'. The leaves of the Lesser Burnet are smaller and more deeply jagged. The flowers in both the saxifrages grow in umbels of white or pinkish flowers. The Burnet Saxifrage has rather the taste and smell of cucumber and has been used in cooling drinks since the time of the ancient Greeks and Romans.

The generic name of the plant, *Poterium*, refers to its use in drinking cups. It was steeped in beer at one time and given as a cure for rheumatism.

It is one of the oldest of the cordial herbs. The seeds used to be made into sugar plums like Caraway comfits; the juice was used for injuries to the head, and the distilled water was a cosmetic for removing freckles and was taken internally for any of these purposes. Country people used it sometimes to cure toothache.

Burnet Saxifrage was the plant that Bacon recommended to be planted with Thyme and Watermint to perfume the air. It is very much liked by cattle and as it grows on the downs where sheep run, it is a useful and nourishing food for them.

The plant resembles the Garden Burnet though the latter belongs to a different order—the Rosaceae. The Garden Burnet is also used in salads like the Lesser Burnet, and in cordials as well. They are both cordial herbs.

TINCTURE OF BURNET SAXIFRAGE

Take of the root of Burnet Saxifrage, sliced, 5 ounces; rectified spirit, 2 pints.

After sufficient extraction, express and filter. Dose: from 36 to 40 drops, or more.

BUTTERBUR

No gemlike sage glitters in thy pale face,
No rich aroma breathes from thy dull lip,
Yet, Petasites, there is that in thee
Which calls emotion from its lurking place
To work upon the brow and tinge the cheek;
A room the sun scarce sees, an atmosphere
Converted into poison, and the couch
The plague spot marks his own: where crowded victims
Mingle their groans, their weeping and despair.

Botanical name	Petasites vulgaris (Desp.)
Natural order	Compositae
Country names	Plague Flower, Butterdock, Umbrella Plant, Flapper Dock, Bog Rhubarb, Bogshorns, Langwort, Capdockin, Blatter-dock
French name	Herbe aux teigneux
Old German names	Pestilenzenwart, Echte Pestwurz
Italian names	Bardana, Erba dei tignosi
Turkish name	Kel-otu
Under the dominion of	Sun
Part used	Root
Natural habitat	England

The Butterbur grows throughout England in marshy ground. It is found by the side of streams and rivers, and because of its enormous leaves gives protection in hot weather to birds, large and small. The plant takes its botanical name from a Greek word meaning 'a hat', in reference to the immense size of its leaves. The umbrella plant is one of its popular names. In some ways it resembles the Coltsfoot, creeping along the ground in the same way and flowering before the appearance of its leaves. The pale flesh-coloured flowers grow in clusters at the top of a round spongy stem, the male and female flowers usually growing on separate spikes. The heart-shaped leaves, irregularly notched, are covered with down, and are white underneath. No larger leaves are found in any British plant, they are often two feet in width.

The plant is very like its near relation the Winter Heliotrope, and the flowers particularly closely resemble each other, except that the Winter Heliotrope has a perfume rather like a Hyacinth.

Butterbur is a favourite remedy among herbalists for a weak heart. It is a tonic and a stimulant and is very useful in cases of dropsy.

In Culpeper's day it was used to allay fevers, and as a disinfectant against plagues and pestilences, and in earlier days still it was one of the herbs used to divine to lovers the true state of each other's hearts.

Nicholas Culpeper recommended gentlewomen to grow the plant for the benefit of their poorer neighbours, adding 'it is fit the rich should help the poor, for the poor cannot help themselves'.

The plant is very attractive to bees. It is a cordial herb and can be used, as all cordial herbs can, to give coolness and fragrance to wine cups and a cheerful spirit to those who drink them.

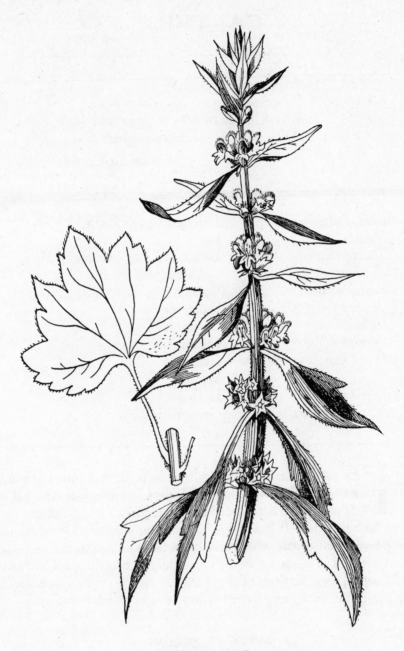

MOTHERWORT

Leonurus cardiaca

CALAMINT

Aromatic plants bestow
No spring fragrance while they grow.
But crush'd or trodden to the ground
Diffuse their balmy sweets around.

Oliver Goldsmith

Botanical name	Calamintha officinalis
Natural order	Labiatae
Country names	Bassil Thyme, Mountain Mint, Calamint Balm
French name	Calamenthe
German name	Kalamint
Italian name	Calaminta
Spanish name	Calamento
Dutch name	Calamint
Under the dominion of	Mercury
Part used	Herb
Natural habitat	Great Britain

This small plant seldom grows more than a foot high and has blue flowers not unlike those of the Catmint—it is closely related to the Thyme. It grows in dry places but can be cultivated. It has a hot scent rather similar to Peppermint and an aromatic taste which makes it a pleasant tisane.

Calamint is a cordial herb, very useful, according to Nicholas Culpeper, for afflictions of the brain. It is made into a syrup which is prescribed for cramps, convulsions and a disordered spleen.

SYRUP OF CALAMINT

Take the flowering stems and put into an earthen jar, covering them with water. Set this in a saucepan of water and let it boil for 2 hours, then strain out the juice, put $1\frac{1}{2}$ pounds of sugar to a pint of the juice. Put it into a skillet, and set it at the fire stirring all the time till the sugar is dissolved. Do not let it boil, then withdraw to the side of the fire and leave to cool, then bottle.

CONSERVE OF CALAMINT

Gather the flowers on a dry day. Strip the flowers from the stems, weigh them and to every pound of the flowers add $1\frac{1}{2}$ pounds of loaf sugar, beating the two together in a mortar and adding the sugar gradually. When well mixed, pot and cover. This is not enough sugar for the conserve to keep more than a year.

CARNATION

The curious choice clove July flower,
Whose kinds hight the Carnation,
For sweetness of most sovereign power
Shall help my wreath to fashion,
Whose sundry colours, of one kind,
First from one root derived,
Then in their several suits I'll bind,
My garland so contrived.

Michael Drayton

Botanical name	Dianthus caryophyllus
Natural order	Caryophyllaceae
Country names	Gillyflower, Clove Gillyflower, Picotee, Clove Pink, Grenadine
French name	Oeillet
German name	Nelke
Italian name	Garofano
Spanish name	Clavela
Dutch name	Angelier
Under the dominion of	Jupiter
Symbolises	Fascination
Parts used	Flowers, leaves
Natural habitat	South of Europe, India

The old-fashioned clove Carnations were deep purple in colour with a spicy aromatic smell of cloves and the leaves were a lovely greyish-green colour.

So popular were these clove gillyflowers in the seventeenth and eighteenth centuries that they were used in soups, sauces, syrups and cordials. The flowers themselves were candied and preserved, and were made into reviving vinegars, decorated salads, and above all, as sops in wine, floated in the drinks of betrothed couples. The Carnations actually known as Sops-in-wine were a small variety of the clove gillyflower. The word 'carnation' is probably derived from coronation because the flowers were so much used in wreaths to celebrate betrothals of marriage. In France there is still a special Carnation Day—the 29th of June, which is dedicated to St. Peter and St. Paul. William Cole was a great advocate for the use of Carnation flowers in medicine. He considered them a very great cordial and a great comforter of the heart. Michael Drayton refers to them as 'Cloves of Paradise' and Culpeper describes them as 'gallant fine temperate flowers, of the nature and under the dominion of Jupiter'.

The flowers themselves were sometimes prescribed dried and powdered, but they were more often made into syrups and conserves.

SIR JOHN HILL'S RECIPE FOR
SOPS-IN-WINE—CARNATION SYRUP

Pour 5 pints of boiling water upon 3 pounds of the flowers picked from the husks and with the white heels cut off—after they have stood 12 hours strain off this clear liquor without pressing and dissolve in it 2 pounds of the finest sugar in every pint.

This makes the most beautiful and pleasant of all syrups.

CLOVE JULY FLOWERS IN MOUNTAIN WINE
FOR THE NERVES

Infuse 3 ounces of Clove July flowers in a quart of Mountain wine for 10 days.

Shake every day except the last and filter through clean white blotting paper.

A wineglassful can be drunk three times a day as a nerve tonic.

The following recipe provided by Miss Cullen of Dundee appears in Miss Florence White's book, *Flowers as Food*.

'Cut off the white ends of the flower petals, and to every pound allow a quart of water and about a dozen cloves.

'Put all into a stone jar. Tie it up close with paper. Place it in a pot of cold water. Boil up and let it boil from 5 to 6 hours, taking care to add more hot water from time to time.

'Be sure not to let the water in the jar boil.

'Then drain the syrup through a sieve into a basin. Squeeze the flowers in a clean cloth so as to extract all the juice. To every pint of liquid add a pound of loaf sugar.

'When cold bottle and cork tightly.'

SYRUP OF CLOVE PINK

Take of fresh flowers, 1 ounce; boiling water, 1 ounce; refined sugar, ½ pound.

Let the water stand on the flowers for 12 hours, strain and add the sugar.

VINEGAR OF CLOVE PINK

Take of flowers, 1 ounce; the best wine vinegar, 16 ounces.

Let them stand for 15 days. Strain and filter.

This is a most excellent and refreshing liquor to smell at by those afflicted with headache. It is also good to sprinkle the room of sick persons.

In both of the above recipes, only the petals must be used.

VIPER'S BUGLOSS

Echium vulgare

MARIGOLD

Hark! how the bashful morn in vain
Courts the amorous Marigold
With sighing blasts and weeping rain,
Yet she refuses to unfold.
But when the planet of the day
Approaches with his powerful ray,
Then she spreads, then she receives
His warmer beam into her virgin leaves.

Carew

Botanical names	Calendula officinalis (Linn.)
	Caltha officinalis
Natural order	Compositae
Country names	Golds, Mary Gooles, Ruddes
French names	Souci des champs, Fleurs de tous les mois
German name	Ringelblume
Italian names	Fior d'ogni mese, Solis sponsa, Oculus Christi, Calendula
Spanish names	Claveton, Flameniquillo
Under the dominion of	The Sun in the sign of Leo
Symbolises	Grief
Parts used	Flowers, leaves, whole herb
Natural habitat	Southern Europe, the Levant

So wonderful is the Marigold as a healing herb that it can hardly be overrated. Nothing else in medicine contributes so much to the making of healthy tissue. It reduces inflammations, expels fevers, and cheers and strengthens the heart. If Marigold tea is taken after an accident it brings out the bruises and prevents internal complications. For burns it not only cures and helps to relieve the pain but it prevents the formation of scars. Where scars already exist it takes them away.

Marigolds can be used internally and externally, with the most perfect safety, by young and old.

In Holland the flowers are much used in broths, and in the England of John Evelyn's time they were put into salads. They are cheerful to look at and the consumption of them cheers the heart.

As a pot herb and as a salad herb they cannot be too much used.

Marigolds are grown in nearly every garden from seed and if, after they bloom, the dead heads are kept cut they will go on blooming into the late summer. They will grow in the poorest soil and I have constantly seen them blooming at Christmas time on the sea shore in Sussex. Their lovely orange colour adds much gaiety to any garden, and nobody can afford to be without them. Under the pretty English name of Marigold it is not always re- cognised as the chemists' Calendula, which can be made at home by soaking the flowers in hot water.

A SIMPLE HEART TONIC CONSERVE OF MARIGOLD

Boil together the petals of the marigolds with loaf sugar, allow- ing three times the weight of sugar to marigolds. First put the marigolds into a pan with water (a pint of marigold to a quart of water) and boil till tender, then add the sugar and keep stirring until they form a syrup, then put into gallipots.

From *The Gentle Art of Cookery*

MARIGOLD CORDIAL

One peck of Marigold petals, 1½ pounds of stoned raisins, 7 pounds of castor sugar, 2 pounds of honey, 3 gallons of water, 3 eggs, 6 oranges, 4 tablespoonfuls of German yeast, 1 ounce of gelatine, 1 pound of sugar candy, 1 pint of brandy.

Take a peck of Marigold flowers and put them into an earthen- ware bowl with the raisins. Pour over them a boiling liquid made of the sugar, honey and 3 gallons of water. Clear this liquid while it is boiling with the whites and shells of 3 eggs, and strain it before putting in the flowers. Cover up the bowl and leave it for two days and nights. Stir it well and leave it for another day and night. Then strain it and put it into a 6-gallon cask which has been well cleansed, and add to it 1 pound of sugar candy and the rinds of 6 oranges, which have been peeled and stripped of all white pith.

Stir into it 4 tablespoonfuls of German yeast and cover up the bung hole. Leave it to work till it froths out; when the fermentation is over pour in a pint of brandy and a $\frac{1}{2}$ ounce of dissolved gelatine. Stop the cask and leave it for several months before bottling.

MARIGOLD CHEESE

Pick the finest petals and pound in a mortar, straining out the juice. Make a junket in the usual way with milk and rennet and add the juice to the milk first. When set, break as gently as possible by stirring and break it as equally as possible—then put into the cheese vat and press with gentle weight so that the whey can pass through the holes at the bottom of the vat.

MELILOT

Bring me an unguent made of scented roots,
Pomander of Green herbs, and scarlet fruits,
Verbena leaves, mallow and melilot
And balmy Rosemary.

Mary Webb

Botanical name	Melilotus officinalis (Linn.)
Natural order	Leguminosae
Country names	Kings Clover, Sweet Lucerne, Wild Laburnum, Hart's Tree
French names	Mélilot, Tréfoil, Couronne royale
German name	Gemeine Steinklee
Italian name	Meliloto, erba cavallina
Spanish name	Meliloto
Under the dominion of	Mercury
Part used	Herb
Natural habitat	Great Britain

Melilot grows wild in parts of England, and was common in Essex, Suffolk and Huntingdonshire. At one time it was cultivated as a crop, but since the sixteenth century, clover has taken its place.

It is a perennial plant, and, being one of the leguminous plants, is a good bearer. The leaves are sweet smelling, set in threes, and have uneven indentation. The flowers are yellow.

The plant contains coumarin, and, when dried, the scent gets stronger.

The word Melilot is derived from *mel*, honey, and *lotus*, denoting its sweetness and scent. The plant is said to have sprung from the blood of the lion which the Emperor Adrian slew.

It is sometimes used to flavour beer, and also cheese. In Switzerland it is put into the green cheese known as Schabzieger; and

Melilot itself is called by the Swiss Ziegerkraut (curd herb). It is also used in Gruyère cheese.

In England it is sometimes an ingredient of herbal snuffs and tobaccos. The juice dropped into the eyes clears the sight and in France is used for ophthalmia.

The herb is put amongst furs and woollens to keep away moths, but it is as a cordial herb that it ranks first. Both in baths to take away melancholy, and in drinks to strengthen the memory and to comfort the brain and the head, it is most effective. It was an old cure for those who lost their senses. A distilled water of the plant was used to wash the head in such cases, and an infusion was administered internally. It was a simple and safe treatment.

Melilot still grows in Cambridgeshire; and a blue variety is found in the mountains near the lovely little town of Gruyère.

TO MAKE A BATH FOR MELANCHOLY

Take Mallowes, pellitory of wall, of each three handfuls; Camomile flowers, Melilot flowers, of each one handful; Senerick seed, one ounce, and boil them in nine gallons of water till they come to three—then put in a quart of milk and go into bloud warm or something warmer.

From *The Fairfax Stillroom*

MOTHERWORT

Then doth the joyful feast of John
The Baptist take his turne,
When bonfires great, with loftie flame,
In everie towne doth burne:
And young men round about with maides
Do dance in everie streete
With garlands wrought of Motherwort
Or else with Vervaine sweet.

Botanical name	Leonurus cardiaca (Linn.)
Natural order	Labiatae
French name	Agripaume, Herbe battudo
German name	Herzgespannkraut
Italian names	Agripalma, Melissa salvatica
Spanish name	Agripalma
Dutch name	Aartgespan
Under the dominion of	Venus and the Sign of Leo
Symbolises	Concealed love
Part used	Herb
Natural habitat	Europe, including Great Britain

Motherwort is the only one of its family which grows wild in England, and it is a disputed point as to whether it grew here naturally or was cultivated in the first instance. It is very easy to grow from seed and requires no special soil or position. The palmate form of its lower leaves distinguishes it from other Labiate plants.

The plant grows about three feet high, the stalk is square, thick and nepryletic, the leaves are arranged in twos at each joint on long foot stalks. They are divided into three parts and are all deeply indented. The flowers grow in prickly cups, and vary in colour from a reddish purple to pink, two of the stamens are longer than the others, and the anthers are covered with hard shining dots. The smell is strong and rather unpleasant. The whole effect of the plant is rather handsome and it bears resemblance to a lion's tail.

The flower blooms in August and the plant increases rapidly if it is left to seed itself.

Like many other herbs, Motherwort has a reputation for warding off evil spirits.

In medicine it is unequalled as a simple heart tonic, especially when fever is present. It drives away melancholy and cures cramp.

CONSERVE OF MOTHERWORT

Gather the flowers on a dry day and strip them from the stems —allowing 2 pounds of sugar to 1 pound of flowers. Beat them together in a mortar, stirring the sugar in gradually, then pot and tie down well.

SYRUP OF MOTHERWORT

Cut the flowering stems into small pieces and put them into an earthen pot and pour over them boiling water, allowing 1 gallon of water to every 3 pounds of the stems. Cover closely and leave for 12 hours, then squeeze the herbs very carefully, heat the liquid and add a fresh lot of herbs; infuse again, covering closely, and continue to do so until the infusion is strong enough. To every quart of the infusion add 4 pounds of loaf sugar and boil to a syrup and when cool bottle.

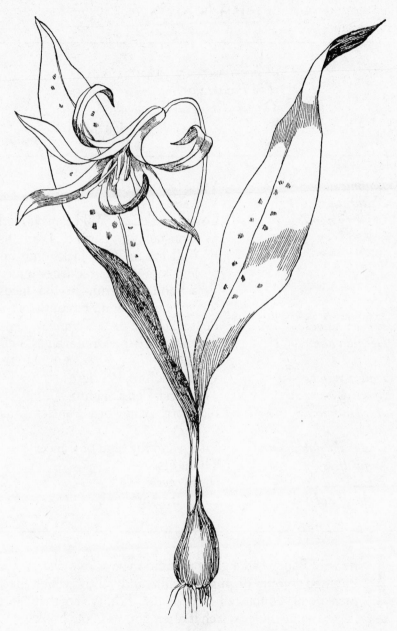

AMERICAN ADDER'S TONGUE
Erythronium Americanum

PANSIES

What flowers are these?
The Pansie this;
Oh! that's for loving thoughts.

Chapman

Botanical name	Viola tricolor (Linn.)
Natural order	Violaceae
Country names	Love-in-idleness, Wild Pansy, Herb Constancy, Herb Trinitatis, Call-me-to-you, Jack-jump-up-and-kiss-me, Three-faces-under-a-hood, Kit-run-in-the-fields, Stepfathers and Stepmothers
French names	Pensée, Herbe de la Trinité
German names	Stiefmütterchen, Dreifärbiges Veilchen
Italian names	Viola tricolore, Pensiero
Spanish names	Trinitaria, Pensamiento
Ancient names	Banwort, Banewort, Pancies (Sussex)
Under the dominion of	Saturn and the Sign of Cancer
Symbolises	Thoughts
Parts used	Herb, seeds
Natural habitat	Great Britain

The wild Pansy had a great reputation as a love charm, and its three colours of purple, white and yellow which mark each petal, connected it with the Trinity, so that Herb Trinitas is the name under which it often figures in old books.

Presumably both the garden Pansy and the wild Heartsease have the same virtues. It is an old remedy for skin diseases in babies, but it has also been used for asthma and for epilepsy. Its properties are cordial and cooling and in this respect it is not unlike the Violet. The herb is demulcent and contains mucilage so it is a useful remedy to allay inflammations of the lungs and chest. The plant contains salicylic acid.

Its country name of Love-in-idleness has been perpetuated by William Shakespeare:

> *Yet mark'd I where the bolt of Cupid fell:*
> *It fell upon a little western flower,*
> *Before milk-white, now purple with Love's wound*
> *And maidens call it Love-in-Idleness.*

SYRUP OF HEARTSEASE

Make an infusion of the flowers by covering them with hot water and letting them simmer gently in a water bath for 24 hours, covered closely, then strain out the flowers and to every pound of the infusion put 2 pounds of loaf sugar and cook in a water bath till dissolved. If the first infusion is not strong enough more flowers can be infused and the process can be repeated as often as wished.

ROSES

RED AND WHITE

There was the pouting rose both red and white.

Leigh Hunt

Old garden rose trees hedged it in:
Bedroft with roses waxen white,
Well satisfied with dew and light,
And careless to be seen.

Elizabeth Barrett Browning

Botanical names	Rosa Gallica, Rosa damascene, Rosa indica
Natural order	Rosaceae
French name	Rose du Midi
German name	Gallische Rose
Italian names	Rosa domestica, Rosa mistica
Spanish name	Rosa
Under the dominion of	Jupiter, Venus, and the Moon. Red Roses ruled by Jupiter; White Roses by the Moon.
Symbolise	Love
Parts used	Petals, leaves
Natural habitat	Northern Persia

It is so long ago since Roses were first introduced into Europe that it has been almost forgotten that they came to us from Persia, which is their real home.

A trade was carried on by the Persians in water distilled from Roses as long ago as the eighth and ninth centuries, and Rose-water was known and written about as early as 140 B.C., when it is first mentioned by Nicander.

Attar of Roses is a much later invention and the traditional story of its discovery is as romantic as everything else concerned with Mogul rule in India.

The Emperor Jehangir and his beautiful bride while walking in the royal garden by the side of the canals filled with Roses to celebrate their wedding, noticed an oily film on the surface of the waters produced by the action of the sun on the Roses. They were so fascinated by the scent of this oil that they ordered it to be bottled, and it became henceforth the most precious scent of emperors.

Long before the reign of the Moguls, Roses had played such an important part at the feasts of Roman emperors that not only were the floors of the palaces strewn with Roses for their scent, and the guests crowned with them, but the food was flavoured with Roses, and Roses floated in their wine. Later still, the rose on the ceiling of the dining room of private houses symbolised the privacy of the conversation (*sub rosa*). Later, the rose on the ceiling lost its meaning, and was used to decorate all ceilings indiscriminately.

Theophrastus' is the first herbal to mention Roses; and the rare oil of Dioscorides was simply olive oil in which Roses had been macerated. Avicenna knew how to make Rose-water, and Provence was famous for its dried Rose petals as early as the thirteenth century. The inhabitants made juleps and conserves of red Roses and considered them valuable in medicine. The Provence Rose (the *Rosa Gallica*) is still the red Rose of medicine. To-day Roses are chiefly used to ease coughs, to comfort the heart and for Eustachian catarrh. They help the hearing, and are useful at the beginning of hay fever; and as a flavour to other medicines they are very much used in pharmacy. The petals contain, as well as other things, glucose, gallic acid, and quercitrinic acid.

In France Roses enter into the composition of such liqueurs as Parfait d'Amour, and the Turks and Greeks make a delicious conserve of Roses which is copied in other European countries.

In England we cultivate the red Rose of medicine in Oxfordshire and Derbyshire; and the hips of the wild Rose are made into a conserve by country people, who give it to consumptives, who derive benefit from it.

The leaves of the wild Rose when dried make a good substitute for tea, and the petals and the fruit were formerly regarded as a useful heart tonic. Red Roses increase the retentive faculty; they can be used as a gargle, and Rose-water mixed with syrup of mulberries is excellent as well as delicious for quinsies and sore throats.

In Europe we only use the red Rose, the damask Rose and the Dog Rose in medicine, but the snow-white Rose contributes its essence to the Bulgarian otto of rose and so does the Moss Rose.

Nicholas Culpeper places the red Rose under the dominion of Jupiter, the damask Rose under Venus, and gives the white Rose to Venus.

The legend of how Roses became red is the story of Venus and Adonis—the tears she shed for the loss of Adonis fell on the white Rose and turned it red. The Moss Rose was introduced from Holland in 1596. This is the Rose that shielded the angel of the flowers from the sun and was given a cloak of moss as a reward.

The Rose was plucked on Midsummer Eve and if it hadn't faded by the beginning of the next month, country maidens knew that their lovers were faithful.

It is the symbol of love and peace. 'What is more tranquil than a moss rose blowing in a green island, far from all man's knowing.'

SYLLABUB OF ROSES

Take the white of a new laid egg, beat well, and beat into it conserve of red Roses till the whole is the consistency of a thick cream.

This is excellent for a sore throat.

CLARET OF ROSES

For a strain

Boil a good handful of red Rose petals in a pint of claret for an hour. Then dip into it a piece of linen or flannel, apply to the strained part and keep it on all night, covering with oiled silk to keep in the moisture.

HONEY OF ROSES

Infuse 4 ounces of the dried buds of red Roses for six hours in a little distilled boiling water; mix 5 pounds of clarified honey into the strained liquor, and boil it to a syrup.

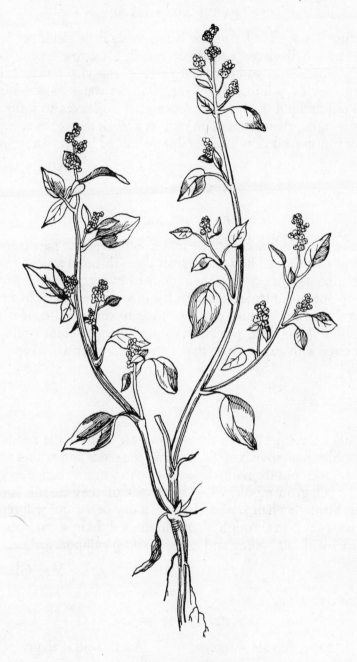

STINKING ARRACH

Chenopodium olidum

SYRUP OF ROSES

Infuse 3 pounds of damask Rose petals in a gallon of warm water in a well-glazed earthen pot with a narrow mouth for 8 hours, which stop so close that none of the virtue may exhale. When they have infused so long, heat the water again, squeeze them out and put in 3 pounds more of Rose leaves to infuse for 8 hours more; then press them out very hard; then to every quart of this infusion add 4 pounds of fine sugar and boil it to a syrup.

Mrs. Glasse

CONSERVE OF RED ROSES

Take Rosebuds and pick them: cut off the white part from the red and part the red flowers and sift them through a sieve to take out the seeds, then weigh them, and to every pound of flowers take 2½ pounds of loaf sugar: beat the flowers pretty fine in a stone mortar, then by degrees put the sugar to them and heat it very well, till it is well incorporated together; then put it into gallipots, tie it over with paper, over that a leather, and it will keep seven years.

CONSERVE OF HIPS

Gather the hips before they grow soft, cut off the heads and stalks. Slit them in halves, take out all the seeds and whites that is in them, then put them into an earthen pan and stir them every day or they will grow mouldy. Let them stand till they are soft enough to put through a hair sieve. They are a dry berry and will require pains to rub them through, then add the weight in sugar, mix well together without boiling and keep it in deep gallipots for use.

Mrs. Glasse

VINEGAR OF ROSES

Roses rouges   100 gr.   Acetic acid   20 gr.
White vinegar   980 gr.

Let the petals macerate for 10 days and then filter.

ELECTUARY OF ROSES

Take of sugar and the juice of red Roses, of each, $1\frac{1}{4}$ pounds, of the three sorts of Sanders, of each, 9 drachms. Let the juice be boiled with the sugar till thick, and then add the other ingredients in powder.

ROSE BUTTER

Put into a stone jar $\frac{1}{4}$ pound of butter and cover it entirely with Rose petals above and below and leave overnight in a cool place with the lid on. This butter can be used for spreading on very thin bread and after a few Rose petals have been placed on the top the bread should be delicately rolled, the Rose petals being allowed to protrude at either end.

VIPER'S BUGLOSS

The Bugloss buds of crimson hue
To azure flowers expand.
Like changeful banner, bright to view
By wild winds fann'd.

Botanical name	Echium vulgare (Linn.)
Natural order	Boraginaceae
Country names	To-day and To-morrow, Blueweed, Soldiers and Sailors
French name	Vipérin
German name	Gemeiner Natterkopf
Italian names	Erba delle vipere, Dente di cane
Spanish names	Buglose, Hierba de la Vibora
Dutch name	Slangenkruid
Russian name	Rumian
Under the dominion of	Jupiter, and in the sign Leo
Symbolises	Falsehood
Part used	Herb
Natural habitat	Great Britain

Viper's Bugloss can be used for the same purposes as its close relation the Borage. It is a cordial herb with demulcent and pectoral properties—very useful in feverish colds and chest complaints; and cooling and cheering, and decorative in wine cups and summer drinks.

Like the Borage, it has rough and prickly leaves, but its flowers range in colour from purple and pink to the palest mauve and blue, and are even sometimes white.

The seeds are formed like the head of a viper and it was from this resemblance that the plant became known as a cure for snake bites.

The word 'Bugloss' is derived from two Greek words meaning 'ox' and 'tongue'.

Viper's Bugloss grows in cornfields and on chalky cliffs and is found in the vicinity of Cambridge and on the cliffs of Dover, where so many flowers, rare and common, grow undisturbed.

WOODRUFF

The Woodruff is a bonny flower, her leaves are set like spurs,
About her stem, and honey sweet is every flower of hers.
Yet sweetest dried and laid aside unkist with linen white,
Or hung in bunches from the roof for winterly delight.

Botanical name	Asperula odorata (Linn.)
Natural order	Rubiaceae
Ancient names	Woodrova, Wuderove, Cordialis
Old French names	Muge-de-boys, Reine des Bois, Aspérule des champs
German names	Waldmeier, Mariengras, Ackermeier
Italian names	Piccolo mughetto, Regina dei boschi, Asperula dei campi, Raspello
Spanish name	Asperula
Under the dominion of	Mars
Symbolises	Modest worth
Part used	Herb
Natural habitat	Europe, including Great Britain

The wild Woodruff with its small white flower grows wild in many parts of England, especially in Kent and Surrey. It thrives in poor soil and likes shade. It does not even mind drippings from trees, and grows well under apple trees. It has a delightful scent which becomes stronger after it is dried. The scent is of the same type as Melilot, they both contain coumarin. The fresh flower imparts a delicious fragrance to wines and liqueurs, and in Germany is infused in a special May Day drink.

When dried, it has a very lasting scent and is most suitable for sachets to put amongst linen, for pot-pourri, and for keeping away moths. It was used for church festivals and it figures in the accounts of the church of St. Mary-at-Hill, London, for garlands on St. Barnabas Day.

The herb is one of the cordial plants. It cools and removes obstructions of the biliary duct. It makes a delicious tisane and the flowers can be infused either in water or wine.

Another species, the *Asperula cyandila*, which has no perfume, grows on chalky hills in England and is sometimes called Squinancywort. Culpeper recommended it for jaundice.

The Field Woodruff, *Asperula arvensis*, with its bright blue flowers and large berries, is much more rare and has only appeared in England recently. It had the reputation of growing in every country *but* England. The Common Woodruff is eaten by most animals and is particularly liked by horses, cows, sheep and goats.

WOODRUFF CAKES

Boil double-refined sugar candy high, and then strew in your Woodruff flowers and let them boil up once—then very lightly strew in a little double-refined sugar and as quickly as possible put into your little pans made of card and pricked full of holes at the bottom. When cold take out.

Chapter III

COOLING HERBS

COOLING HERBS

Chapter III

COOLING HERBS

The phrase 'Greater and Lesser cold seeds' runs through all medical pharmacopoeias and books on medicine belonging to the past centuries. There were four greater cold seeds and four lesser. The four greater were the seeds of Cucumber, Gourds, Melon and Cittral and the four lesser were seeds of Endive, Succory, Purslane and Lettuce. These were the cooling medicines of those days, and are still used for cooling the blood. There are a dozen or more others, of which the Violet is one of the most important. It is so pleasant in flavour that people are apt to deride its medicinal value as an old wives' tale.

Sarsaparilla is another valuable cooling medicine made popular as a summer drink at fairs, and among bank holiday crowds.

The Stonecrops of our rockeries are all cooling; and so is the canary's food, Groundsel.

The fern (Adder's Tongue) and a herb called Stinking Arrach come under the same category. Coolwort speaks for itself; the Docks, which cure the burns of the stinging nettle; the Horsetail, used for scouring pots and pans because it contains so much silica; the Ragwort, the Purslane, and the Beech tree, all cool blood that is overheated.

Melons of all kinds are the same, and in hot countries the melon carrier is as necessary as the water carrier; in fact the Melon is much safer than his unboiled water is.

ADDER'S TONGUE

For them that are with newts, or snakes or adders stung
He seeketh out a herb that is called adders tongue.

Michael Drayton

Botanical name	Ophioglossum vulgatum (Linn.)
Natural order	Filices
Country name	Christ's Spear
French name	Herbe sans couture, Langue de serpent
German name	Echte Natterzunge
Italian name	Lingua di serpe
Turkish name	Yilan dili
Under the dominion of	The Moon, in the sign of Cancer
Part used	Fern
Natural habitat	Great Britain

This curious fern, quite unlike any other and somewhat resembling the Arum plant in appearance, was once a famous cure for wounds.

It was cooked in oil, which was strained and became known as 'The Green oil of Charity'. A water was also distilled from it for inflamed eyes, and the juice of the leaves was drunk for internal wounds.

From its names it was undoubtedly also used to cure the sting of serpents.

GREEN OIL OF CHARITY

Boil 2 pounds of the leaves of the fern called Adder's Tongue with 1½ pounds of suet and ½ pint of linseed oil till crisp, then strain and use. Or the fern can be boiled in linseed oil alone, and then strained.

The American adder's tongue, Erythronium Americanum belongs to the Lily family and is used as medicine for Dropsy.

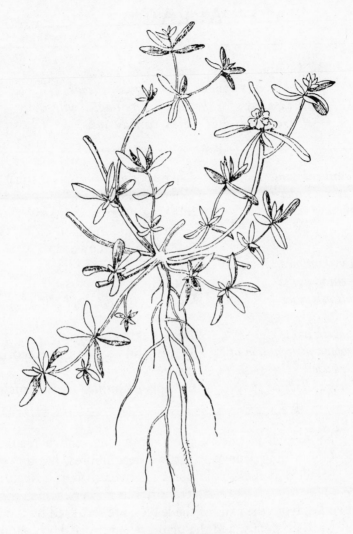

PURSLANE
Portulaca sativa

ARRACH

With vinegar, honey, and salt, the arrach
Made hot, and applied, cures a gouty attack;
Whilst its seeds for the jaundice if mingled with wine
—As Galen has said—are a remedy fine.

Botanical name	Chenopodium olidum (Linn.)
Natural order	Chenopodiaceae
Country names	Stinking Arrach, Stinking Mother-wort, Stinking Goosefoot, Goat's Arrach, Netchweed
French names	Vulvaire, Ansérine fétide
German name	Stinkender Gänsefuss
Italian names	Chenopodio fetido, Atriplice puzzolana
Turkish name	Fena kokulu raz ayaḡi
Under the dominion of	Venus, and in the sign of Scorpio
Part used	Herb
Natural habitat	Europe, including Great Britain

The Arrach is one of the Goosefoots, and a relation of Good King Henry. It grows near houses, has an odious smell, and the whole plant is covered with a dusty substance which gives it a greyish colour. The flowers, which grow in green spikes from the axils of the leaves, are fertilised by the wind as they have no petals, and the plant, when bruised, gives out the most objectionable scent.

As a nerve tonic the plant is unequalled, and it formed the basis of a famous anti-hysterical electuary which was a good deal prescribed in the eighties.

The plant can be cooked and eaten in the same way as Spinach, and need not even have water added, if it is placed in a screw jar and boiled in a saucepan of water.

The anti-spasmodic properties of Stinking Arrach are proverbial. The Garden Arrach and the Halberd-leaved Arrach are different varieties.

BEECH

Botanical name	Fagus sylvatica
Natural order	Corylaceae
Country names	Buche, Buke, Boke, Bog, Bok, Hetre
French name	Hêtre, Fonteau
German name	Buche
Italian name	Faggio
Spanish name	Haya
Under the dominion of	Saturn
Symbolises	Prosperity
Part used	Leaves, bark
Natural habitat	England, but cultivated in Europe, Palestine, Asia Minor, Japan

The Beech tree is one of the glories of England, which is its native country. Its beauty is hardly surpassed by any other tree and its salutary effect on the ground is so great that wherever it grows the soil becomes enriched and well drained. The leaves contain a large amount of potash and when they are shed they provide excellent food for the soil.

The trees often grow to an immense size, especially if they have been planted on chalk or sand, and some of the famous English Beeches, like the ones at Burnham and Penshurst, are said to be nearly a thousand years old.

The Beech tree has the reputation of being a non-conductor of lightning and Indians choose it to shelter under during a thunderstorm.

The wood of the tree is not particularly durable, but it makes excellent fires and is very much used for chairs and, on the Continent, for parquet flooring. It was used extensively for the panels of carriages in pre-motor days. Its early use was for books and some of the first books were written on Beech, hence its early English names of Buche, Buke, Boke.

In medicine, Beech leaves have a cooling effect on the blood and a tisane of them is good for the skin and the lungs. The tar from the tree is also used externally in skin complaints for its stimulating and antiseptic properties.

Beech nuts make excellent food for poultry and deer and also for pigs.

CUCUMBER

Cold herbes in the garden for agues that burn
That over strong heats to good temper may turn.

Tusser, 1573

Botanical name	Cucumis sativus (Linn.)
Natural order	Cucurbitaceae
Country name	Cowcumber
French name	Concombre
German names	Kukumer, Gurke
Italian names	Cetrinola, Cocomero
Spanish name	Cohombro à pepino
Under the dominion of	The Moon
Symbolises	Extent
Part used	Fruit
Natural habitat	East Indies

The Gourd tribe are conspicuous for their cooling, agreeable, pulp-like fruit which cools and nourishes at the same time.

The Cucumber has a history thousands of years old, just as the Melon and the other Gourds have. They come from the Orient where, because of their thirst-quenching powers, they are almost a necessity to the life of the people.

When the children of Israel left Egypt they missed Cucumbers and Melons as much as they missed Onions, and one of the things Moses had to contend with in the wilderness was the complaints of his people at losing the foods that they had become accustomed to and bewailed.

The Greeks and Romans were just as partial to them and we are told by Pliny that the Emperor Tiberius had them on his table every day. The Greek name for Cucumber was Siknos.

In England, though the cucumber ceased to be popular for several centuries, it was eaten in the time of Edward III and was introduced again in the reign of Henry VIII but not really grown in the vegetable garden till the latter end of the seventeenth century.

Cucumber seeds figured in medical pharmacopoeias of the eighteenth century as one of the four greater cold seeds, and were used for their cooling and anthelmintic properties.

The juice is universally used as a cosmetic, for whitening and softening the skin.

DOCKS

Out nettle; in dock;
Dock shall have a new smock.

Nettle out; dock in;
Dock remove the nettle sting.

Botanical names	(Yellow Dock) Rumex crispus; (Red Dock) Rumex aquaticus; (Great Water Dock) Rumex Hydrolapathum; (Sharp-pointed Dock) Rumex acetus; (Round-leaved dock) Rumex obtusifolius; (Patience Dock) Rumex alpinus; (Sharp Dock) Rumex conglomeratus
Natural order	Polygonaceae
French names	Herbe britannique, Oseille d'Eau, Patience aquatique
German names	Flussampfer, Wasserampfer, Alpenampfer
Italian names	Erba britannica, Romice acquatico
Spanish name	Bandana
Under the dominion of	Jupiter
Symbolises	Patience
Parts used	Root, leaves
Natural habitat	Europe, including Great Britain

The Docks as a family are excellent for the blood. Rhubarb is one of them, and the reason it has the bad reputation of causing rheumatism is because after it is eaten it begins to stir up the acid in the blood in order to neutralise it or get rid of it.

William Cole said: 'Rhubarb is so effectual for the liver that it is called the Life, Soul, Heart and treacle of the liver, purging from thence choler, phlegm and watery humours.'

Its sour taste is due to oxalic acid which is also found in a still greater degree in another Dock—the Sorrel.

Rhubarb was introduced from Russia and has been cultivated in England since 1573.

All the Docks make wholesome vegetables and pot herbs, and the Yellow Dock in particular is of great value in purifying the blood.

It contains, in common with other docks, a valuable alkaloid known as Rumicin, and also chrysophanic acid, both of which are used in the cure of liver complaints and scrofulous skin diseases.

The Red Dock has good tonic properties and is sometimes mixed with spinach in France and eaten as a vegetable.

The Great Water Dock is said to be Pliny's *Herba Britannica*. It derives its botanical name from three Teutonic words meaning to 'tighten a loose tooth'. It is used in Sweden as a tooth paste, to fasten loose teeth, and to cure spongy gums.

Monk's Rhubarb, *Rumex alpinus*, is a capital pot herb. As Herb Patience it grows sometimes in kitchen gardens, and if cooked with meat will make the toughest animal tender.

The ordinary wayside Dock or Round-leaved Dock, which only flourishes in good soil, is an excellent food for deer, and the leaves are used to wrap round butter to keep it cool.

The Sharp Dock makes a good greenish-brown dye.

It has always been said that meat cooks more quickly if Docks are boiled or cooked with it. Culpeper scathingly says about house-wives who refused to put Docks into their pots because it made their soup black in colour: 'pride and ignorance, a couple of monsters in their creation, preferring nicety before health'.

SYRUP OF YELLOW DOCK

Boil $\frac{1}{2}$ pound of the crushed root in a pint of syrup and take it in teaspoonful doses.

RAGWORT

Senecio Jacobæa

GROUNDSEL

With venerable locks the groundsel grows;
Hard care more quick than years white head-gear shows.

Botanical name	Senecio vulgaris (Linn.)
Natural order	Compositae
Country names	Ground Glutton, Grundy Swallow, Simson, Sention
French name	Seneçon
German names	Kreuzpflanz, Gemeines Greiskraut
Italian names	Senecione, Cardoncello, Erba Calderina
Spanish name	Hierbe Cana
Russian name	Krestownik
Dutch name	Krunkskruid
Under the dominion of	Venus
Part used	Herb
Natural habitat	Russian Asia. Europe, including Great Britain

Only nine of the large family of Senecios grow in England, three of which are used in herbal medicine—viz. the Golden Groundsel of America which is more usually called Life Root, a herb called Ragwort, and the Common Groundsel.

We associate the ordinary Groundsel with caged birds like canaries, because it is popularly believed to be the best green food for them. Actually Groundsel is an excellent medicine.

William Cole says: 'It has mixt faculties; it cooleth and moisteneth, and withall digesteth. It reduces swollen joints and sinews and has discutient properties in gravel and knots in the body.'

It is given to rabbits when they are pot-bellied to make them healthy.

In wars when old-fashioned weapons were used in fighting, it had a reputation for curing wounds caused by iron.

The plant is sometimes used in the same way as Ragwort as a poultice for painful limbs. A decoction of the herb cures chapped hands, and if the root is smelt when it is first taken out of the ground it will remove a headache.

The word senecio, from *senex*—an old man, probably refers to the white woolly heads of the flowers after the petals have fallen off.

HORSETAIL

Here horsetail round the water's edge
In bushy tufts is spread,
With rush and cutting leaves of sedge
That children learn to dread.

John Clare

Botanical name	Equisetum arvense
Natural order	Equisetaceae
Country names	Bottle Grass, Shave Grass, Pewterwort, Paddock pipes, Dutch Rushes
French names	Prêle des champs, Équisette
German names	Kannenkraut, Ackerschachtelhalm
Italian names	Equiseto, Rasperella
Spanish name	Equiseto
Russian name	Cherostak
Dutch name	Akkerig paardestaart
Under the dominion of	Saturn
Part used	Herb
Natural habitat	Great Britain, Northern regions

The horsetails, though allied to the ferns, are in a class by themselves.

They are a relic of the gigantic Horsetails of the Carboniferous age.

The Equisetums have no leaves. The stems, which spring from a root stock, are jointed and hollow, the joints terminating in toothed sheaves.

The stems bear a cone-like catkin head, round the outer margins of which are found the spores. Propagation is from the spores in the same way as in ferns and also in an entirely different way by subterranean stolons and tubers. They grow near water and at the edges of streams.

The stems contain so much silica that in the country they are often used for cleaning saucepans.

Galen recommended Horsetails for healing sinews, and today, on account of their silica, they are used to strengthen the lungs, and to strengthen generally.

Silica is grit, and without silica plants droop and can't hold their heads up; in the same way when the human body lacks silica there is a general loss of strength.

As Horsetail contains more silica than any other plant it is a good form in which to supply this mineral salt.

KIDNEYWORT

Venus challengeth the herb under Libra. The juice or distilled water being drank, is very effectual for all inflammations and unnatural heats.

Culpeper

Botanical name	Cotyledon umbilicus
Natural order	Crassulaceae
Country names	Wall Pennywort, Navelwort, Penny Pies
French names	Cotylet, Cotylier, Nombril de Vénus
German name	Venusnabelkraut
Italian names	Orecchio d'abate, Ombrellini, Cappelloni, Erba bellica, Sesselini
Turkish names	Yer, Göbeği, Saksi Güzeli
Under the dominion of	Venus, and in the sign of Libra
Part used	Herb
Natural habitat	Europe, including Great Britain

This plant is confined almost entirely to the west and southern parts of England where it is quite common and is generally seen covering stone walls. It is rather like a Nasturtium and very effective with its spikes of greenish-white drooping bell flowers and circular leaves. The plant is very succulent, and the juice of the leaves or an infusion of the leaves is cooling to the spleen and the liver, and also to the eyes.

It is an old-fashioned West Country cure for epilepsy, and also for stone in the kidney.

SARSAPARILLA

Smilax ornata

MELON

Whither is gone the boy?
He had pierced the melon's pulp,
And clothed with wax the wound;
And he had duly gone at morn,
And watched the ripening rind.
And now all joyfully he brings
The treasure now matured.

Botanical names	(Musk Melon) Cucumis melo; (Water Melon) Citrullus vulgaris; (Cantaloup Melon) Cucumis Cantalupensis; (Serpent Melon) Cucumis flexuosum; (Wild Melon) Cucumis chate
Natural order	Cucurbitaceae
French names	Melon, Pastèque
Italian names	Popone, Melone
Spanish name	Melón
Under the dominion of	The Moon
Symbolises	Bulk
Part used	Fruit, seeds
Natural habitat	South Asia from the Himalayas to Cape Comorin, Tropical Africa, East Indies

Melons are an Asiatic fruit with a long history behind them. In all tropical climates where they are cultivated they have become almost a necessity of life. The Melon carrier, like the water carrier, is one of the usual everyday street sights, and in countries where the water is often unsafe to drink, Melons satisfy thirst as well if not better, and provide nourishment at the same time.

The finest Melons grow at Khorassan and are often so big that it is only possible for a man to carry two or three.

In the East they grow in woods, where the camels feed on them, and they are planted in the fields and used by the Arabs as their staple food, or turned into a delicious drink by a process of piercing a hole in the partially ripe fruit and then stopping it with wax. After a few days of attention it has become ready for use and the Melon is then gathered, and the juice drunk.

The Cantaloup Melon is much valued for its flavour as a dessert fruit, and it takes its name from the district near Rome where it was first cultivated as a market fruit, having been brought there from Armenia.

Today most of the Cantaloup Melons come from France.

The seeds of the Melon with the seeds of the Pumpkin, the Gourd and the Cucumber, constitute the four greater cold seeds of medical pharmacopoeias of the eighteenth and nineteenth centuries. In America today various varieties of Gourds are cultivated, and they are not only extremely decorative but they make excellent soup purées and pies. Some of them, such as the Ohio Squash and the Golden Bush, will keep for six or eight months after being cut. In a hot summer they do quite well in England, and the decorative species such as Hercules Club and the Powder Horn Gourds make a magnificent show, but these are not fit for food.

The only example of the Gourd family that grows wild in England is the White Bryony.

PEAR

Botanical name	Pyrus communis
Natural order	Rosaceae
Country name	Pyrrie
French name	Poirier
German name	Birnbaum
Italian name	Pero
Spanish name	Pera
Under the dominion of	Venus
Symbolises	Affection, comfort
Parts used	Fruit, leaves
Natural habitat	Europe

Perry is much less drunk than cider, except in Normandy, but in the seventeenth century, when the Barland Pears were first planted in Herefordshire, there was as much demand for perry as for cider. Today, though three hundred years have elapsed, these trees or many of them are still bearing fruit. Perry was drunk by the Romans after eating mushrooms to antidote any poisonous mushrooms, and perry still remains the right drink to take with mushrooms.

It is made from a combination of wild and cultivated Pears. It is slightly more alcoholic than cider, and has cordial and stimulating properties which make it a wholesome drink.

Pears were very much grown in the old monasteries, where they knew the best way of planting and cultivating them. For a very long time it was thought that Pear trees would not yield fruit for many years after they had been planted, but it has now been found that if they are grafted on a quince stock they will fruit much more quickly. This is probably an old secret that has been rediscovered.

144

There were three different Pears known to Virgil—the Berga-mot, the Pounder and the Volemus. The Wardon Pear, because of its keeping well, has been grown since the time of Henry VI and Wardon pies take their name from the pies made with baked Pears at the Cistercian monastery of Wardon in Bedfordshire.

Pears are particularly suitable for those suffering from diabetes because they contain less sugar than most other fruit; and it has been discovered that water from a well sunk close to a wild Pear tree cures gout.

The only Pear tree that attracts bees and insects for cross ferti-lisation instead of depending on birds to disperse the seeds, is the *Pyrus Japonica*, and in consequence it has ceased to bear eating Pears and has developed a brilliant scarlet blossom which is grown as a decoration. In the language of flowers it symbolises 'Fairies' Fire'.

PURSLANE

Camerarius saith, that the distilled water took away the pains in the teeth when all other remedies failed.

Botanical names	(Green Purslane) Portulaca oleracea; (Golden Purslane) Portulaca sativa
Natural order	Caryophyllaceae
Country names	Pigweed, Garden Purslane
French name	Pourpier, Pourcellaine
German name	Gartenportulak
Italian name	Porcellana, Portulaca
Spanish name	Verdolaja
Under the dominion of	The Moon
Parts used	Herb, juice, seeds
Natural habitat	Europe, East and West Indies, China, Japan

The Purslanes are wholesome salad herbs growing rather like Samphire, with succulent leaves and a cooling juice that will subdue heat in any part of the body. The young shoots of either the green or the golden variety can be used, and also the seeds. They improve the appetite.

SUCCORY

Cichorium intybus

RAGWORT

Botanical name	Senecio Jacobaea (Linn.)
Natural order	Compositae
Country names	St. James-wort, Cankerwort, Staggerwort, Stammerwort, Stinking Willie, Jacoby Fleawort, Yellow Top, Ragweed
French names	Jacobée, Séneçon, Herbe de St. Jacques
German name	Jakob's Greiskraut
Italian name	Giacobea, Senecione di San Giacopo
Spanish name	Zuzón
Under the dominion of	Venus
Parts used	Leaves, flowers, juice
Natural habitat	Europe, including Great Britain

In Ireland the Ragwort is known as the Fairies' Horse and the fairies are said to gallop about at night on its golden blossoms.

The plant is closely allied to the Common Groundsel, has golden daisy-like flowers, and a smell of honey. The flowers give place, when they fade, to a hairy pappus or clock like the Dandelion. The plant is bitter and aromatic and the juice makes a cooling lotion for inflamed eyes.

The whole plant is sometimes used fresh as a poultice to relieve painful sciatica and is often very helpful.

The flowers yield a good yellow dye for wool, and the leaves a green dye.

The plant is poisonous to cattle, but was used as a cure for staggers in horses, to which some of its country names apply.

The plant contains lime and has been found useful in treating cancer.

SARSAPARILLA
SMILAX

*Crocus and smilax may be turn'd to flowers
and the curetes spring from bounteous showers.* Ovid

Botanical name	Smilax ornata
Natural order	Liliaceae
Country name	Red-bearded Sarsaparilla
French name	Salsepareille
German name	Sarsaparille
Italian name	Salsapariglia
Spanish name	Zarzaparilla
Part used	Root
Natural habitat	Central America, Costa Rica

The great value of Sarsaparilla as a cooling medicine for the blood has been taught us by the American Indians. Even in the days of Nicholas Culpeper the plant was unknown in herbal medicine, though it figures in the Herbal of (Sir) John Hill a century later.

The Jamaica Sarsaparilla, which acquired its prefix because it was imported via Jamaica, has the greatest reputation, but there are several varieties with similar properties, and the American Sarsaparilla, *Aralia nudicaulis*, which belongs to the order of *Aralias* and not to the lilies, is constantly used as a substitute or combined with the Jamaican variety. It has a pleasant aromatic spicy taste.

The wild Sarsaparilla (another *Aralia*) is also used in America by the Indians; and in India itself a plant known as Indian Sarsaparilla, *Hemidesmus Indica*, which belongs to an entirely different order, the *Asclepiadaceae*, is considered the best. It was not introduced into England till 1831. The popularity that Sarsaparilla acquired among the masses as a cooling drink has never died, and the Sarsaparilla cart is still to be seen among bank holiday crowds.

Sarsaparilla root is made into a wine, and a decoction of the root is good iced.

STONECROPS

The stonecrops spread a mantle bright
Like cloth of gold or silver white
Powder'd with spots of garnet red.

Bishop Mant

Botanical names	(Common Stonecrop) Sedum acre; (White Stonecrop) Sedum album; (Crooked Yellow Stonecrop) Sedum reflexum; (Orpine Stonecrop) Sedum Telephium
Natural order	Crassulaceae
Country names	(Orpine) Life Everlasting, (Common) Biting Stonecrop, Wall Pepper, Wall Ginger, Bird Bread
French names	(Common) Pain d'oiseau, Orpin brûlant, Trique madame, Poivre de muraille, (Orpine) Herbe aux 'Charpentiers'
German names	(Common) Maverpfeffer, (Orpine) Grosse Fetthenne
Italian names	(Common) Fabaria ardente, (Orpine) Telefio commune, Erba a Calli
Under the dominion of	The Moon
Symbolises	Tranquillity
Parts used	Herb, juice
Natural habitat	Europe, including Great Britain

The Sedums are among our most useful rock-garden plants. Their thick, succulent leaves, which make them of so much value in salads and cooling medicines, also add greatly to their decorative value; and the *Sedum spectabile*, with its lovely pale green leaves and flowers which become pink as the Summer advances is a great standby in the garden in the early Autumn, when the flowers come to perfection and are almost deep rose in colour.

The White Stonecrop is called by Culpeper, Small Houseleek in contradistinction to the ordinary Houseleek, to which a separate chapter has been devoted.

It is sometimes pickled like Samphire, and is excellent in salads, as is also the Crooked Yellow Stonecrop which, unlike the White Stonecrop, is indigenous to England.

The Common Stonecrop usually goes by the name of Biting Stonecrop. It is more potent than the other Stonecrops, and Nicholas Culpeper warns his readers against using it in medicine or in food.

Pliny recommended it to be placed in a black cloth underneath the pillow, to induce sleep in those who suffered from insomnia.

It is a quickly spreading plant and is often seen covering old roofs. When it is in flower in June and July, a mass of it is a very lovely sight, but it has a short flowering season. Country people sometimes call it 'Money' but the real Money is quite a different plant.

The *Sedum Telephium*, which is often called Orpine or Life Everlasting, is said to have been discovered by Telephus, the son of Hercules. It is the largest British species of Sedum. It probably contains mercury as well as sulphur, and for that reason has been recommended in the treatment of cancer. It has an ancient reputation as a magical herb, and its leaves used to be arranged in pairs, representing lovers, on the Eve of St. John. After shuffling the leaves, those that remained together augured well for the future happiness of the couples to whom they belonged.

SUCCORY

On Upland slopes the shepherds mark
The hour when to the dial true
Cichorium to the towering lark
Lifts her soft eyes serenely blue.

Botanical name	Cichorium intybus (Linn.)
Natural order	Compositae
Country names	Blue Succory, Chicory
French names	Chicorée, Barbe à Capucin
German name	Chicorie
Italian name	Cicoria
Spanish name	Achicoria
Russian name	Zikorifa
Dutch name	Suikerey
Under the dominion of	Jupiter
Symbolises	Frugality
Parts used	Herb, root
Natural habitat	Europe, including Ireland and England

This plant with its lovely blue star-like flowers is so much better known to country people as Succory that they do not recognise it as the Chicory with which French people adulterate their coffee. The flower opens so regularly at 7 a.m. and closes so precisely at noon that it has been placed by Linnæus in his floral clock.

The flowers die soon, so it is rare to see a stem that does not contain a few withered flowers, while others are beginning to come out, and this to some extent spoils its appearance. The lovely blue colour of the petals is changed into a brilliant red by the acid of ants, if placed on an ant-hill.

Pliny and Theophrastus say that the root was in great vogue in Egypt as a vegetable, and the Romans introduced it to Europe to

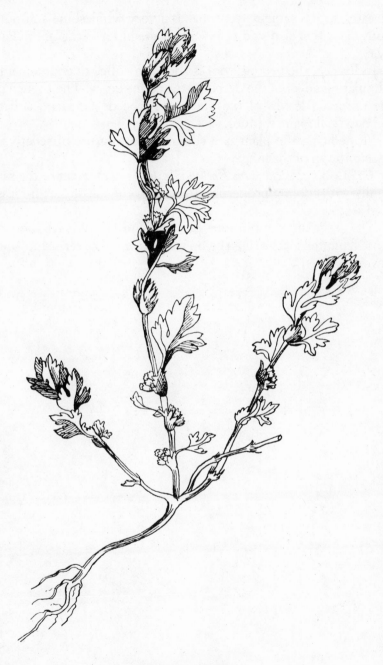

PARSLEY PIERT

Alchemilla arvensis

be eaten in the same way. It makes a very wholesome and nutritious dish. It is also said to be one of the bitter herbs of the Passover.

In France, the ground root is added to coffee to counteract the stimulating effect of the caffein in the coffee berry. The French call the unforced leaves of the Succory Barbe de Capucin, and the Belgians call them Witloof.

In medicine the plant is recommended as a useful sedative in consumption of the lungs.

The Endive, *Cichorium Endivia*, is another member of the same family with cooling properties. Its seeds were one of the four lesser cold seeds.

The seeds are used in love philtres, and legend says the plant arose from the tears of a girl who waited for her lover's ship which never returned.

VIOLET

*That which above all others, yields the sweetest smell in the air,
is the violet especially the white double violet, which comes twice a
year, about the middle of April, and about Bartholomew tide—Next
to that is the musk rose and then the strawberry leaves drying with a
most excellent cordial smell.*

Francis Bacon

Botanical name	Viola odorata (Linn.)
Natural order	Violaceae
French name	Violette
German name	Marzveilchen
Italian names	Mammola, Violetta
Spanish name	Violeta
Under the dominion of	Venus
Symbolises	Constancy
Parts used	Flowers, leaves, root
Natural habitat	Europe, including Great Britain

Jupiter was said to have created Violets upon the earth as food for Io, whom he had turned into a white heifer to protect her from the jealousy of Juno. The Greeks wore wreaths of Violets, and took Violets medicinally to induce sleep, to comfort the heart, to assuage anger and to cure dizziness and headaches. The Romans made it into wine. Since then Violets have been prescribed for every sort of complaint from epilepsy to pleurisy, but they have, in the last hundred years, been found of great value in subduing acute inflammation and have even been recommended with success in the treatment of cancer of the tongue. The leaves are so harmless that they can be used with safety; they contain glucosidal principles with definite antiseptic properties.

In salads they are decorative and wholesome, and the flowers can be used as well as the leaves. They give their colour as well as their flavour to liqueurs and conserves. The lovely colour of the syrup is maintained if it is not boiled. Violet sugar, under the name of Violet Pâté, was popular in the reign of Charles II, and Violet vinegar is used for headaches, and as a liniment for gouty joints.

FRANCIS BACON'S RECIPE

Take violets and infuse a good pugil in a quart of vinegar, let them stand three quarters of an hour and take them forth and repeat the infusion with like quantity of violets seven times and it will make a vinegar so fresh of flower, as if a twelve months after it be brought you in a saucer, you shall smell it before it comes to you.

Note: It smelleth more perfectly of the flower a good while after than at first.

A useful laxative for children

VIOLET SYRUP

Infuse 2 ounces of Violets in 1 pint of boiling water and leave it 12 hours in a low heat; mix it well into 1 pound of sugar in caramel and bring it to caramel.

SYRUP OF VIOLETS

Pour $2\frac{1}{2}$ pints of boiling water over 1 pound of freshly picked sweet Violets in a china jug and leave it to infuse for 24 hours. Then strain it through muslin and add double its weight of white loaf sugar and stir into a syrup without allowing it to boil.

Chapter IV

REFRESHING HERBS

REFRESHING HERBS

Chapter IV

REFRESHING HERBS

In France 'tisane rafraîchissante' is a popular blend of herbs for thirsty people, whether the thirst is induced by fever or a hot day.

These 'herbs' are usually the products of fruit trees, like the Lemon, the Lime, the Orange, the Apple, the Pomegranate or the Tamarind; but there are other plants which have the same properties of alleviating thirst, and these are included in this chapter with the fruit trees I have mentioned.

It is acids such as citric acid, tannic acid, tartaric acid, malic acid and others that give to these plants their particular refreshing properties; but it is probably something else as well as a particular combination of acids and salts, because all plants containing these acids cannot be classed under this head.

Hesperidin is a constituent of both Lemon and Orange, in addition to citric acid. The Pomegranate has a special acid of its own known as Punico-tannic acid. Tamarinds contain tartaric, citric and malic acids. Red Currants contain citric and malic acids. The leaves of the Houseleek have malic acid combined with lime, Sorrel has tartaric and tannic acid but its peculiar sourness is due to oxalate of potash.

All refreshing herbs are used in fevers, but all fever herbs do not come under the heading of 'Herbes Rafraîchissantes'. Some of the herbs used in fevers have mucilaginous and pectoral properties, others are diaphoretic and tonic—Viper's Bugloss, Balm of Gilead, Peruvian Bark, Maidenhair and Liquorice are none of them refreshing, but they all have febrifuge properties of some kind.

The refrigerant herbs are few in number compared with the number of herbs that come under other heads. The Lemon will always take the first place, principally for its thirst-quenching powers, but also because it is as essential in cooking as the onion.

Sydney Smith uttered a *cri de cœur* when he wrote to a friend in London, from a remote country living, that he was living 'ten miles from a lemon'.

APPLE

Eat an apple going to bed
Make the doctor beg his bread.

Eat an apple going to bed
Knock the doctor on the head.

Botanical name	Pyrus Malus
Natural order	Rosaceae
French name	Pommier
German name	Apfelbaum
Italian names	Pomo, Melo
Spanish name	Manzana
Symbolises	Temptation
Parts used	Fruit, bark
Country of origin	Europe and temperate regions of the Northern Hemisphere

Actually all Apple trees are descended from the wild Crab by having been grafted on its stock. There are two varieties of the crab, one has a smooth calyx tube and the other a downy one, and the smooth one, *Pyrus acuba*, was adopted by the French for their cider trees. This little French cider Apple goes by the name of Pomme d'appui, and there are several French restaurants called after it, such as the restaurant at Malmaison.

The Custard, the Nonpareil, the Oslin and the Arbroath are among the very earliest Apples cultivated in England and most of them came from France. Pippins were introduced from France in the reign of Henry VIII and were so called because they grew from seed instead of being grafted.

The only Apple of English origin is the Reinette d'Angleterre, which was first grown in Lord Zouch's garden at Parham in Sussex. It was given to Catherine of Russia who introduced it from England.

The cider orchards of Herefordshire were planted at the same time as the perry orchards in the reign of Charles I, and are still in existence.

The life of the Apple tree, however, cannot compare with that of the Pear but it bears fruit earlier.

Chemically, the fruit contains chlorophyll, phosphorus, albumen, sugar, gum, lime, and malic and gallic acids. It is very easily digested, and its acids neutralise with the acids in the body and leave an alkaline deposit, so that the old saying about an apple a day keeping the doctor away is a true saying and can be carried further, because it keeps the dentist away as well—the juice having a most beneficial action on the teeth and the mouth.

In cider counties like Herefordshire and Devonshire calculus complaints are almost unknown.

There are many legends about the Apple tree, and the wassailing of the Apple trees on New Year's Day is an old pagan custom which goes back many hundreds of years and is still practised in remote parts of the country. It was a deeply rooted belief that until the Apple trees had been toasted they would not bear fruit.

The Apple was the food and medicine of the gods, and in Jewish, classical and northern literature it is used symbolically as the fruit of the tree of knowledge: the Apple of Eden—the golden Apples of the Hesperides—the Apple that Paris awarded to Helen.

APPLE CANDY

Bake half a dozen large cooking Apples and after removing the skins, pass them through a sieve and beat into them half a pound of sifted sugar, or more if too sour. Beat well, and then add the white of an egg. Then cover a board with a linen cloth and spread the Apple purée over it about half an inch thick and leave overnight in a half-warm oven. Cut into squares the next day and powder with sugar.

JELLY OF CRAB APPLES

To each pound of Crab Apples add six cloves and half a salt-spoonful of ginger and cook together till the fruit is soft.

Then strain and boil again with $\frac{3}{4}$ pound of sugar to each pint of strained liquid adding the sugar just before the liquid boils.

Boil till it jellies, and pot.

PELLITORY OF THE WALL
Parietaria officinalis

CATMINT

Botanical name	Nepeta cataria (Linn.)
Natural order	Labiatae
Country names	Catnep, Catnip
French name	Chataire
German name	Nept
Italian name	Cataria
Spanish name	Calaminta
Under the dominion of	Venus
Parts used	Herb, leaves
Natural habitat	Europe, including Great Britain, North America, temperate Asia

The Catmint is known to all garden lovers as one of the most useful herbaceous edging plants. When it first comes out in June its lovely deep lilac sprays are almost startling in their beauty, especially as an edging to a long border. The plant grows wild in most parts of England, particularly the south, and prefers chalky or gravelly soil. The wild flowers are usually almost white, with corollas dotted with crimson, and the leaves have the downy appearance that they have when cultivated. The appearance of the greyish plant is as if it had been covered with dust. The scent is strongly aromatic.

A tisane of Catmint is not unlike Mint tea, and in France the young shoots are used in salads and in the flavouring of dishes.

Catmint tea is excellent in feverish colds drunk hot on going to bed and conserve of Catmint is a cure for nightmare. The tea also induces peaceful sleep.

Strip the flowers from their stems, weigh them and to every pound of the flowers take 2 pounds of loaf sugar. Crush it, and beat it gradually into the flowers in a mortar. When thoroughly incorporated, pot and tie down for use.

CHICKWEED

The chickweed cures the heat that in the face doth rise,
For physic some agree he inwardly applies.

Michael Drayton

Botanical name	Stellaria media
Natural order	Caryophyllaceae
Country names	Chickweed, Starweed
French names	Stellaire, Langue d'oiseau, Mouron blanc
German name	Augentrosgräs, Vogelmiere
Italian names	Stellaria, Budelina, Paperina, Centone
Turkish names	Cam otu, Serçe dili
Under the dominion of	Moon
Symbolises	Rendezvous
Part used	Herb
Natural habitat	Nearly all over the world

The Chickweed provides food for little birds all over the world.

What is not nearly so well-known is that it is so nutritious —on account of its abundance of potash salts—that if it is given to consumptive people and children who suffer from malnutrition, they very quickly gain strength. It is also a rheumatic medicine of great potency, the indication for its use being shifting pains and enlarged finger joints. It was used at one time in cramps and palsy. If it is taken internally in large doses it produces a static condition, which points to it as a cure for paralysis if taken in minute doses.

The principles of Chickweed are two; an oil and an acid. For skin diseases it can be taken internally or used externally. It is excellent for asthma, for wounds, for peritonitis, and for all internal inflammation.

The young stems can be cooked and eaten in the same way as Spinach. It makes a very wholesome vegetable.

The starlike flowers of the Chickweed open at nine in fine weather and remain open for twelve hours. The plant is closely allied to the Stitchworts.

CURRANTS—WHITE, RED, AND BLACK

The currant bushes spicy smell
Homely and honest, likes me well,
And while on strawberries I feast,
And raspberries the sun hath kissed.

Katherine Tynan Hinkson

Botanical names	Ribes Alba, nigrum, rubrum (Linn.)
Natural order	Saxifragaceae
Country names	Quinsy Berries, Squinancy Berries, Wineberry, Garnetberry, Gayles
French name	Groseiller
German names	Johannisbeere, Schwarzeribsel
Italian name	Ribes grossularia
Spanish names	Grosellero, Grosella
Under the dominion of	Jupiter
Symbolises	Thy frown will kill me
Parts used	Fruit, leaves, bark, root
Natural habitat	Russia, Siberia, North of Great Britain, Appenines, Alps

Currants do not appear to have been cultivated by the Anglo-Saxons or the Normans. The Black Currant grows wild in the northern parts of England and in Scotland but is considered to be indigenous only in Yorkshire and the Lake District. The acids which the fruit contains make it of great use in feverish complaints and in coughs and colds. It has a refreshing quality which makes it even more valuable than the Red or the White Currant. The leaves of the Black Currant secrete an aromatic fluid, and, either dried or fresh, they make a very pleasant substitute for ordinary tea.

The fruit makes a good rob and a good wine, and the French make from it an excellent liqueur called Cassis.

ALEXANDERS

Smyrnium olusatrum

Red Currants and White Currants also have refrigerant properties and make excellent wine. In the north of England the Red Currant is called Wineberry. They contain pectin and malic and citric acids which makes them cooling in drinks in health or in sickness. Red Currant jelly is the traditional accompaniment to venison, saddle of mutton, game and veal. It also is one of the ingredients of Cumberland Sauce. Red Currants and Raspberries are excellent cooked together, and Red Currant wine is the right thing to drink with Cherry pie, as we know by the nursery rhyme.

White Currants are more exotic, and they are usually kept for dessert, or for making into a *compote de luxe* such as we associate with Bar-le-Duc.

In the Alps Red Currants grow wild and are very plentiful; in the north of England they are also found but not so abundantly.

CASSIS PUNCH

Mix together a pint of cold tea and half a pint of Black Currant syrup made from fresh Black Currants and sugar. The Currants should be lightly pressed through a sieve. Add before serving two bottles of ginger beer and a small glass of the cassis liqueur.

BLACK CURRANT SHRUB

To each pint of Black Currants allow a pound of loaf sugar. Remove the stems and wash the fruit and put into a large jar with the sugar.

Cover the jar and place it in a saucepan of hot water and boil for 2 hours. Then strain through a jelly bag and boil the syrup for 10 minutes.

Pour into bottles and cork tightly.

GOOSEBERRY

Nor chestnuts shall be wanting to your food,
Nor garden fruits, nor wildings of the wood.

Dryden

Botanical name	Ribes grossularia
Natural order	Grossulariaceae
Country names	Feverberry, Goosegogs, Feaberry, Honeyblobs, Carberry Fea
French names	Groseille verte, Groyet
German names	Stachelbeere, Ribsel
Italian name	Grossularia rossa
Spanish name	Grosellero
Under the dominion of	Venus
Symbolises	Anticipation
Parts used	Fruit, leaves
Natural habitat	Central and Northern Europe, Morocco

Gooseberries are such a useful corrective of rich foods, and on account of their citric acid are so refreshing, that, next to the Lemon, they hold a very important place in traditional cookery. Gooseberry sauce is eaten with mackerel; Gooseberry jam is indispensable in the kitchen, in trifles, as sauce, for puddings, pies and chutneys. The leaves are very good in salads, and the yellow Gooseberries are delicious dessert and make a really excellent wine.

GOOSEBERRY WINE

Gather the Gooseberries in dry weather when they are only partially ripe. Put them into a tub and bruise them with a wooden mallet—then take a horse-hair cloth and press them as much as possible without breaking the seeds. When all the juice has been

171

pressed out, add to every gallon of Gooseberries 3 pounds of loaf sugar. Stir together till the sugar is dissolved, then fill a cask with the mixture. It must be entirely filled. If 10 gallons is the amount it must stand a fortnight—if 20 gallons, 5 weeks. Set it in a cool place, then draw it off the lees, clear the vessel of the lees, and put in the clear liquor again. If it be a 10-gallon cask, let it stand 3 months; if a 20-gallon, 4 months, then bottle it.

HOUSELEEK

The clay built wall with woodbine twisted o'er,
The houseleek clustering green above the door.

Botanical name	Sempervivum tectorum (Linn.)
Natural order	Crassulaceae
Country names	Sengreen, Jupiter's Beard, Bullock's Eye, Thor's Beard, Ayegreen
French name	Joubarbe des toits
German names	Donnersbart, Hauswurz
Italian name	Semprevivo
Under the dominion of	Jupiter
Symbolises	Vivacity, Domestic industry
Part used	Fresh leaves
Natural habitat	Central and Southern Europe and the Greek islands

From time immemorial a Houseleek was planted above the porch of a house as a protection against lightning; and this is why, though the plant is not indigenous to England, it is so common everywhere throughout England and Scotland. It has been grown on porches, or, where there was no porch, on the roofs themselves. The Romans grew it in vases in front of their houses.

The word 'houseleek' means house plant; 'leac' being an Anglo-Saxon word for plant. Sempervivum—'never dying', refers to its vitality and tenacity of life. The leaves are so succulent and full of mucilage that it is almost impossible to kill it. For this reason the Greeks used it as an aphrodisiac, and as a protection against witchcraft.

In medicine, either taken internally or used externally, it is extremely useful in skin diseases, inflamed eyes, corns, warts, cuts, ulcers, shingles, burns and scalds, and enlarged glands.

It is sometimes boiled in milk and the strained milk is given in fevers, and the juice is mixed with cream and made into a paste for applying to erysipelas. It takes away the pain of bee stings and mosquito bites.

The Dutch use the leaves in salads. The plant was dedicated to Jupiter, under whose dominion it is.

For other sedums *see* Stonecrops.

LEMON

Into an oval form the citrons rolled
Beneath thick coats their juicy pulp unfold.
For some the palate feels a poignant smart,
Which, though they wound the tongue, yet heal the heart.

Botanical name	Citrus limonum (Risso)
Natural order	Rutaceae
French names	Limonier, Citronnier
German name	Limonenbaum
Italian names	Limone, Citrino
Spanish name	Limón
Symbolises	Zest
Parts used	Rind, juice, oil
Natural habitat	Northern India, Persia, cultivated in the countries bordering the Mediterranean

In the language of flowers the Lemon's symbol is Zest, because Zest actually signifies a strip of Lemon peel which is added to drinks to flavour them. We can hardly exaggerate the importance of Lemon in cooking and in medicine. The salts and acids it contains are not only powerfully antiscorbutic but of the greatest assistance to the digestion of the bile. A squeeze of Lemon or a small piece of the rind in cooking will make a dish that would otherwise be sickly, deliciously refreshing.

It is the refreshing power of the Lemon that makes it so welcome, not only in fevers but in all illnesses. Every ounce of the juice contains about forty grains of citric acid. The juice of a Lemon mixed with a saltspoonful of bicarbonate of soda will almost immediately relieve the worst attack of indigestion. Lemon juice not only liquifies bile but has a sedative effect on the nerves of the heart, and its continuous use has been known to soften arteries that were beginning to harden. It also contains a reducing sugar which keeps down weight.

The rind of the Lemon gives an even better flavour in cooking than the juice, though both are needed in many dishes. Barley water is never as good in flavour as it is when cooked with the rind of a Lemon.

The Lemon tree came originally from Persia, and was cultivated first in Greece and then in Italy. Messina is now the centre of the industry and Messina Lemons are considered the best.

Lemon is very much used in perfumes, and a scent which has a Lemon flavour never grows stale, and is pleasing to men as well as to women.

A special variety of the Lemon (for which a large price is paid to secure a perfect example) is handed round at the Jewish Feast of Tabernacles in accordance with the Mosaic Law, for the congregation to smell and to praise God for the sweet odours He has given to man.

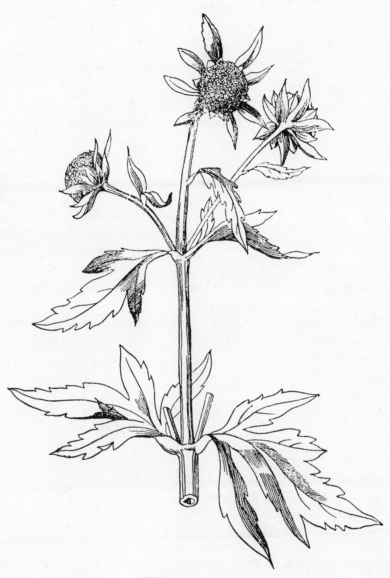

BUR MARIGOLD

Bidens tripartita

MINTS

Botanical name	Mentha viridis
Natural order	Labiatae
Country names	Spearmint, Heartmint, Mackerel Mint, Sage of Bethlehem, Lamb Mint, Spire Mint, Garden Mint, Our Lady's Mint
French names	Menthe de Notre Dame, Menthe verte
German names	Frauenmussatze, Grüne Rossmünze
Italian names	Erba Santa Maria, Menta verde
Spanish name	Menta
Under the dominion of	Venus
Symbolises	Virtue
Parts used	Herb, leaves, oil
Natural habitat	Mediterranean countries

The Mints were not actually introduced into England until the Roman conquest; but they grow better and smell sweeter in England than they do anywhere else.

The Mint that we grow in gardens for Mint sauce is the Spearmint, and the Mint that we call Peppermint is the *Mentha piperita* which used to be cultivated almost exclusively at Mitcham, from which it takes its commercial name. Peppermint is cultivated in the districts where Lavender is grown, and the same stills are used for both, the Peppermint harvest preceding the Lavender. English Peppermint oil is far superior to that of any other country. The Mints like our damp climate, and it brings out the aromatic camphor-like scent that is so pronounced in the Peppermint.

Spearmint is used chiefly as a flavouring for cocktails and wine cups, and to make Mint sauce. It is more grown in the kitchen garden than other varieties; though the *Mentha cardiaca* and the *Mentha crispa* are sometimes cultivated for culinary purposes.

The Greeks and the Romans used Spearmint as a relish to meat dishes, and it is mentioned by several of their writers, including Pliny. It was said to represent the maiden Pluto loved. Pliny says of it: 'As for the garden mint, the very smell of it alone recovers and refreshes our spirits as the taste stirs up the appetite for meat, which is the reason that it is so general in our acid sauces where we are accustomed to dip our meat.'

The Horsemint is a wild Mint of a coarser type, but it belongs to the same family. There was a tradition in the seventeenth century that if it were given to a wounded man he would never recover.

Other varieties are the round-leaved Mint which is generally known as Egyptian Mint, and the Water Mints.

In the rock garden we have the Bergamot Mint, *Mentha citrata*, which has a very pleasant Lemon scent and taste, and the miniature Requieni which makes a beautiful blue carpet in July.

In medicine, *Mentha Pulegium* is the popular Pennyroyal—a country remedy for coughs and colds, said by some to be the Dictannus of the ancients; Virgil tells us that deer who had been hurt sought it out to cure their wounds.

Peppermint also has a reputation in medicine, and the oil is considered one of the best aids to a weak digestion, and one of the pleasantest. It is also used to keep away rats.

All the Mints have cordial and carminative properties, and are also extremely refreshing. Their reviving power makes them particularly suitable for summer cups, either wine or fruit.

COMPOUND INFUSION OF SPEARMINT

Take of the leaves of Spearmint dried, 2 drachms; boiling water, as much as will afford 6 ounces of the infusion, when filtered. Digest for half an hour in a covered vessel; strain the liquor when cold, and then add of double refined sugar, 2 drachms; oil of Spearmint, 3 drops dissolved in Compound Tinctum of Cardamoms half an ounce. Mix.

This is stimulating and diaphoretic and very agreeable.

PEPPERMINT WATER

Take of the herb of Peppermint, dried, 1½ pounds; water, as much as is sufficient to prevent burning. Distil off 1 gallon. This will prevent sickness. A wineglassful can be taken 3 times a day.

For spirit of Peppermint, a gallon of proof spirit is used in addition to the water, and a gallon is distilled off.

CRYSTALLISED MINT LEAVES

Wipe the fresh Mint leaves, remove from the stems, brush each leaf with white of egg stiffly beaten. Then dip each leaf in granulated sugar to which a few drops of oil of Spearmint have been added.

Place the leaves closely together on a tray, cover them with waxed paper, and leave them in a very slow oven till dry.

The process must be repeated if the leaves are not sufficiently covered with sugar.

GREEN PEPPERMINT JELLY

Add to a quart of sweetened calf's foot jelly a few drops of Mitcham Peppermint essence and a liqueur glass of crême de menthe and you will have when cold and turned out a lovely bright emerald jelly.

FRESH MINT PUNCH

Crush 12 fresh sprigs of Mint; squeeze the juice of 6 oranges and 3 lemons over them and add ¾ cup of white sugar. Stir well— put a lump of ice in punch bowl, pour the mixture over, add 1 pint of cider, 1½ quarts of sugar ale, and green colouring matter.

MULBERRY

The mulberry found its former whiteness fled,
And ripening, saddened into dusky red.

Botanical name	Morus nigra (Linn.)
Natural order	Artocapaceae
Other names	Common Mulberry, Black Mulberry
French name	Mûrier
German name	Maulbeerbaum
Italian names	Moro, Gelso
Spanish name	Moreas
Under the dominion of	Mercury
Symbolises	(white) Wisdom, (black) I shall not survive you
Parts used	Fruit, juice, leaves
Natural habitat	Northern Asia Minor, Armenia, Southern Caucasus as far as Persia

The black Mulberry tree with its luscious fruit, regal in colour, and juicy almost beyond other fruit, was dedicated to Minerva.

The legend of how it was changed from the Chinese white Mulberry into the black is told by Ovid: Pyramus and Thisbe were slain under its branches, and the fruit became dark in colour through absorbing their blood. The Mulberry tree was probably introduced from Persia, but from the earliest times it has been held in the greatest esteem in the countries of the East, and in Greece, Rome and Italy, as we know from such chroniclers as Virgil, Horace, Ovid and Pliny.

The Mulberry was not introduced into England till 1548 when the first tree was planted in the Duke of Northumberland's garden at Syon House; it is still alive.

Mulberries are very slow in growth and live to a great age.

Many of the famous English Mulberry trees date from the reign of James I, when they were planted systematically throughout the country to encourage the cultivation of the silk worm which feeds on the tree. The Mulberry is the last fruit to bud and so it avoids the spring frosts and has been called in consequence the wisest of fruit trees.

The Mulberry grows easily in England, especially in the southern counties, once it has become established; but the ground needs constant hoeing.

There is a famous Mulberry tree in Hogarth's garden at Chiswick, in the Chapter's garden at Canterbury, and in the Dean's garden at Winchester.

The fruit has a great and an ancient reputation in medicine. It contains glucose abundantly as well as citric and malic acids. The Romans prescribed it for diseases of the throat and the windpipe.

The traditional way to eat Mulberries is as an *hors-d'œuvre*, though according to the poet Francis they were at one time more popular as dessert.

> *He shall with vigour bear the summer's heat,*
> *Who after dinner, shall be sure to eat*
> *His mulberries of blackest, ripest dye*
> *And gathered ere the morning sun arise.*

TO PRESERVE MULBERRIES WHOLE

Set some Mulberries over the fire in a skillet and draw from them a pint of juice, when it is strained; then take 3 pounds of sugar beaten very fine, wet the sugar with the pint of juice; boil your sugar and skim it and put in 2 pounds of ripe Mulberries, letting them stand in the syrup till they are thoroughly warm; then set them on the fire and let them boil very gently: do them but half enough so put them by in the syrup till next day; then boil them gently again and when the syrup is pretty thick and will stand in a round drop when it is cold, they are enough. Put all together in a gallipot for use.

BUTCHER'S BROOM

Ruscus aculeatus

ORANGE

'Mid orange boughs of polished green,
With glowing fruit, and flowers between
Of purest white.

Charlotte Smith

Botanical name	Bitter Citrus vulgaris, var. Bigaradia; Sweet Citrus Aurantium (Linn.) var. dulcis.
Natural order	Rutaceae
Other names	Seville Orange, Portugal Orange, China Orange
French names	Oranger, Bigaradier, Bergamotier
German names	Orangenbaum, Bergamottenzitrone
Italian names	Arancio, Melarancio, Bergamotta
Spanish name	Naranja
Symbolises	Generosity, Chastity
Parts used	Leaves, fruit, flowers, peel, oil
Natural habitat	India, China, Spain, Madeira

The Orange needs a tropical climate to ripen the fruit thoroughly. It came to us originally from India, and, though most of the imported Oranges reach us now from Spain and Portugal, it was quite unknown to the Spaniards until the sixteenth century. Before that time, it was generally believed that the Orange was the special reward of the Mahommedans and must not be eaten by individuals of other religious sects unless they intended to become Mahommedans.

The China Orange contains the most juice, and this is the variety which is cultivated in the South of Europe. Medicinally, the bitter Seville Orange is valued most. Both the leaves and the flowers are used in convulsive complaints in the form of a tisane. Orange buds make a delicious tea to take at night to induce sleep, and confection of bitter Orange peel has a sedative effect on the digestive organs.

All Oranges contain a reducing sugar, and the fresh juice assists in keeping down weight and in counteracting an acid condition.

The fruit is antiseptic, and for this reason in the days when plagues spread rapidly, an Orange stuffed with cloves was carried by nearly everyone as a pomander to ward off infection.

The oil extracted from Orange flowers is called Oil of Neroli and is extremely useful in making perfumes. Eau de Cologne and other refreshing scents are made from it. Oil of petit grain is made from the leaves, and Orange flower water from the flowers after the oil has been extracted. It is used in cooking and flavouring. A few drops added to an infusion of China tea often greatly improves its flavour. Orange peel is crystallised and used in puddings, and in China and Greece the tiny green Oranges that drop from the trees are preserved in syrup and eaten as dessert.

The Arabs restore the colour to grey hair with an Orange cut in half and dried and then soaked in oil for a month or longer. Oranges and Lemons have been coupled for us in the old nursery rhyme, and though they do not quite replace each other, they are both universally necessary for their antiscorbutic properties, and their thirst-quenching powers. As John Evelyn says: 'The orange sharpens appetite, exceedingly refreshes and resists putrefaction.'

PARSLEY PIERT

It is a good salad herb. The whole plant is to be used, and it is best when gathered fresh.

Nicholas Culpeper

Botanical name	Alchemilla arvensis
Natural order	Rosaceae
Country names	Parsley Breakstone, Parsley Pierce-stone, Field Lady's Mantle, Honewort
French names	Alchimille des champs, Perce-pierre
German names	Feldsinau, Steinbrech
Italian names	Spaccapietra, Erba ventaglina piccola
Turkish name	Ova arslan pençesi
Part used	Herb
Natural habitat	Europe, including Great Britain, North Africa

The Parsley Piert belongs to the same family as the Lady's Mantle, and is not in any way allied to the garden Parsley with which we are so much more familiar.

The Parsley Piert grows on the tops of walls and in waste places and prefers a sandy, moist soil. It used to be common on Hampstead Heath and in the old Tothill fields. It is easy to recognise because the leaves are so arranged that they appear to be lying on the ground and the foot stalks are so covered with leaves that they are hardly visible. The leaves are broad and deeply dented round the edge—the flowers are almost too small to be perceptible. It is an old remedy for dissolving stones, and its country names, Parsley Breakstone and Parsley Piercestone, are a testimony to this.

An old way of taking the herb medicinally was as an infusion in sherry; or it was used in salads, which is perhaps the best use to make of it; or pickled in the same way as samphire and eaten with cold meats.

PELLITORY OF THE WALL

*. . . A good old woman did cure me with sodden ale and pellitorie
o' the wall.*

Ben Jonson

Botanical name	Parietaria officinalis (Linn.)
Natural order	Urticaceae
Country name	Lichwort
French name	Pariétaire
German name	Glaskraut
Italian names	Parietaria, Erba da vetro
Spanish name	Yerba del Muro
Polish name	Noc-i-Dyien
Dutch name	Glaskruid
Under the dominion of	Mercury
Part used	Herb
Natural habitat	Europe, including Great Britain

Pellitory of the Wall, so called because it is found growing on
old walls, is a bushy plant with stalkless, purplish, hairy
flowers growing from the axils of narrow, hairy leaves. It is
in flower all through the summer. The stems are a brownish red,
and the filaments of the stamens are jointed and so brittle that the
moment they are touched they spring and scatter the pollen.

The plant is an old cure for dropsy, and was also used for dissolving stone. It contains a large supply of nitre and will ignite
very easily.

The old way of taking it was either in the form of an electuary
made with honey, or a water was distilled from it and given medicinally. As a poultice it was mixed with mallows and boiled in
wine with wheat bran and bean flour. Partridges feed on the plant.

Pellitory of Spain is an altogether different plant and is one of
the pyrethrums. It is used to keep away mosquitoes and to cure
their bites. If the root is taken internally, it produces great warmth,
and it is sometimes nibbled to cure toothache or to create saliva.
It has been known to help a paralysed tongue.

PINEAPPLE

Oft in humble station dwells
Unboastful worth, above fastidious pomp,
Witness, thou best Anana, thou the prior
Of vegetable life, beyond what'er
The poets imaged in the golden age.
Quick let me strip thee of thy tufty coat,
Spread thy ambrosial stores, and feast with love!

James Thomson

Botanical name	Ananas sativus
Natural order	Bronxhiaceae
Other names	Ananas, Bronchia Ananas
French name	Ananas
German names	Ananas, Fichtenapfel
Italian name	Ananasso ordinario
Spanish name	Piña
Symbolises	Perfection
Parts used	Fruit, juice
Natural habitat	South America, West Indies. Cultivated in tropical Asia and Africa

In its wild state the Pineapple is found near the seashore, growing in the sand. Though it has been introduced into the Malay Archipelago and into tropical Asia and Africa, it grows in these countries in wonderful profusion and the fruit acquires an immense size and an excellent flavour; but it favours most sandy plains formed by the receding of the sea where nothing else will grow and where the temperature hardly varies from 70° to 80°. In these places the fruit with its refreshing, cooling juice must be a gift from heaven.

Pineapples were rare in England until a hundred years ago, but are now grown fairly successfully, at great expense. They can never, however, equal those of tropical climates.

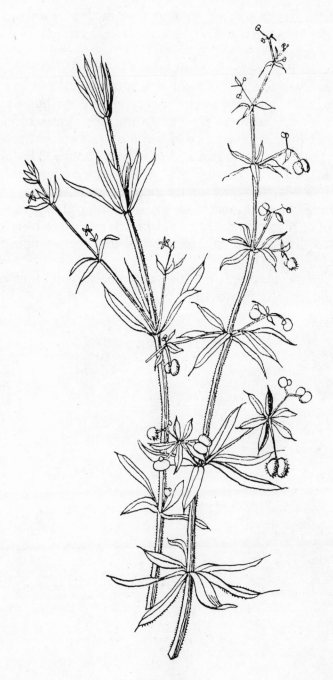

CLIVERS

Galium Aparine

Charles II was painted holding the first Pineapple said to be grown by his gardener Rose, but in all probability it was an imported example.

Though Pineapple juice can hardly be excelled as a refreshing drink in fevers and in hot weather, its greatest value is as a digestive agent. It is said to resemble very closely the human gastric juice, with its discutient powers. In the worst cases of gastritis, Pineapple juice will bring relief because of its solvent properties and its power of making an acid condition alkaline. This makes it valuable used with animal food. Cooked with meat or laid on the top of it, Pineapple will make the toughest joint tender.

Externally it is of great value in dissolving painful corns and in the cure of distressing skin complaints. It is used in cases of diptheria to dissolve the false membrane that that complaint produces.

An average Pineapple produces about half a pint of juice, but if cooked it loses its digestive principle.

POMEGRANATE

... Nor on its slender twigs
Low bending, be the full pomegranate scorned.

James Thomson

Botanical name	Punica granatum (Linn.)
Natural order	Lythraceae
Other name	Carthaginian apple
French name	Grenadier
German name	Granatbaum
Italian name	Granato (Melagrano)
Spanish names	Scorzo del Melogranato, Cortezade Granada
Under the dominion of	Mercury
Symbolises	Foolishness, Elegance
Parts used	Root, bark, fruit, flowers, rind, seeds
Natural hatitat	Western Asia, China, Japan, cultivated in Spain and the countries of the Mediterranean

Pomegranate appears in one of the earliest medical papyri (the Papyrus Ebers) as a medicine of importance. The bark, which was recommended by Dioscorides and Hippocrates as a vermifuge, is still regarded as one of the most useful remedies for tape worm; the rind is used for chronic dysentery; and the fruit is astringent and refrigerant and is made into cooling drinks. It quenches the thirst and gives relief in feverish complaints. The seeds make good conserve and the flowers have much the same properties, and are often combined with the leaves and the seeds in astringent medicines. The flowers yield a good red dye.

In Java, the bark of three species of wild Pomegranate—the red flowered, the white flowered, and the black flowered—are mixed and used in medicine. The Pomegranate, on account of the beauty of its fruit, has been very much reproduced in sculpture and needlework. It was carved on the pillars of brass in the porch of King Solomon's Temple, and when the Israelites were in the wilderness it was chosen to be embroidered on the robe of the High Priests. It is constantly seen as a design on church altar cloths, and in the carving of elaborate ecclesiastical monuments.

The tree grows to a height of about twenty feet, the bark is brown, the leaves opposite and pointed at both ends, and the flowers are large, of a rich scarlet colour, and are either solitary or grow two or three together at the end of the young branches, flowering from June to September; the fruit is the size of an orange, globular and somewhat compressed. It contains immense seeds enveloped in a rose coloured pulp, and is crowned with the limb of the calyx, and covered with a tawny rind.

The lovely avenue of Pomegranates at Granada is said to have been planted by the Moors, who also made a split Pomegranate the arms of the town.

The Pomegranate is one of the favourite fruits of ancient mythology. The first tree is said to have been planted by Venus in Cyprus. The food that Proserpine ate when in Hades was seven Pomegranate seeds; and the Scythian maid who was seduced by Bacchus was turned by him into a Pomegranate tree, on the fruit of which he placed a crown to compensate her for the crown he had promised her before her seduction.

The rareness and the exotic beauty of the tree make it a fitting subject for legends and fairy tales.

The seeds are used in syrups and conserves.

SYRUP OF POMEGRANATE

After extracting the juice, clarify it by standing it in the sun or before the fire. To every 4 ounces take 1 pound of loaf sugar and bring the sugar to boiling point before adding the juice of the Pomegranates—if the adding of the juice checks the boiling too much, boil till it becomes pearled—then take off the fire and, when cool, bottle.

RASPBERRY

Our last thanksgivin' dinner we
Ate at Granny's house, and she
Had—just as she allus does—
The bestest pies as ever wus.
Canned blackberry pie, an' luscious goose
Bury squashin' full of juice,
And rosburry, an' likewise plum,
Yes, an' cherry pie! Yum! Yum!

Botanical name	Rubus Idaeus (Linn.)
Natural order	Rosaceae
Country names	Bramble of Mount Ida, Hindberry, Raspbis
French name	Framboisier
German name	Himbeerstrauch
Italian names	Lampone, Lampine
Spanish name	Frambueso
Under the dominion of	Venus
Symbolises	Remorse
Parts used	Leaves, fruit
Natural habitat	Europe, including Great Britain

The Raspberry grows wild in parts of Great Britain and the wild berry is almost as good as the cultivated fruit though it is not quite as large. The plant has been named botanically the Bramble of Ida, because it grew in profusion on Mount Ida, where Paris awarded the Apple to Venus for her beauty.

Raspberries almost rival Strawberries in their popularity. They are more refreshing; and Raspberry vinegar is invaluable in domestic medicine, not only for feverish colds and sore throats but for its astringent and stimulating properties.

Raspberry conserve can be made without being boiled and is delicious. It will keep quite well in a dry place.

Pour a quart of white wine vinegar over a pound of the fresh fruit and leave it to stand in a large china milk bowl for 24 hours. Then carefully strain the liquid, without squeezing the fruit, on to another pound of fresh fruit and repeat the process until the desired amount of liquid has been obtained.

Then strain and put into a stone jar with a pound of broken white loaf sugar to every pint of juice. Stir when dissolved and gently cook in a bain-marie, only allowing the juice to simmer. Take off any scum that rises and when cold bottle it and cork well.

The author's recipe for

UNBOILED RASPBERRY CONSERVE

Crush the Raspberries with a wooden spoon. Set them in a pan on the fire and stir till they nearly boil, then remove them.

Heat the same weight of sugar in the oven and add it to the Raspberries. Put them on the fire and just bring to the boil. Then remove and fill the jars and tie them down while hot. Though the jam will be liquid at first, it will get stiffer and keep for a long time.

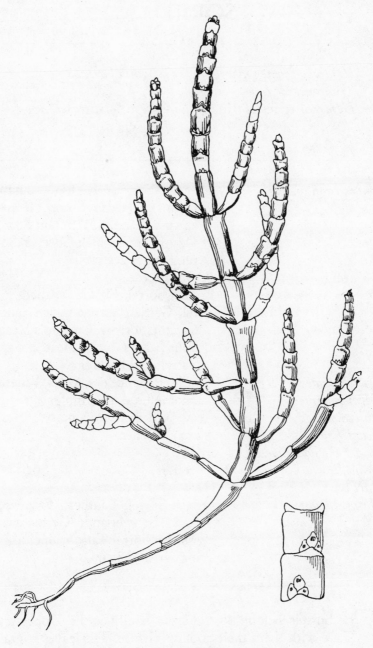

GLASSWORT

Salicornia herbacea

SORREL

Here wholesome plantain that the pains of eyes and ears
    appeases:
Here cooling sorrel that again we use in hot diseases.

                              Michael Drayton

Botanical names	French Sorrel, Rumex scutatus (Linn.); Garden Sorrel, Rumex acetosa (Linn.); Mountain Sorrel, Oxyric reniformis; Sheep's Sorrel, Rumex acetosella
Natural order	Polygonaceae
Country names	French Sorrel: Buckler-shaped Sorrel. Garden Sorrel: Green Sauce, Cuckoo Sorrow, Cuckoo's Meate, Sour Sabs, Gowke-Meat. Sheep's Sorrel: Field Sorrel
French names	Oseille, Patience des Alpes, Vinette
German names	Sauerampfer, Alpenampfer
Italian names	Acetosa, Rubarbaro alpino
Spanish names	Alazan, Acedera
Under the dominion of	Venus
Symbolises	Affection
Part used	Herb
Natural habitat	French Sorrel: Southern France, Italy, Switzerland, Germany. Garden Sorrel: Europe, including Great Britain

The Sorrels belong to the same family as the Docks and share with them their cooling virtues. The leaves contain oxalate of potash, which gives them a sharp acid taste which adds a relish to salads when they are used.

Sorrel leaves are used by the French in several distinctive dishes such as: *Potage du maigre aux herbes à la bonne femme, sauce à la purée d'oseille* and *purée d'oseille au maigre, purée d'oseille au gras*, etc.

In France they do not use the Garden Sorrel, but another species, *Rumex scutatus*, which does not grow in England. It is less acid than the Garden Sorrel, and more succulent.

The Garden Sorrel is indigenous to England and is an old pot herb. It generally grows in soil containing iron, and the plant does not acquire its acid taste till the summer advances, when the flowers become a deep purple and the leaves almost a rusty red in colour.

The Sheep's Sorrel is a smaller variety and is also noticeable in fields in the summer because of the red colour of the leaves.

The Mountain Sorrel is found in the Alps and it grows by streams in Wales and in the north of England. It is also used as a pot herb, and in Sweden has been made into bread.

TAMARIND

. . . Say we reclined
Beneath the spreading tamarind, that shakes,
Fanned by the breeze, its fever cooling fruit.

James Thomson

Botanical name	Tamarindus Indica (Linn.)
Natural order	Leguminosae
Eastern name	Imlee
French name	Tamarinier
German name	Tamarindenbaum
Italian name	Tamarindo
Spanish name	Tamarindo
Part used	Fruit stripped of the outer pericarp
Natural habitat	Tropical Africa, India, cultivated in West Indies

The Tamarind is a beautiful tree growing to a height of forty feet. The flowers are large, partly white and partly yellow, with red and purple filaments, and are very sweet smelling.

The Indians have a prejudice against sleeping under the tree, and a dampness in the tree affects the canvas of camps which are pitched near it.

Tamarind pods contain an unusual proportion of acids and are particularly useful in fevers. The Arabians introduced them to Europe, and they remained popular until this century. They are sometimes made into whey—two ounces of the fruit being boiled in two pints of milk and, when strained, the milk is drunk.

The fruit possesses traces of gold and contains citric, tartaric and malic acids. It is, therefore, extremely useful in septic fevers, especially if jaundice is present.

The Tamarind fruit was at one time known as Oxyphoenice,

YELLOW GOAT'S BEARD
Tragopogon pratensis

which means 'Sour Date'. Its more modern name Tamir Hind means 'Indian Date'. It is often imported without its outer pod in the form of a pulpy jam which is quite as useful as pods, but the pulp has to be separated from the strings and seeds before it is made into a drink.

Chapter V

POT HERBS

POT HERBS

Chapter V

POT HERBS

The expression 'pot herbs' has come down to us from very primitive stages of cookery. The 'pot' was one of the earliest of cooking utensils, and the simplest, and survives into civilised ages in the form of the cauldron suspended over the fire from an iron bar in the chimney. It is the simplest way of preparing a meal, for into the pot goes meat, vegetables, bread and every available edible substance, animal and vegetable. Man soon found out that nearly every herb that produced tuberous roots, even if poisonous in the raw state, could by cooking be made wholesome and nutritious. Cooking takes the poisonous element out of most plants, with a few exceptions, and the salts they impart to the water provide the minerals needed for the blood.

Until quite lately the vitamins in plants and the mineral salts had not been scientifically discovered, but man knew by instinct that vegetables were necessary to avoid scrofulous complaints and they were always part of his diet.

Life in town has deprived us of many of these edible herbs, and we now use only those that are cultivated for the market, so that the knowledge of many of the wild ones has been lost, except to a few.

Out of the seventy-five vegetable substances named by John Evelyn in his *Acetaria*, only about thirty-seven can be bought to-day from a greengrocer, and of these such herbs as Cornsalad, Sweet Cicely, Tarragon and a few others are not generally distributed.

John Evelyn includes, in addition to those that will be found in this chapter, the young roots of Daisies, and the buds and tender leaves of Elder.

The leaves of all salad herbs should be used in the Spring, or when they first appear, otherwise they are bitter and stringy.

Young Spinach leaves are excellent in salads, and provide iron in its best form. Watercress and Horse Radish give sulphur; Nettles and Dandelions, calcium as well as iron. All green plants contain chlorophyll, mineral salts, and vitamins, and if freshly gathered and eaten uncooked have vitamin B—which cooking destroys.

Some of the old-fashioned herbs, such as Good King Henry, Jack by the Hedge, Goat's Beard, Wild Rocket and Pimpinella make an ordinary salad much more interesting. Good King Henry is one of the goosefoots, and is sometimes called English Mercury.

Jack by the Hedge was so much used at one time by itself as a relish to cold meat that its popular name was Sauce-alone. Goat's Beard is not unlike Salsify, and Wild Rocket is hotter and sharper even than Jack by the Hedge, so must be used sparingly.

Pimpinella is the great Wild Burnet that used to grow near St. Pancras Church in Culpeper's time and was described by him as 'a friend to the heart, liver and other principal parts of a man's body'.

A salad can be gathered from the hedges, and vegetables also. There is an inexhaustable supply in the country, and even the brooks and streams have Cresses and other cruciform plants equal in flavour to the cultivated Watercress.

All cruciform plants are safe to eat.

ALEXANDERS

My flower is sweet in smell, bitter my juice in taste
Which purges choler, and helps lives that else would waste.

Botanical name	Smyrnium olusatrum (Linn.)
Natural order	Umbelliferae
Country names	Black Lovage, Alisanders, Black Potherb, Horse Parsley
French name	Maceron
German name	Smyrnerkraut
Italian name	Macerone
Turkish name	Yaban kereviz
Under the dominion of	Jupiter
Part used	Herb
Natural habitat	Europe, including Great Britain

Black Lovage was one of the everyday salad herbs when John Evelyn wrote his *Acetaria*. It had a reputation among the Greeks and Romans for its myrrh-like flavour which is recorded in its botanical name of Smyrnium.

It is an umbelliferous plant which grows in waste places near the sea and in salt marshes. It has a taste and smell not unlike Celery and the young shoots can be eaten like Asparagus, or used in soups.

At one time it was cultivated in European gardens and the seeds were used in medicine to remove obstructions from the spleen.

ARROWHEAD

Broad water lilies lay tremulously,
And starry river buds glimmered by,
And around them the soft stream did glide and dance
With a motion of sweet sound and radiance.

Percy Bysshe Shelley

Botanical name	Sagittaria sagittifolia (Linn.)
Natural order	Alismaceae
Other names	Wapatoo, Is'-ze-kn
French names	Herbe à la flèche, Sagittaire
German name	Pfeilkraut
Italian names	Sagittaria, Barba silvana, Freccia d'acqua
Turkish names	Su otu, Su oki
Under the dominion of	Jupiter
Part used	Bulbs
Natural habitat	Europe, including Great Britain

The Arrowhead is a water plant recognisable at once by its numerous arrow-shaped leaves floating on the top of the water and its exotic-looking lilylike flowers with three snow-white petals bearing at their base a purple blotch and three outer sepals. The flowers rise direct from the root and are often seen growing wild in brooks and streams. I have seen it very often in tributaries of the river Arun in Sussex.

The Chinese use the tubers powdered as a substitute for Arrowroot, and Europeans boil the bulbs and eat them as a vegetable. They have a taste rather like dried peas.

In commerce the Sagittarias are used to make ink.

GOOD KING HENRY

Chenopodium bonus Henricus

ASH

Its buds on either side opposed
Its couples each to each enclosed
In casket black and hard as jet,
The ash trees graceful branch beset:
The branch which clothed in modest grey
Sweeps gracefully with easy sway,
And still in after life preserves
The bending of its infant curves.

Bishop Mant

Botanical name	Fraxinus excelsior (Linn.)
Natural order	Oleaceae
Country name	The Husbandman's tree
French name	Frêne
German name	Echte Esche
Italian name	Frassino
Spanish name	Fresno
Under the dominion of	Sun
Symbolises	Grandeur
Parts used	Leaves, bark, fruit
Natural habitat	Europe, including Great Britain

The Ash tree has been called the Venus of the Forest. Certainly very few trees, except Poplars, reach so near the heavens. The wood is more useful than that of almost any other tree because of its toughness and elasticity. It is strong and hard and takes a good polish. In early days it was used for spears and bows, and today the best carriage shafts and the best oars are made from it. It is also used in the making of aeroplanes.

The Ash and the Privet are the only two members of the Olive family that are indigenous to England.

Apart from the commercial value of the Ash tree, it is a very useful medicine for dropsy and rheumatism. William Cole says:

'There is scarce any part about the Ash but is good for the dropsy.'
It was sometimes used in the form of a distilled water, or a decoction of the leaves in white wine was taken medicinally.

Pliny recommended it for snake bites, and later herbalists regarded it as a good substitute for Peruvian bark in fevers. It has all the tonic properties of quinine.

The Romans used the leaves as fodder for cattle, and in Queen Elizabeth's reign it was used in England as food for sheep and cows.

The keys of the Ash tree are excellent in salads, or can be eaten alone with oil and vinegar as John Evelyn recommends in his *Acetaria*. An old idea prevails that when the Ash tree shows an unusual abundance of keys, a severe winter will follow, and country people in England regard this as an infallible sign.

BASIL

A chaplet of herbs I'll make
With Basil then I will begin
Whose scent is wond'rous pleasing.

Michael Drayton

Botanical name	Ocimum Basilicum (Linn.)
Natural order	Labiatae
Country name	Sweet Basil
French name	Basilique sauvage
German names	Kleine Bergmünze, Basilikum
Italian name	Bassilico
Spanish name	Albahaca menor
Dutch name	Vol Mynte
Under the dominion of	Mars and the sign Scorpio
Symbolises	Hatred
Part used	Herb
Natural habitat	India

There are as many varieties of Basil as there are of Thyme. One is Lemon scented, another smells rather like Tarragon, and another like Fennel; but the Common Basil, known more often as Sweet Basil, has a clove-like smell when it is bruised, and the leaves are cool to the touch. It has white flowers which grow in whorls in the axils of the leaves.

The Basil plant came originally from India, and, though it has been growing in England since the sixteenth century when it was first introduced, it will not live through an English winter.

Legends connect the Basil with scorpions, possibly because scorpions like to lie under the plant and even to breed under it. Another possible explanation may be that the plant comes under the sign of the zodiac—Scorpio. At any rate nearly all the old herbals refer to this relation between the two.

In India the plant is sacred to Krishna and to Vishnu. Its name is derived from the Greek word meaning king—a herb fit for a king.

The Basil plant has an aromatic scent and taste which makes it useful in cooking, and it is the herb that is specially used to flavour fish.

In medicine it has pectoral properties, and is cordial, cleansing, and comforting. Dr. Chambers says: 'It is a cordial which raises the spirits and re-establishes the movement of the humours which compose the blood.' Both the flowers and the seeds are used as well as the leaves to relieve pains in the head, to cleanse the lungs, and to comfort the heart and expel melancholy. It was the custom to sow Basil seeds with a curse, and this is the derivation of the French expression for slander, 'Semer le basilic.'

Two other species, the Bush Basil, *Ocimum minimum*, which came from India, and the Wild Basil, *Calamintha Clinopodium*, which resembles Calamint, are also used in the same way. The former is good in salads, and so is the Wild Basil which is extremely fragrant.

BAY

Look on my leafy boughs, the crown
Of living song and dead renown.
William Morris

Botanical name	Laurus nobilis
Natural order	Lauraceae
Country names	Sweet Bay, Noble Laurel, Daphne, Roman Laurel
French name	Laurier d'Apollon
German name	Edler Lorbeerbaum
Italian names	Lauro franco, Lauro poetico, Lauro regio
Spanish name	Bahia
Under the dominion of	Sun and the sign Leo
Symbolises	Glory
Natural habitat	Shores of Mediterranean

French cooking may almost be said to be founded on a Bay leaf, for it enters into the bouquet of herbs without which no truly French dish can be properly flavoured.

The Bay tree is the nearest approach to a spice tree that grows in Europe, and even in the cold climate of Great Britain it often reaches a height of twenty-five feet.

Its leaves are not unlike those of the tropical spice trees, and they exude a delicious scent which gives an excellent flavour to meat dishes and to sweetmeats.

Branches of Bay leaves were used for strewing in the days when scented plants disinfected and perfumed the floors and furniture of the rich.

As a protection against the devil the Bay tree was pre-eminent. Culpeper says: 'It is a tree of the sun, and under the celestial sign Leo, and resists the witchcraft very potently as also all the evils old Saturn can do the body of man, and they are not a few; for it is the speech of one and I am mistaken if it were not Mizaldus, that neither witch nor devil, thunder nor lightning will hurt a man where a Bay tree is.'

Galen recommends the fruit as being even more healing than the leaves and the bark, but every part of the tree, and the oil extracted from it, has healing properties. The fruits have been used in hysterical complaints, the oil for sprains, and the berries and leaves for restorative baths.

The Bay tree is the emblem of Glory, and wreaths of Bay leaves were worn by the victorious. The Bay leaf symbolises, 'I change but in death'.

BROOKLIME

Veronica, namesake of the woman blest
With love's true image.

Newman Howard

Botanical name	Veronica beccabunga (Linn.)
Natural order	Scrophulariaceae
Country names	Becky Leaves, Water Pimpernel, Housewell, Cowcress, Lime-wort, Wall-ink, Water-Pumpy, Well-ink
French names	Beccabunga, Cressonnière
German name	Bachbunge ehrenpreis
Italian names	Veronica crescione, Beccabunga
Turkish name	Yavsan otu
Scotch name	Water Purpie
Under the dominion of	Mars
Symbolises	Fidelity
Part used	Herb
Natural habitat	Great Britain

This water-loving Veronica with which Scotsmen are familiar by the name of Water Purpie, is an excellent substitute for Watercress. It has all the valuable antiscorbutic properties of the Cresses and is generally found growing with them in streams and by the edges of ponds.

Brooklime was one of the ingredients of the famous Spring Juices—the much vaunted cure for scrofulous complaints. Culpeper says it is 'a hot and biting martial plant'.

The plant has a creeping root, and the small blue flowers grow on long foot stalks which shoot forth from the root. The leaves are deep green and thick.

MUGWORT

Artemisia vulgaris

BUR MARIGOLD

You may look for them in cold grounds by the sides of ponds and ditches, as also by running waters: sometimes you shall find them grow in the midst of the waters.

Nicholas Culpeper

Botanical name	Bidens tripartita (Linn.)
Natural order	Compositae
Country names	Water Agrimony, Water Hemp, Bastard Hemp, Bastard Agrimony, Hepatorium
French names	Chanvre aquatique, Cornuet
German names	Sumpfzweizahn, Wasserhanf
Italian names	Canapa acquatica, Eupatoria acquatica
Turkish name	Su keneviri
Under the dominion of	Jupiter and the sign of the Crab
Part used	Whole plant
Natural habitat	Europe, including Great Britain, though not common in Scotland

Water Agrimony is the old name for this plant which is quite common in England by the sides of ditches and ponds, especially in the north. It has dark, almost purple coloured stalks which grow to about two feet in height. The leaves are winged, much indented, and the flowers which grow at the top of the branches are a yellowish brown colour with black spots and a composite centre. The seeds adhere to wool, and the flowers when crushed have a smell of burnt cedar.

It is an old remedy for 'the third day ague'. It is particularly valuable in dropsy, not as a diuretic but because it thins the secretions. It is also a useful styptic, healing wherever there is haemorrhage.

As a styptic a strong infusion can be taken warm every half

hour till relieved. The plant is chiefly used by herbalists who understand it. Nicholas Culpeper said that in his day it was given to cattle who were broken-winded, and he himself regarded it as a cure for an enlarged spleen and a great strengthener of the lungs.

Another species, *Bidens cernua*, is known as the Nodding Marigold.

BUTCHER'S BROOM

Mid barren heaths the Butcher's Broom
On thorn tip't leaves its lovely bloom
Infixes. When the central eye
Shoots to a purple nectary;
Bright mid the greenish petals shows
A dark green leaf wherever it blows.

Bishop Mant

Botanical name	Ruscus aculeatus (Linn.)
Natural order	Liliaceae
Country names	Kneeholly, Kneeholy, Sweet Broom, Kneeholm, Jew's Myrtle, Pettigree
French names	Fragon piquant, Petit-houx, Buis pointu
German name	Echter Mäusedorn
Italian names	Brusco, Rusco pungente
Turkish name	Yaban mersini
Under the dominion of	Mars
Parts used	Leaves, berries
Natural habitat	Europe, including South of England

Butcher's Broom is the only Liliaceous shrub growing in Great Britain. It is quite different from ordinary Broom and belongs to a totally different order of plants. Its barkless stems send out short branches with rigid leaves and are really only an expansion of the stem. They terminate in a sharp spine, and the greenish white flowers which grow from the centre of the leaves have their stamens and pistils on different plants. The fertile flowers are followed by red berries as big as Cherries which remain on the plant right through the winter.

The young shoots can be eaten like Asparagus; and a decoction and poultice of the berries and leaves knits broken bones. A decoction of the root is used in jaundice and is good for pulmonary diseases.

The young branches are sold to butchers for sweeping their blocks. The Butcher's Broom is the badge of the Earls of Sutherland.

BUTTERCUP

There is the daisy, so prim and white,
With its golden eye and its fringes white,
And here is the golden buttercup,
Like a miser's chest with the gold heap'd up.

Calder Campbell

Botanical name	Ranunculus bulbosus (Linn.)
Natural order	Ranunculaceae
Country names	Goldcup, St. Anthony's Turnip, Frogsfoot, Crazy
French names	Jauneau, Bouton d'or
German name	Hahnenfuss
Italian names	Piè Corrino, Ranuncolo
Spanish name	Ranunculo
Under the dominion of	Mars
Symbolises	Riches
Part used	Root
Natural habitat	Europe, including Great Britain

The prevailing idea that cows feeding in a field of Buttercups produce cream and butter of a yellow colour is entirely erroneous. Cows show great discrimination in avoiding the Buttercups, and if they make a mistake suffer in consequence from a blistered mouth. Buttercups and all the plants allied to them—like the Crowfoots and the Spearworts—have an acrid juice in their stems which burns and raises blisters. This is used sometimes for external use as a counter-irritant in sciatica and rheumatic pains, and a homeopathic tincture of Buttercup taken internally is a cure for shingles.

In the west country the Buttercup is called Crazy and believed to provoke insanity.

Boiling destroys the acrid principle of all species of Buttercups and the boiled roots have been used in the past as a vegetable.

These plants are placed under the order of Ranunculaceae which takes its name from the Latin for 'a frog', because they grow in damp places beloved of frogs.

CAMPANULAS

Among the heath furze still delight to dwell,
Quaking as if with cold, the Harishbell.

John Clare

Botanical name	Campanula rotundifolia
Natural order	Campanulaceae
Country names	Harebell, Witches' Thimble
French name	Clochette
German name	Weisenbusch
Italian name	Campanella
Spanish name	Campanula
Symbolises	Aspiring
Part used	Root
Natural habitat	Europe

The Campanulas range from the tiny delicate blue Harebell known to everyone to the giant blue, pink and white Canterbury Bells of herbaceous borders. The family also includes the wild Rampions, which have been used as man's food in many countries. The *Campanula rapunculus* is cooked as a vegetable in France where it is called Raiponce. In Germany its name is Rapunzel and the Italians call it Raperonzola. It contains a large amount of starchy nutriment.

Another edible species, the Spiked Rampion (*Phyteuma orbiculare*) with cream-coloured flowers, was at one time cultivated for salads and is still occasionally found in England and much eaten in Switzerland, where it is common.

Even the root of the tiny Harebell is edible.

Apart from their nutritious properties, the Campanulas have a commercial value for the ink that is made from their juice and the rich green dye that can be obtained by mixing the juice with alum.

GARDEN ROCKET

Hesperis matronalis

CLIVERS

The lowly bird with its delicate tinge,
The azure Succory's silken fringe,
The modest Scabious of deeper blue,
And silvery Galium of virgin hue.

Botanical name	Galium Aparine (Linn.)
Natural order	Rubiaceae
Country names	Cleavers, Goosegrass, Robin-run-in-the-Grass, Everlasting Friendship, Catchweed, Mutton Chops, Barweed, Goosebill, Grip Grass, Hayriffe, Eriffe, Hedgeheriff
French names	Aparine, Grateron
German name	Klebenabkraut
Italian names	Cappello dei tignosi, Aparine
Turkish name	Çoban süzegi
Under the dominion of	Moon
Part used	Herb
Natural habitat	Europe, including Great Britain, North America

This is one of the Bedstraws, the plants with roots which, like the Madder, supply us with a good red dye. It is an old wives' remedy for keeping thin and was taken in the form of a soup to lose weight.

It is also a cure for sunburn and freckles and the seeds are sometimes used as a substitute for coffee. The plant is very common in English hedges. It has white star-like flowers which spring from the axils of the leaves and are followed by bristly, globular seed vessels which stick to anything they come in contact with. These bristly capsules account for some of its popular names, such as Everlasting Friendship, Beggar's Lice, etc. Other names relate to the serrated leaves of the plant which are not unlike the bill of a goose.

In herbal medicine this plant has a reputation for curing cancer, used internally and externally. It contains a special acid known as rubichloric acid, and there are several authentic cases of cures of cancer, or what has been diagnosed as cancer, that have resulted from the use of it.

The botanical name Galium comes from a Greek word meaning 'milk' and is applied to the Bedstraw because it was used to curdle milk in the same way that rennet does.

COCHLEARIA

It hath a very hot, aromatical and spicy taste.

Nicholas Culpeper

Botanical name	Cochlearia officinalis (Linn.)
Natural order	Cruciferae
Country names	Scurvy Grass, Spoonwort, Scruby Grass
French names	Cranson, Cochléaire
German name	Löffelkraut
Italian names	Coclearia, Erba a cucchiaino
Dutch name	Lepelkruid
Danish name	Skeawurt
Under the dominion of	Jupiter
Part used	Herb
Natural habitat	Sea coasts of Northern and Western Europe

This anti-scrofulous plant is said to be the Herba Britannica of the ancient Greeks. Its leaves are so hollow that they are almost like the bowl of a spoon, and Spoonwort is a translation of Cochlearia, its botanical name.

Of all the Cruciferous plants this is probably the best for purifying the blood. The succulent leaves can be eaten in salads, or the juice can be added to Orange juice to make what is known as 'Spring Juices'.

It has a salt taste which is sometimes disguised with pepper and aniseed. It is put into beer.

The juice is also made into gargles or into a conserve or syrup.

The plant has whitish flowers with yellow threads surrounding a green head which becomes the seed vessel. It grows at Lymington in Hampshire, on the banks of the Avon, and in Cumberland and other places.

COLEWORT

The Colewort, colliflower and cabbage in the season,
The rounce fall Greek, beans, and early ripening peason;
The onion, scallion, leek which housewives lightly rate,
Their kinsman's garlic then the poor man's mithridate.

Michael Drayton

Botanical name	Brassica campestris
Natural order	Cruciferae
French name	Chou champêtre
German name	Feldkohl
Italian names	Cavolo, Colza
Spanish name	Col-verde
Under the dominion of	Moon
Symbolises	Profit
Part used	Herb
Natural habitat	Europe, including Great Britain

The Colewort, of which there are several varieties, is the wild Cabbage from which our garden Cabbage and its varieties are derived. It grows on sea cliffs throughout Europe and has a salty flavour which becomes less pronounced after it is washed. It can be used as a vegetable.

The Sea Cabbage, *Brassica oleracea*, with panicles of sulphur-coloured flowers, is found on the cliffs of Devonshire and Cornwall and as far north as Yorkshire and as far west as Wales. It is collected from the Dover cliffs and sold as a vegetable.

Another species, the *Brassica monensis*, also has bright yellow flowers but they are streaked with purple, and a third variety, the *Brassica napus*, is cultivated for its seed which is known as Rape seed.

All the Coleworts contain a good deal of nitrogenous matter and a certain amount of sulphur. This gives them their unpleasant smell when they are cooked, but they are so wholesome that they can't be dispensed with.

We are told by Cato and by Pliny that the Romans had no other medicine for six hundred years but the Cabbage. In Greece and Rome the Cabbage was as much revered as the Onion was in Egypt. It was said to have sprung from the tears of Lycurgus. The Greeks called it Amethustos because it was the colour of an amethyst and also because it prevented drunkenness. Even John Evelyn refers to the power of the Colewort to prevent intoxication, and through the ages herbals refer to the Colewort and the Ivy as herbs to cure drunkenness.

The Coleworts and Cabbages belong to the Cruciferous order of plants and all the plants belonging to this order are antiscorbutic and wholesome.

The Red Cabbage is made into a syrup to be used medicinally, and the Germans make their well-known Sauerkraut from it. The ordinary Cabbage is sometimes used as a poultice and the water in which it is boiled is a useful remedy for rheumatism.

Cato's Cabbage was introduced into England by Sir Anthony Ashley, whose monument in the Church at Wimborne has a Cabbage carved on it.

LOHOCH OF COLEWORTS

Take a pound of the juice of Coleworts, clarified; Saffron, 3 drachms; clarified sugar and honey, of each, ½ pound. Make into a lohoch.

This we recommend to be eaten off the end of a stick of liquorice. Prescribed for the after-effects of a drunken orgy.

CORN SALAD

Botanical name	Valerianella olitoria
Natural order	Caryophyllaceae
Country names	Lamb's lettuce, White potherb
French names	Loblollie, Salade de Chanoine, Mâche, Doucette
German name	Gemeiner Feldsalat
Italian names	Valeriana ortense, Valerianella
Spanish name	Canonigo
Part used	Herb
Natural habitat	Great Britain

Corn salad was much cultivated in the herb gardens of the monasteries as a salad plant. Today it is seldom seen except in expensive greengrocers' shops; but it makes the best of all salads to eat with game, and it has a particularly attractive appearance because it looks like the leaves of Daisies. It is allied to the Valerian, and Little Valerian is one of its names.

It was at one time classed with the Lettuces under the name of *Lactuca aquina*. It grows wild throughout Great Britain in waste ground and in cornfields, but it is cultivated also, and if sown through the autumn, winter and spring, produces successive supplies for salads all through the year.

CROWFOOTS

The azure violet scents the breeze
Which shakes the yellow crowfoot's bell.

Leyden

Botanical names	Celery-leaved Crowfoot, Ranunculus sceleratus (Linn.); Upright Meadow Crowfoot, Ranunculus acris (Linn.)
Natural order	Ranunculaceae
Country names	Marsh Crowfoot, Gold Cup
French names	Grenouillette, Renoncule scélérate
German name	Gifthahnenfuss
Italian name	Ranuncolo scellerato
Spanish name	Ranunculo
Under the dominion of	Mars
Symbolises	Ingratitude
Part used	Herb
Natural habitat	Europe, including Great Britain

Both these Crowfoots are common in England in meadows, but the Celery-leaved Crowfoot is found chiefly in marshes and by water. All the Crowfoots, except the Wood Crowfoot, *R. auricomus*, in common with Spearworts and Celandines, have an acrid juice which can be used for removing warts and corns and to raise blisters. When boiled they become harmless and have been used as pot herbs. The Water Crowfoot, *R. aquatilis*, is sometimes given to cattle as fodder.

Nicholas Culpeper, in writing of the Common Meadow Crowfoot, said 'Many are the names this furious, biting herb hath obtained, almost enough to make up a Welshman's pedigree'.

He recommended it for external use in ointments and plasters and spoke highly of it as a substitute for cantharides.

SAMPHIRE

Crithmum maritimum

GLASSWORTS

They are under the dominion of Mars, and are of a cleansing quality, without any great or manifest heat.

Nicholas Culpeper

Botanical name	Salicornia herbacea (Linn.)
Natural order	Chenopodiaceae
Country names	Saltwort, Jointed Glasswort, Sea Grass, Crab Grass, Marsh Samphire, Salsola Kali, Frog Grass
French names	Salicorne, Crestmarine
German name	Echtes Glasschmalz
Italian names	Salicornia erbacea, Erba kali
Turkish name	Salikorn
Dutch name	Zondkruid
Under the dominion of	Mars
Part used	Herb
Natural habitat	Syria, Egypt, Spain, Italy, Great Britain

The Glassworts contain much soda and on that account were used in the making of glass and soap. There are references to their use in this way in the Bible. When, hundreds of years later, a method of extracting soda from salt was discovered, Barilla, the name given to the Glassworts, ceased to be imported from Africa and the South of Europe and the plant has been almost forgotten.

Cattle like their salty taste, and when the salt is washed out of them they make a wholesome and useful vegetable, and are closely allied to the Goosefoots. Their old name is Saltwort; and the two varieties that grow in Great Britain are the Small Glasswort, *Kali minus album*, and the Jointed Glasswort, *Salicornia herbacea*.

GOAT'S BEARD

The goat's beard, which each morn abroad does peep
But shuts its flowers at noon and goes to sleep.

Abraham Cowley

Botanical name	Tragopogon pratensis (Linn.)
Natural order	Compositae
Country names	Jack-go-to-bed-at-noon, Noon Flower, Star of Jerusalem
French name	Salsifis
German name	Bocksbart
Italian name	Barba di Becco
Spanish name	Barba cabruna
Dutch name	Boksbeard
Under the dominion of	Jupiter
Part used	Root
Natural habitat	Great Britain

The Goat's Beard is easily distinguished from other Compositae plants by its thin wheat-like leaves. It has large single yellow flowers in which the anthers are sometimes brown, and they fade into a fluffy clock like the dandelion. The roots can be cooked in the same way as Parsnip and make an excellent vegetable rather like Salsify, which is another species of the same plant known as the Purple Goat's Beard.

In medicine, Goat's Beard liquefies bile that has become too thick.

The botanical name is a literal translation of the English name, Goat's Beard.

The Purple Goat's Beard, *Tragopogon orientalis*, has the same properties. The flowers are purple instead of yellow and they are surmounted by long green cups which gives them an unusual appearance.

GOOD KING HENRY

With vinegar, honey and salt, the orrach,
Made hot and applied cures a gouty attack;
Whilst its seeds for the jaundice if mingled with wine
As Galen has said—a remedy fine.

Botanical name	Chenopodium Bonus Henricus
Natural order	Chenopodiaceae
Country names	English Mercury, Fat Hen, Mercury Goosefoot, All Good Smearwort, Blite
French names	Bon Henri, Epinard sauvage
German names	Fetthenne, Heinrichsgänsefuss
Italian names	Tutta buona, Mercorella lunga
Spanish names	Bono Enrique, Spinachio selvatico
Under the dominion of	Moon
Part used	Herb
Natural habitat	Europe, including Great Britain

Good King Henry is one of the Goosefoots and is said to have been so called to distinguish it from Bad King Henry, another Goosefoot but a poisonous one. I think it is more likely that the name arose because it was used in France to first fatten and then stew the Sunday fowl that Henry IV of France made possible for every Frenchman. Until the time of their Good King Henry the French people as a whole were too poor ever to eat chicken, and with their gastronomic art, the French regarded this bird as the *pièce de résistance* of any meal. Therefore when Henry IV promised every peasant a weekly fowl, he became immensely popular with the masses, and to this day is remembered by every peasant.

The herb Good King Henry was at one time cultivated instead of Spinach, and is still preferred by some people because it hasn't such a pronounced flavour as Spinach though it is closely related to it. The plant grows in waste places in Great Britain. It has arrow-shaped leaves and the flowers grow in close spikes of yellow green sepals, and are succeeded by a bladder-shaped fruit.

The plant probably contains mercury, and English Mercury is one of its country names. In common with another Chenopodium known as Stinking Goosefoot, *Chenopodium Vulvaria,* it is extremely good for the blood, and both of them are regarded as valuable pot herbs. The Stinking Goosefoot is sometimes called Orrach, and is used for poultices.

Conserve of Orrach was also known as Dr. Fuller's Hysterical Electuary because it was found useful in hysterical complaints.

The white and the red Goosefoot, *Chenopodium album* and *Chenopodium rubrum,* have the same properties as Good King Henry; and in Peru the seeds of *Chenopodium Quinoa* are used instead of oatmeal and are called Petty Rice.

MARJORAM

The thyme strong scented 'neath our feet,
The Marjoram beds so doubly sweet,
And pennyroyal's creeping twine
These, each succeeding, each one thine.

Botanical name	Origanum Majorana (Linn.)
Natural order	Labiatae
Country names	Knotted Marjoram, Sweet Marjoram
French name	Marjolaine
German name	Majoran
Italian name	Maggiorana
Spanish name	Majorana
Under the dominion of	Mercury and the sign of Aries
Symbolises	Blushes
Parts used	Herb, leaves
Natural habitat	Asia, North Africa, Europe, including Great Britain

The Sweet Marjoram, the Winter Marjoram and the Pot Marjoram are all cultivated for their use in the kitchen, but the Wild Marjoram, *O. vulgare*, from which the others are derived, is the only one used in medicine. The oil expressed from it relieves the painful swellings of rheumatic joints, and a bag stuffed with the herb and plunged into boiling water and applied locally will have the same effect. A tisane, or tincture, of Wild Marjoram will also act as a sedative to prevent sea sickness.

The word Marjoram comes from two Greek words which mean 'the joy of the mountain'. The wild plant likes a mountainous chalky soil, and is to be found on chalky cliffs in England. It has a strongly aromatic scent and taste, and can be used as a substitute for the Garden Marjorams.

Marjoram is used in stuffing for meat and poultry; the dried leaves are sometimes substituted for ordinary tea, and they make

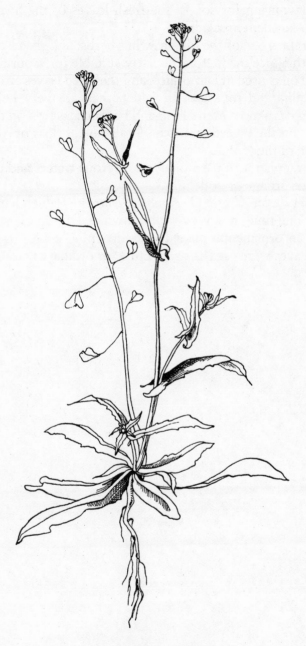

SHEPHERD'S PURSE

Capsella Bursa-pastoris

a good flavouring for soups; the fresh leaves of the Sweet Marjoram are excellent in salads.

Marjoram is one of the old strewing herbs; and the clean, spicy smell of the juice made it particularly suitable for scouring furniture. The oil is used in hair tonics; and the dried leaves are put into herbal snuffs and tobaccos, in which they are very helpful, as Marjoram has a most nourishing and beneficial action on the brain as well as on the digestive organs. It also helps 'loss of speech by resolution of the tongue'.

'Marjoram is much used in all odoriferous waters and powders that are for ornament or delight.'

A variety from Crete, *Origanum Dictamnus*, which had a great vogue at one time, was very well known as Dittany. It was cultivated as an ornamental plant for its drooping spikes of flowers, and the leaves were used as a substitute for ordinary tea.

MUGWORT

There is my moly of much fame,
In magic often used;
Mugwort and nightshade for the same,
But not by me abused.

Michael Drayton

Botanical name	Artemisia vulgaris (Linn.)
Natural order	Compositae
Country names	Felon Herb, St. John's Plant, Maiden Wort, Mother's Wort
French name	Armoise commune
German names	Beifuss, Mugwurz
Italian names	Artemisia, Erba di San Giovanni
Spanish names	Zona diri Johannis, Artemisa común
Under the dominion of	Venus
Symbolises	Happiness, tranquillity
Parts used	Leaves, root
Natural habitat	Europe, including Great Britain

Mugwort in many ways resembles Wormwood which is also one of the Artemisias, herbs dedicated to Diana. The external difference lies in the leaves, which are white underneath and have pointed segments instead of being blunt. The small yellow flowers consist of small flat oval heads like buttons. It is taller and more slender than Wormwood, and does not emit an odour until it is bruised. It grows in hedges and on shingly beaches.

The name Mugwort is probably a survival of its use in flavouring drinking 'cups', though Dr. Ferine attributes it to a derivation of the word 'moughte' or moth, because it was recommended by Dioscorides to keep away moths—a use to which it is still put.

In cooking it is used particularly as a stuffing for roast goose, but it is not strongly aromatic like Wormwood because it has no aromatic volatile oil, as Dr. Ferine points out.

As a medicinal herb it has mysterious properties which are not fully understood. It is anti-epileptic and probably has an action on the pineal gland. It has always been known as a herb that induces, or increases, clairvoyance and it is said to be a good remedy for excessive opium-smoking. Like many other herbs it has been used by magicians on the Eve of St. John. Pliny was of opinion that it relieved fatigue, and for that reason it was put into baths and worn in the soles of shoes. It was even tied round the neck of wayfarers. There is a tradition that St. John the Baptist wore a girdle of Mugwort when he was in the wilderness.

There is an old saying in the North of England and in Scotland: 'If nettles were used in March and Muggins in May—many a bra' lass wudna' turn to t' clay.'

NETTLE

Tender handed stroke the nettle
And it stings you for your pains
Grasp it like a man of mettle
And it soft as silk remains.

Aaron Hill

Botanical name	Urtica dioica (Linn.)
Natural order	Urticaceae
Country name	Stinging Nettle
French name	Grande Ortie
German name	Brennessel
Italian name	Ortica
Spanish name	Ortiga
Under the dominion of	Mars
Symbolises	Spitefulness
Parts used	Herb, seeds
Natural habitat	Europe, including Great Britain; Africa, Australia

The word 'net' means something spun, and in Scandinavia thread was made from Nettles; and tablecloths and sheets, until quite lately, were made in Scotland from Nettle fibre. The botanical name, Urtica, relates to the stinging power of the Nettle. The Nettle contains formic acid in the hairy covering of the plant and this gives it its irritating property.

Stinging Nettles are sometimes used to produce a counter-irritation in rheumatic complaints and in Nettle rash, and also to revive lost vitality, as in the case of paralysis or loss of muscular power.

In domestic medicine the Nettle is extremely valuable as a blood purifier, if the Nettles are used when they first come out in the spring. Such old dishes as Nettle Pudding, or Nettles cooked in the same way as Spinach, are of decided benefit to the health, and Nettle beer is a wholesome drink.

The Roman Nettle, *Urtica pilulifera*, is said to have been introduced by the Romans to keep them warm in the English winters by flogging themselves with it. It burns more severely than either the greater or lesser stinging nettles, *Urtica Didica* and *Urtica urens*. It is only found now in parts of Essex and on the East coast.

Nettles have other economic uses besides making thread. In Siberia they are made into paper, an oil can be expressed from them to use as a green dye and this is sometimes mixed with alum in dying Easter eggs yellow. The oil can also be burned instead of paraffin. The leaves preserve the bloom on plums if they are packed with them, and a decoction of Nettles can be used instead of rennet to turn milk sour. A rennet is made of a strong decoction, and a spoonful of the liquor coagulates a large bowl of milk, according to Lightfoot.

The juice of Nettles prevents wooden tubs from leaking; it coagulates and fills up the interstices. Nettles make good fodder for cows, and the seeds mixed with food given to poultry increase the hens' laying power. The seeds are also sometimes put into hair tonics.

Altogether the Nettle, troublesome as it is as a weed, can be put to great use economically and medicinally. Cooling Docks nearly always grow somewhere in its neighbourhood and are ready to hand to antidote its stings. Hence the old rhyme,

Nettle in, dock out,
Dock rub nettle out.

ELECTUARY OF NETTLES

Take of powdered Nettles an ounce and a half with their double weight of honey clarified in white wine. Mix together and make into an electuary.

NETTLE CLARET

Put into a bottle of claret an ounce of Nettle seeds. Cork the bottle and immerse it in a saucepan of hot water, keeping the water boiling for 15 minutes to enable the wine to become impregnated with the virtues of the seeds.

This can be taken once or more daily in wineglassful doses to remove cholic.

ONION

This is every cook's opinion,
No savoury dish without an onion.
But lest your kissing should be spoiled,
Your onions must be fully boiled.

Dean Swift

Botanical name	Allium Cepa, var. aggregatum
Natural order	Liliaceae
Country name	Egyptian onion
French name	Oignon
German name	Zwiebel
Italian name	Cipolla
Spanish name	Cebolla
Under the dominion of	Mars
Part used	Bulb
Natural habitat	Egypt

The Onion is the groundwork of nearly all cookery, especially French cooking. It is as useful as the Lemon and both are almost indispensable.

The Onion comes to us from Egypt, where the Children of Israel learned to like it. It was so popular in Egypt, we are told by Herodotus, that when the Pyramids were being built, Onions to the value of nine tons of gold were bought for the workmen.

The Onion has the power of absorbing poison and in Latin countries a string of onions is hung outside cottage doors, or inside, to keep the inmates free from infectious diseases.

This is why Onions should be so carefully examined before they are eaten or cooked, because a bad onion nearly always means that it is poisoned.

A raw Onion is a quick cure for a cold because the germ is at once absorbed by the Onion. The bulb contains a good deal of sulphur and also phosphorus.

Onions have decided soporific power, and Onion gruel is a very helpful and safe remedy to take at night to induce sleep.

Onions have a most beneficial action on the mucous membranes of the body, and in asthmatical and catarrhal complaints they are very useful. They stimulate and give warmth internally.

The acrid volatile oil in a raw onion brings tears to the eyes, even in handling it.

> *Mine eyes smell onions,*
> *I shall weep anon.*

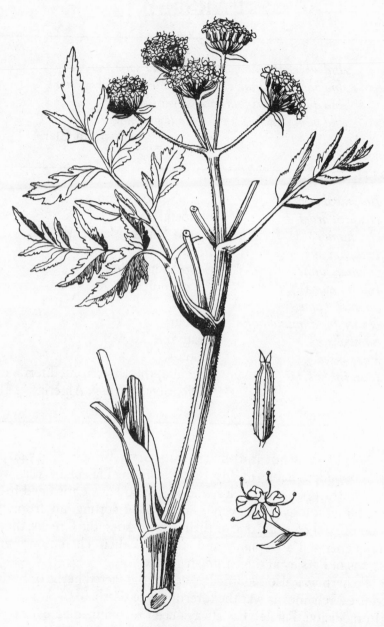

SWEET CICELY
Myrrhis odorata

PARSLEY

And where the marjoram once, and sage and rue
And balm and mint, with curl'd leaf parsley grew.
And double marigolds and silver thyme,
And pumpkins 'neath the window climb.

John Clare

Botanical name	Carum petroselinum
Natural order	Umbelliferae
Old names	Anglo-Saxon: March, Marish
French name	Persil
German name	Gartenpetersilie
Italian name	Prezzemolo
Spanish name	Perejil
Under the dominion of	Mercury
Symbolises	Festivity, To win
Parts used	Root, seeds
Natural habitat	Sardinia, the Eastern Mediterranean districts, Turkey, Algeria

Parsley was not introduced into Great Britain till 1548. Its botanical name means Rock Selinon. The plant was well known to Dioscorides who is said to have christened it. In Greek mythology Parsley is said to have sprung up from the blood of Archemorus, one of their great heroes; the Greeks, therefore, venerated the plant, and crowned their champions with wreaths of Parsley at the Isthmian games.

The herb was also regarded as one of the sacred herbs of burial, because Archemorus was the forerunner of death.

In medicine, Parsley has always been recommended ever since the time of Galen as a good remedy for obstructions. It was one of 'the five opening roots' according to Culpeper. Galen used the boiled roots for epilepsy; and Gerard recommended it to get rid of poison; and we know that it removes all trace of onions or garlic from the breath if it is eaten after either of these. Parsley has an influence on the nerve centres of the head and the spine. Sheep, hares and rabbits seek the plant, but it poisons parrots and chickens.

In cooking it is used for sauces and as a flavouring, and as a decoration for cold dishes and butter.

The old saying, 'We are at the parsley and rue'; meaning the very beginning of a project, arose from the habit of bordering Greek gardens with Parsley and Rue. Two other old sayings, with regard to Parsley are entirely contradictory. One is, 'Fried parsley brings a man to his saddle and a woman to her grave,' and the other is, 'Poison to men and salvation to women.' The latter probably refers to its use in women's complaints.

Parsley must not be confused with Fool's Parsley which is a poisonous plant, but the wild Parsley has all the properties of the garden variety.

PEONY

The lilacs browned, a breath dried the laburnum,
The swollen peonies scattered the earth with blood,
And the rhododendrons shed their sumptuous marbles
And the marshalled Irises unsceptred stood.

J. C. Squire

Botanical name	Paeonia officinalis (Linn.)
Natural order	Ranunculaceae
Other name	Paeonia Corallina
French name	Pivoine
German names	Echte Pfingstrose, Paonie
Italian name	Peonia
Spanish name	Peonia
Under the dominion of	Sun and the sign Leo
Symbolises	Bashfulness
Parts used	Root, seeds, flowers, leaves
Natural habitat	China

The Peony is a very ancient medicinal plant, every part of which has some healing virtue. It was called after Paeos who cured Philo when he was wounded in the Trojan war. The ancients believed it to be an emanation of the moon, and lunatics were given Peony roots to cure them of their madness. The seeds were also strung into necklaces which were worn round the neck as an antidote to witchcraft.

A distinction is drawn in medicine between the male and female roots, the former being only given to men and the female roots to women.

Nicholas Culpeper and all the herbalists make a point of this, and the root was regarded as of the first importance, then the seeds, after this the flowers and last of all the leaves.

The seeds are used as tea by the Mongolians, and they make the roots into broth. The kernels are eaten as a condiment, and were used in cooking to decorate creams in the same way as sliced almonds.

Peonies were introduced from China and only grow wild in England on the island in the Severn called Steep Holme, where they are probably an escape from some former monastery garden.

SYRUP OF PEONY FLOWERS

Take of fresh Peony flowers 1 pound, infuse them in 3 pints of hot water for the space of 12 hours, then let them boil a little and press them out, adding the like quantity of fresh flowers and use as the former up to 5 times, then add to the infusion 2½ pounds of loaf sugar and boil to a syrup.

PEONY WATER

Take of Peony flowers 1½ pounds; Spanish wine, 12 pints. Infuse the petals in the wine for 24 hours, then distil them in an alembic. Draw out 3 pints of strong water. Sweeten with sugar and keep for use.

RADISH

A Roman meal,
Such as the mistress of the world once found
Delicious, when her patriots of high note
Perhaps by moonlight at their humble doors,
Under an ancient oak's domestic shade,
Enjoy'd spare feast—a radish and an egg.

                                                    Thomson

Botanical name	Raphanus sativus
Natural order	Cruciferae
French name	Radis
German name	Rettig
Italian name	Rafano
Spanish name	Rabano
Dutch name	Tamme radÿs
Under the dominion of	Mars
Parts used	Root, seed pods
Natural habitat	China, Cochin China, Japan. Culti-vated in Europe, including Great Britain, Temperate Asia

The Radish is a cultivated variety of the Horseradish. It was so reverenced by the ancient Greeks that in the Temple of Delphi a Radish was represented in gold, whereas Beetroots were only carved in silver and Turnips in lead. The plant was cultivated in Egypt during the reign of the Pharaohs. It was one of the herbs that Dioscorides praised most highly and so did Pliny.

It was not introduced into England till 1548, and it has been popular ever since. The large amount of phosphorus it contains gives it exceptional tonic properties; and its other salts, such as sulphur, make it a very valuable blood purifier.

Radishes, like Pears, are good food to follow Mushrooms; because if the Mushroom should be poisonous, Radishes and Pears antidote the poison.

A preparation of Radish juice and honey makes the hair grow; and the juice alone is a quick cure for corns if it is applied on several successive days.

The Wild Radish, *Raphanus Raphanistrum*, from which the garden variety is derived, is quite common in English cornfields. It is sometimes called Jointed Charlock and its roots are used instead of Horseradish.

William Cole says, 'Radishes doth manifestly heat and dry, open and make thin by reason of the biting quality that ruleth in it.'

Radishes are still an old wives' remedy for keeping a young figure.

REST HARROW

In grey-green leafage, dewy and downy, lay a little blossom of delicate pink, chalice-shaped, with a lip of flushed white.

'Rest Harrow', Maurice Hewlett

Botanical name	Ononis arvensis
Natural order	Leguminosae
Country names	Land Whin, Cammock, Wild Liquorice, Stinking Tommy, Ground Furze.
French name	Bugrane
German name	Hauhechel
Italian name	Ononide serpeggiante
Spanish name	Detienebuey
Dutch name	Stalkruid
Under the dominion of	Mars
Part used	Herb
Natural habitat	Europe, including Great Britain

Rest Harrow is one of the vetches. The flower is like a Sweet Pea in appearance but the plant has rough woolly leaves and thorns. It is very common on arable land, hence its name.

It was well known to the Greeks, who used it to cure delirium tremens. Pliny said it was obnoxious to snakes. Donkeys like it and it is one of their favourite foods.

The young shoots can be boiled as a vegetable or they can be eaten raw in a salad or they can be pickled and eaten with cold meat.

The plant is said to dissolve stone.

In the eighteenth century the bark was made into a conserve with sugar, or the root was steeped in Canary wine.

There is a legend that Rest Harrow was the plant used to make the crown of thorns at the Crucifixion of Our Lord.

CARAWAY

Carum Carvi

ROCKET

Blest is thy lesson, vestal of the flowers—
Not in the sunshine is our whole delight;
Some joys bloom only in love's pensive hours,
And for their fragrance on the breeze of night.

Botanical name	Hesperis matronalis
Natural order	Cruciferae
Country names	Dame's Rocket, Vesper Flower, Dame's Violet
French names	Roquette, Julienne
German name	Ruckbette
Italian names	Cruccia sativa, Giuliana
Spanish name	Jaramago
Under the dominion of	Mars
Symbolises	Deceit
Part used	Whole plant
Natural habitat	Central and Southern Europe, including Great Britain

The Garden Rocket is one of those flowers that keeps its perfume for the night. In the daytime it is scentless. The flowers are white, purple, or variegated. The spear-like leaves are hot to the taste, and take the place of Cress in salads, but they should be gathered before the plant has flowered.

The Garden Rocket must not be confused with the Wild Rocket, which is too strong to be used in salads or even in medicine.

The seeds, however, were said to be a most efficacious cure for stings and bites of serpents and they were sometimes mixed with vinegar to cure freckles.

SAGE

Sage strengthens the sinews, feaver's heat doth swage,
The palsie helps and rids of mickle woe,
In Latin (salvia) takes the name of safety,
In English (sage) is rather wise than craftie;
Sith then the name betokens wise and saving,
We count it Nature's friend and worth the having.

From 'The Englishman's Doctor', 1607

Botanical name	Salvia officinalis
Natural order	Labiatae
French name	Sauge officinale
German names	Salbei, echte Salvei
Italian name	Salvia
Spanish name	Salvia
Under the dominion of	Jupiter
Symbolises	Domestic virtue
Parts used	Leaves, herb
Natural habitat	Northern shores of Mediterranean

Sage is so wholesome that it is not surprising that at one time it was regarded as a panacea for every disease under the sun. Even the Chinese once preferred its leaves to their own tea. The botanical name is derived from Salvere—to save, in reference to its great healing power.

After its introduction into England in the sixteenth century, it became so popular that it was universally drunk as we drink tea today. It was made into wine, pressed into cheeses, eaten between bread and butter, and made into stuffing for turkey and goose and veal; and in the eighteenth century, sage butter was one of the Church's great fasting dishes.

Today it is still used to flavour sausages, and to make stuffing for veal, duck and Christmas goose, but the marbled cheeses of our grandmothers are only rarely seen.

There are many varieties of Sage and they are some of the most popular of our garden plants. They are delightfully aromatic and the oil distilled from them is strongly antiseptic. Sage has a marked effect on the brain and the head. It strengthens the sinews and has been used with success in palsy. In Germany and Dalmatia a large industry is carried on in Sage oil.

Sage apples are produced by the puncture of insects in one of the Sages which grow in the Greek islands. The natives preserve the apples in syrup and make them into conserves.

Two other varieties of Sage much used in herbal medicine are the Wood Sage, *Teucrium Scorodonia* and the Clary Sage, *Salvia Sclarea*. The Wood Sage is used in gargles, and Clary, because of its mucilage, is helpful in clearing foreign matter from the eyes. This is why it is called Clary, which means Clear Eye.

FRIED SAGE PANCAKES

Make a batter in the usual way. Dip the Sage leaves in it and fry in butter till crisp.

SAMPHIRE

And there the emerald samphire oft
Appears a tempting sight,
And lures the venturous boy aloft
To scale the height.

Botanical name	Crithmum maritimum (Linn.)
Natural order	Umbelliferae
Country names	Sampier, Sea Fennel, Crest Marine
French names	Herbe de S. Pierre, Crête marine
German name	Meerfenchel
Italian names	Sanpetra, Erba di San Pietro, Erba corda
Spanish name	Finochio marino
Under the dominion of	Jupiter
Part used	Herb
Natural habitat	Europe, including Great Britain

Samphire grows on rocks near the sea and is found on the coasts of England, and in Scotland. It puts forth big branches from the root and the leaves are deep green, full of sap, and have a hot spicy pleasant taste. The flowers grow in white umbels and are followed by seeds which are larger than Fennel seeds. The whole plant is powerfully aromatic. It can be boiled as a vegetable or made into a pickle to eat with cold meat. Preserved with vinegar and spice it makes one of the most wholesome of all pickles.

At one time it was so much collected and sold that it was cried in the streets of London.

PICKLED SAMPHIRE

Take the Samphire that is green, lay it in a clean pan. Throw over it a few handfuls of salt and then cover it with spring water. Let it lie 24 hours, then put it into a clean saucepan, throw in a handful of salt and cover it with vinegar. Cover it tightly and set it on a slow fire and leave it till it is green and crisp: then take it off at once, for if it stands long enough to get soft it will be spoilt. Then put it in the pickling pot and cover it closely. When cold tie it down and keep for use—or it can be kept all the year in a strong salt brine and water and thrown into vinegar before using.

SAVORY

Botanical names	(Summer) Satureia hortensis (Linn.),
	(Winter) Satureia montana (Linn.)
Natural order	Labiatae
French name	Sarriette
German name	Bohnenkraut
Italian names	Savoria, Santoreggia
Spanish name	Ajedrea
Under the dominion of	Mercury
Part used	Herb
Natural habitat	Europe, including Great Britain

These plants of the Satyrs, as their botanical names denote, were known to Virgil who recommended that both varieties, the summer and the winter, should be planted close to beehives.

They are strongly aromatic and the leaves are wholesome and comforting in salads.

The Romans made a sauce of them with vinegar corresponding to our Mint sauce of today.

Summer Savory has a reputation for preserving the sight and also the hearing. It was made into conserves and syrups.

CONSERVE OF SUMMER SAVORY

Take together equal quantities of the fresh leaves of Summer Savory and white sugar and beat to a conserve.

SAXIFRAGES

His disk of white on upland wolds
The pretty saxifrage unfolds
With lucid spots of crimson pied
Hence brought, and hail'd the city's pride.

Botanical name	Chrysoplenium oppositifolium
Natural order	Saxifragaceae
Country name	Golden Saxifrage
French name	Dorine
German name	Goldmilz
Italian name	Sassifraga
Dutch name	Goudveil
Danish name	Gylden Steenbreck
Swedish name	Gul Stenbråck
Under the dominion of	The Sun
Symbolises	Affection
Part used	Herb
Natural habitat	Europe, including Great Britain

There are several Saxifrages used in medicine including the Greater and Lesser Burnet Saxifrages, which as Umbelliferous plants, belong to another order.

The golden Saxifrage, which is a true Saxifrage, is better known in the Vosges mountains as Cresson de Roche. It must not be confused with *Alyssum saxatile compactum*, which belongs to the Cruciferae, and is one of the gayest of our spring flowers because its yellow leaves and clusters of sulphur-coloured flowers give it the effect of gold. This comes out at the same time as the purple Aubretias and the white double Arabis, and the effect of the three together in rockeries is startlingly beautiful. The yellow Saxifrage is often called by its country name of Gold Dust, a name by which it is also known in other countries.

CASCARILLA
Croton eluteria

In medicine it is used to cure a disordered spleen and to drive away melancholy.

The white Saxifrage, *Saxifraga alba*, which is governed by the moon, is also used in medicine for its seed, root and flowers, from which a water was at one time distilled and found useful in dissolving stone in the kidney.

A Canadian plant belonging to the same order, *Tiarella cordifolia*, with white spiral-like flowers, has lately become popular as an anti-acid cure which is taken internally in the form of a tisane of the whole herb. Its English name is Coolwort. It will grow in England in rich light soil and makes a good border edging. It grows wild from Canada to Virginia.

SHEPHERD'S PURSE

To him that hath a flux, of Shepherds purse be given,
And Mouse Ear unto him whom some sharp rupture grieves.
Michael Drayton

Botanical name	Capsella Bursa-pastoris
Natural order	Cruciferae
Country names	Lady's Purse, Shepherd's Scrip, Shepherd's Bag, Pepper and Salt, Witches' Pouches, Sanguinary, Mother's Heart, Pick Pocket, St. James's Wort, Clapper Pouch
French names	Bourse de Pasteur, Fleur de S. Jacques
German name	Hirtentäschel
Italian name	Borsa di Pastore
Spanish name	Bolsa de Pastor
Under the dominion of	Saturn
Symbolises	I offer you all
Part used	Herb
Natural habitat	Europe, including Great Britain, Asia

Shepherd's Purse, the great specific for haemorrhages of all kinds, is found all over the world. In China and North America it is cooked and eaten as a vegetable, but it has not a very pleasant taste and this is against it, even as a medicine. Herbalists combine it with Pellitory of the Wall and Juniper to get over this difficulty.

It contains a special acid, known as bursinic acid, which probably chiefly contributes to its great use in medicine. An added factor is that it can be used with perfect safety.

The plant takes its name from its seed pods, which are in the form of a purse.

It grows in hedges and ditches and is in flower from early spring to late autumn. It thrives in heat or in cold and in damp or dry climates. Nothing thwarts it.

SPURGES

Botanical name	Euphorbia Helioscopia
Natural order	Euphorbiaceae
Country names	Churnstaff, Wart Weed, Cat's Milk, Wolf's Milk, Little Good, Sun Tithy Male
French name	Euphorbe
German name	Wolfsmilch
Italian name	Euforbio
Spanish name	Euforbio
Dutch name	Wolfsmelk
Under the dominion of	Mercury
Parts used	Root, juice
Natural habitat	The slope of the great Atlas range in Morocco

The Spurges, which take their name of Euphorbia from Euphorbus, one of the physicians of Juba, King of Mauretania, are characterised by an acrid milky juice which can be used externally for removing warts, but which makes the plants unsafe for internal use until the roots have been boiled. The exception to this rule is the Caper Spurge, *Euphorbia Lathyrus*, the seeds of which can be pickled and eaten with meat.

The most deadly of all the Euphorbias in its fresh state is the South American Spurge known as Manioc; but, after the acrid juice has been taken from it, the root can be made into a nourishing and wholesome bread, and from the pulp we get Tapioca. Two other important Euphorbias are the Castor Oil Plant and the India-rubber tree. Most of the Euphorbias contain Caoutchin in some form.

Two other species, the Wood Spurge and the Petty Spurge, *Euphorbia Peplus*, are common in English woods and are conspicuous by their long bright-green blossoms. The Petty Spurge turns its flowers to the sun, and its botanical name literally translated means 'Welcome to the Home'.

STITCHWORT

And the Stitchwort with its pearly star
Seen on the hedge bank from afar.

Calder Campbell

Botanical names	(Greater Stitchwort) Stellaria Holostea, (Lesser Stitchwort) Stellaria Graminea
Natural order	Caryophyllaceae
Country names	Milkmaid, Adder's Meat, Satin Flower, Miller's Star, Shirt Buttons, Bird's Tongue, White Sunday, Devil's Eyes, Devil's Ears, Snapjack, Snapcrackers, Snappers
French name	Stellaire
German name	Sternmiene
Italian name	Stellaria
Spanish name	Stellaria
Under the dominion of	The Moon
Symbolises	Hermitage
Parts used	Herb, juice
Natural habitat	Europe, including Great Britain

The Greater and Lesser Stitchworts are closely allied to the Chickweed. As their name suggests, they were at one time used generally as a cure for stitch in the side. The herb was drunk in wine with powdered acorns, according to Gerard. The juice is said to help the sight when it has become dim, and this is probably explained by the fact that it contains silica, which is known to be good for restoring sight. The Stitchworts are very wholesome and can be boiled and eaten as a vegetable in the same way as Chickweed.

There are three other varieties of Stitchwort—the Marsh Stitchwort, the Bog Stitchwort and the Wood Stitchwort.

266

STOCKS

But the few lingering scents
Of streaked pea, and gillyflower and stocks
Of courtly purple and aromatic phlox.

Robert Bridges

Botanical name	Matthiola incana
Natural order	Cruciferae
French names	Giroflée, Quarantaine
German names	Stock, Winterlevkoje
Italian names	Fiorbarco, Tronco di Cavolo
Symbolises	Lasting beauty
Part used	Leaves, flowers
Natural habitat	Southern Europe

The leaves of all the Stocks can safely be used in salads or stews. The plant from which the garden varieties are derived is called after the great Italian herbalist Matthiolus. It is sometimes found growing wild on the southern shores of the Isle of Wight near the sea. It has light purple flowers and the strong scent that we associate with Stocks.

The Virginia Stock which is so popular as a garden edging also grows wild near Dover, but it is really a Mediterranean coast plant.

SYRUP OF STOCKS

Take of the fresh petals of the Stocks, 2 pounds; boiling distilled water, 5 pints. Macerate for 24 hours; afterwards strain the liquor, without pressing, through thin linen. Add enough double-refined sugar to make into a syrup.

SUNFLOWER

The flower enamoured of the sun
At his departure hangs her head and weeps
And shrouds her sweetness up and keeps
Sad vigils, like a cloistered nun.
Till his reviving ray appears
Waking her beauty as he dries her tears.

Botanical name	Helianthus annuus
Natural order	Compositae
Country name	Marigold of Peru
French name	Hélianthe
German name	Sonnenblume
Italian name	Elianto
Spanish name	Helianto
Under the dominion of	The Sun
Symbolises	Haughtiness
Parts used	Seeds, leaves, oil
Natural habitat	Peru and Mexico

The Sunflower is called after the Sun, Helios. Every part of the plant is useful either medicinally or economically. The oil can be burnt instead of paraffin and has been very much used in this way in the past; the seeds are eaten on the Continent; the buds are used in salads and cooked as a vegetable, the leaves are smoked, and the flowers make an excellent yellow dye.

As food for cattle, Sunflower seeds are so useful that their use is general in most countries.

As a medicine, Sunflower seeds are considered a specific cure for whooping cough; the seeds are so emollient that they have a soothing effect on the mucous membrane and most coughs are relieved by them.

For economic purposes the giant Sunflower of Russia is the best variety to cultivate.

CORIANDER

Coriandrum sativum

Boil 2 ounces of the seeds in a quart of water till it is reduced to a pint. Strain and add six ounces of Hollands and sugar to taste.

A teaspoonful can be taken at a time for coughs and whooping cough.

SWEET CICELY

And Nature holds, in wood and field,
Her thousand sunlit censers still;
To spells of flower and shrub we yield
Against or with our will.

John Greenleaf Whittier

Botanical name	Myrrhis odorata
Natural order	Umbelliferae
Country names	British Myrrh, Chervil, Sweet Cus, Smooth Cicely, The Roman Plant, Shepherd's Needle, Sweet Fern, Sweet Hemlock, Cow Chervil, Beaked Parsley
French name	Cerfeuil
German names	Kerbel, Spanische Süssdolde
Italian names	Cerfolio, Mirride
Spanish name	Perifolio
Under the dominion of	Jupiter
Symbolises	Sincerity
Parts used	Root, herb
Natural habitat	Europe, including Great Britain

Sweet Cicely is better known as Chervil. It is generally associated in cookery with Tarragon, because together they form almost the best flavouring for salads and omelettes. Chervil has the sympathetic property of improving the flavour of other herbs with which it is blended.

It stands alone, however, as a tonic. It is so safe that its use can hardly be abused. It gives back strength and courage to those who have lost both. It cures flatulence, and its fragrance makes it a very pleasant drink. In parts of France its seeds are macerated in brandy, which is taken medicinally. The leaves are excellent in salads. The roots can be boiled and eaten with oil and vinegar. They are good, like Eryngo, for people who are no longer young.

Sweet Cicely grows in pastures in the North of England and in the Lowlands of Scotland. It is a perennial herb, somewhat resembling the dangerous Hemlock. It's feathery leaves turn almost purple in the autumn and the whole plant has a very pleasant smell of aniseed. It is the cultivated plant that is used and this variety differs from the wild by having its stems swollen beneath the joints.

In the sixteenth and seventeenth centuries, the seeds of the Chervil were used to scent and polish floors and furniture in France, where the plant has always been a favourite. The botanical name, Choerophyllum, means 'a leaf which rejoices the heart'. It was one of the aromatic herbs used in making the holy oil of the Tabernacle with which Moses anointed the sacred vessels.

TARRAGON

The Greenherbs
Stir in the summer's breath; a thousand flowers
By the roadside and the borders of the brook
Nod gaily to each other; glossy leaves
Are twinkling in the sun, as if the dew
Were on them yet.

Botanical name	Artemisia dracunculus (Linn.)
Natural order	Compositae
Country names	Little Dragon
French names	Herbe au dragon, Estragon
German name	Dragon
Italian names	Serpentaria, Dragontea
Spanish name	Estragon
Under the dominion of	Mars
Symbolises	Share
Parts used	Leaves, herb
Natural habitat	Siberia

Tarragon is closely allied to two other plants which grow in England—Wormwood and Mugwort. It is a perennial aromatic herb growing about one-and-a-half to two feet in height, with long narrow leaves which, unlike those of other members of the same family, are undivided. The flowers, which appear as yellow and black heads, rarely open. The plant grows best in an open position with a good deal of sun, but it likes a poor soil.

It is called Dragon because it has the power of curing the bites and stings of venomous reptiles.

The herb is cooling as well as aromatic and carminative and is generally combined with Chervil as a flavouring for salads and omelettes.

The combination of Chervil and Tarragon is essentially French, and is used in the cooking of many French dishes. Tartare sauce depends on Tarragon, so does Béarnaise sauce and also Ravigote sauce.

Tarragon is also largely used to make Tarragon vinegar.

The herb has a cordial effect on the head and on the liver. There are two varieties, the French and the Russian, but the latter has not the same sharp flavour as the French, which is certainly to be preferred.

THYME

What time the mighty moon
Was gathering light
Love paced the thymy plots
Of Paradise.

Tennyson

Botanical names	(Garden Thyme) Thymus vulgaris (Linn.), (Wild Thyme) Thymus serpyllum (Linn.)
Natural order	Labiatae
French name	Thym
German name	Thymian
Italian name	Timo
Spanish name	Tomillo
Under the dominion of	Venus and Aries
Symbolises	Courage
Part used	Herb
Country of origin	Europe, including Great Britain

Thyme will grow wherever Lavender and Rosemary thrive, so in England it does better than almost anywhere else. The wild Thyme, which is called Serpyllum because of its creeping habit, grows best on light soil and is found in great clumps on moors and other dry places. The honey of Hymettus is collected by the bees from the wild Thyme which grows on the mountain of Hymettus in Sicily.

Those who eat it are said to become more courageous, because the wild Thyme has had from time immemorial the reputation of increasing courage.

In the Middle Ages a sprig of Thyme was given to knights by their ladies to keep up their courage, and even scarves embroidered with a bee alighting on a sprig of Thyme were supposed to produce the same effect.

In appearance the wild Thyme is very similar to the common garden Thyme. It has purple flowers and is in bloom from May to October.

In herbal medicine it is a cure for melancholy, for nightmare, for insomnia; and is said to strengthen the lungs and improve digestion. It also helps the sight; and it makes delicious baths which improve the skin and tone up the nervous system.

The garden Thyme provides us with the antiseptic oil which is known as Thymol. The whole plant has disinfectant properties and can be used in medicine much in the same way as the wild Thyme. It is a favourite plant in rockeries and paved walks because of its scent, which becomes stronger the more it is trodden on. There are other scented varieties which are even more decorative and more sweet smelling, such as the Lemon Thyme, the Caraway Thyme (*Thymus baronna*), the Basil Thyme, and the Orange Thyme. Their leaves are beautiful, so the Silver Thyme and the Variegated Thyme make lovely clumps in the rock garden, as do also the broad-leaved and the narrow-leaved varieties. It must always be remembered, however, that all the Thymes extract the goodness from the soil they grow in, so that it becomes impoverished in time.

Thyme has such a pleasant, wholesome scent and it is so cleansing to the blood that its use in cookery is valuable. When sheep feed on it the mutton is considered specially tender and succulent. Vinegar of Thyme is a useful form in which to use the plant as a disinfectant and it can be used like smelling salts to alleviate a nervous headache.

VINEGAR OF THYME

Infuse a pound of the flowers in light sextaries of vinegar and set it for 40 days in the sun, then strain and keep the vinegar. It will be still stronger if the process is repeated a second time.

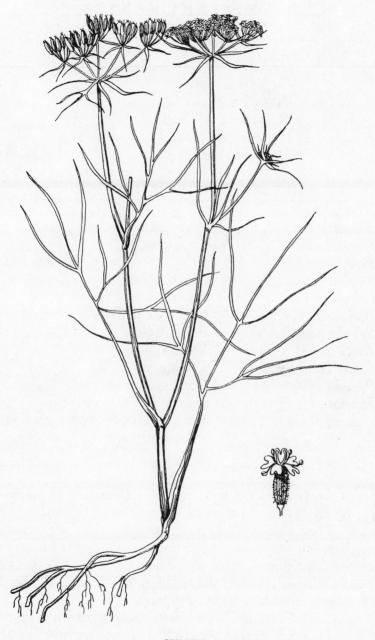

CUMIN

Cuminum cyminum

WATERCRESS

Lord, I confess too when I dine,
The pulse is Thine:
And all these other bits that be
There placed by Thee:
The wurts, the perslane, and the mess
Of watercress.

Robert Herrick

Botanical name	Nasturtium officinale
Natural order	Cruciferae
French names	Cresson au poulet, Cresson de fontaine, Nasilord
German name	Brunnenkresse
Italian name	Crescione di fonte
Spanish name	Berro di agua
Dutch name	Waterkers
Under the dominion of	The Moon
Symbolises	Stability, power
Parts used	Leaves, flowers, seeds
Natural habitat	Russian Asia, Europe, including Great Britain

'Eat Cresses and get wit' was a Greek tribute to the whole family of Cresses, of which Watercress is the most popular. They all share the same pungent, biting and warming properties; and, in the days when Eastern spices were a luxury the poor could not afford, some of the Cresses, such as Pepperwort, *Dittanda sativus*, obtained the name of Poor Man's Pepper because it was a substitute for real pepper.

The Garden Cress, or Town Cress, has been grown in England for three hundred years and is rarely grown apart from the Mustard with which it is always associated. This is the Cress that is so often grown in nurseries, to the delight of children, on white flannel in a soup plate, and then eaten for tea.

Of all the Cresses, however, Watercress surpasses them all, not only in flavour but also because of its extraordinary value in giving and restoring health.

It contains so much sulphur and nitrogen, combined with other useful mineral salts like iodine, that it is not only a great promoter of appetite, but a cleansing food that few can do without. Fortunately it is very largely cultivated by market gardeners today and is accessible to everyone, but the curative value of the wild Watercress which grows in brooks and streams in many parts of England is greater.

Watercress pottage is an excellent spring medicine, and Watercress juice is one of the best cosmetics to remove blemishes from the skin.

The garden Nasturtium, which has a monograph to itself, is also one of the Cresses and every part of it is wholesome.

WILLOW HERB

O'er her light skiff of woven bulrush made
The Water Lily lends a polished shade;
White Galium there, in pale and silver line,
And Epilobium on the bank that grew
From her soft couch.

Botanical name	Epilobium angustifolium (Linn.)
Natural order	Onagraceae
Country names	Purple Rocket, French Willow, Wicopy, Wickup, Persian Willow, Blooming Sally
French names	Laurier de S. Antoine, Épilobe à épi, Osier fleur
German name	Weiderich
Italian names	Epilobio a spighe, Lauro roseo
Turkish name	Mukaddes defne
Russian name	Xipree Karamuk
Under the dominion of	Saturn
Symbolises	Pretension
Parts used	Herb, leaves, root
Natural habitat	Europe, including Great Britain

This very decorative, tall, purple-flowering plant grows in great profusion in copses and open spaces and by rivers, and is in flower in the late spring. It springs up in towns where houses are demolished and open spaces are left for a season or two, and in woods where trees are cut down and on river banks. There are large patches of it in the old parts of Hampstead at Frognal, and in woods all over the country. Sheep, cows and goats all like it, and the young shoots are sometimes boiled and eaten in the same way as Asparagus. It is a demulcent tonic with astringent properties and the leaves contain mucilage and tannin.

In medicine the plant is a cure for whooping cough and asthma.

The leaves are very much used in Russia to adulterate ordinary tea and the Russians call it Kaporie tea. It is also used by them to flavour ale.

The plant, in France, is called after St. Antony. Laurier de Saint Antoine is a favourite herb with the French.

Chapter VI

SPICES

SPICES AND CONDIMENTS

Chapter VI

SPICES

S pice trees, like Orange trees, need a tropical climate to ripen their fruit. Jamaica, Ceylon, the West Indies, India and China are the home of most of them. They are among the most beautiful of all fruit trees, but in the case of the Clove trees, their beauty in many cases never reaches maturity because the calyces are beaten off the tree before the fruit ripens, otherwise the seeds— or Cloves as we know them—lose their pungent taste and scent. The best Cloves are grown in the Molucca Islands, particularly in Amboyne, and the old saga of the Amboynese refers to the history of the Clove plantations. The leaves of the Clove tree are like Bay leaves. The tree is evergreen and grows to about thirty feet in height. The flowers grow at the end of long green buds, and are a lovely rose colour. The tree does not bloom until it is nine years old, and then for a hundred years or more it continues to produce flowers and fruit without requiring attention of any kind.

The Nutmeg tree grows in the same islands, and in Malay and other places. Its leaves also are not unlike Bay leaves, but its flowers resemble Lilies of the Valley.

The evergreen Allspice tree with its greenish-white flowers hanging in bunches, is a feature of the Jamaican landscape. It grows to about the same height as the Clove tree, but it begins to bear fruit when it is three or four years old, and at seven years has reached maturity.

The Cinnamon tree is a native of Ceylon and grows best in pure sand. It is cultivated in the East Indies and also in the West Indies, but it is confined to the torrid zone. It has white flowers which grow in panicles.

The Canella tree often grows to a height of fifty feet. It is also a native of the West Indies, and has purple flowers which hang in bunches and rarely open. The tree is so aromatic that it scents the whole neighbourhood.

The Cassia tree is the Cinnamon of China. It is of all spice trees perhaps the most beautiful because of its flame-coloured leaves and exquisite blossoms.

The history of spice trees is most ancient and romantic. It starts long before the journey of the Wise Men to the manger at Bethlehem. Moses obtained Cinnamon from Arabia (where it was probably imported from Ceylon) for the holy anointing oil; and the Old Testament has constant references to Cinnamon, Calamus, Myrrh and Frankincense. Solomon burnt them as incense in the Temple. Pliny speaks of Cinnamon as growing in Syria. Nero burnt Cinnamon and Cassia at the funeral of Poppaea.

Venice was the centre of the spice trade at the height of its prosperity under the Doges; but by the end of the fifteenth century the Portuguese monopolised the Cinnamon industry; then it got into Dutch hands through an alliance between the Dutch and the King of Candy, and when the Chinese entered into competition with them with their Cassia (which some prefer to the Indian Cinnamon) the Dutch made plantations of Cinnamon in Ceylon before it passed into our possession in 1796.

The wealth of nations has been founded upon spices as it has upon Olives. Oils and spices were the oldest international trading commodities.

It is not only for their scent that spices are so valuable, but also for their antiseptic properties in medicine. The value of Cinnamon as an antiseptic is now generally acknowledged, and the oil of all spices has powerful disinfectant properties.

Some of the smaller spice trees or shrubs grow successfully in Europe. Caraway, Coriander, Dill and Juniper ripen their fruit easily in England.

Cumin is now grown in the countries near the Mediterranean, although the plant was in the Middle Ages cultivated throughout Europe.

Cardamom seeds come from India and need a hot climate to ripen them. Ginger is a native of China and the West Indies. Cascarilla is grown in the Bahama Islands.

The Mustard plant, both black and white, is indigenous to Eng-

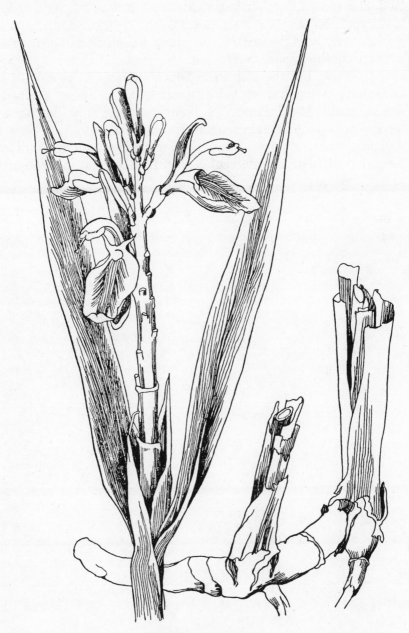

LESSER GALANGAL

Alpinia officinarum

land, and the yellow Mustard fields are a feature of the English landscape. Mustard is *par excellence* the English condiment. Nasturtium seeds and the seeds of the biting Persicaria can be used as a substitute for Pepper and are our English equivalents. They are easy to grow, but the Capsicum which yields Cayenne Pepper must have a tropical or sub-tropical climate. Sweet Peppers, *Croton annum*, is the Pepper of Hungary; the Pepper known as 'grains of paradise' comes to us from Ethiopia.

All these are the stimulants of the vegetable kingdom. Without them our circulation would suffer, for they keep up the temperature of the body, and increase appetite.

ALLSPICE

Botanical name	Pimenta officinalis
Natural order	Myrtaceae
Other names	Jamaica Pepper, Pimento
French name	Piment
German name	Pimentbaum
Italian name	Pimento
Spanish name	Pimiento
Under the dominion of	Mars
Symbolises	Compassion
Part used	Fruit
Natural habitat	West India, Jamaica, South America

The Jamaica Pepper tree in its native country is a beautiful tree growing to a height of often thirty feet in huge forests near the sea. The trunk is covered with a smooth brown bark, and the many branches are closely spread with shiny green leaves, oblong and broad, growing in pairs on long pedicles.

The small flowers grow at the very end of the branches in June, July and August. The fruit is gathered before it is ripe, otherwise it would lose its strongly aromatic scent and its oil. In the process of drying the colour changes to a red brown, which is the colour the berries become if they are left on the tree to ripen naturally.

The rind of the berries contains the aromatic properties. The chief constituent of the berries is Phenol Eugenol, and good Allspice should contain 60 per cent. of this alkaloid.

Allspice is a favourite ingredient for mulled wines. It is used as a condiment in curries, and is a comforting and warming medicine for chills, and colic arising from chills.

It makes a very pleasant drink, rather like Clove tea, and the flavour is extracted by water or alcohol. An old fashioned way of taking it was in powder form mixed with sugar. It strengthens the stomach and gets rid of nausea.

The Carolina Pimento, *Calycanthus floridus*, which grows in the mountainous districts of Northern Carolina, is still more perfumed. It is called in America, Sweet Bush, and when crushed has a scent of Strawberries.

Allspice is nearly always an ingredient of pot-pourri and sweet jars. Its scent improves with keeping.

ALLSPICE WATER

Take of Allspice, bruised, ½ pound; water sufficient to prevent empyreuma.

Macerate for 24 hours and draw off 1 gallon.

ANISEED

Botanical name	Pimpinella anisum (Linn.)
Natural order	Umbelliferae
French name	Anis
German names	Anissamen, Anis
Italian name	Anise
Spanish name	Simiente de anis
Parts used	Seeds, oil distilled from the seeds
Natural habitat	Egypt, Greece, Asia Minor

This elegant annual umbelliferous plant with bright-green feathery-looking leaves was well known to the ancients, and was cultivated largely in Tuscany by the Romans. From there it was introduced into other European countries in the Middle Ages. It has been grown in England since the fourteenth century, but the seeds only ripen in a hot summer.

The commercial Aniseed comes from Germany, Russia and Spain; but the kind known as Alicante Aniseed which is grown in Spain is considered much the best.

In England the seeds and the distilled oil are chiefly used in medicine as warming and comforting carminatives, and for coughs and colds; but on the Continent no kitchen is complete without them, and Aniseed is used in broths and sauces and as a decoration for cakes and bread. The Latin phrase, 'Solamen intestinorum', is a tribute to its medicinal value.

The Romans used it in the digestive cakes which came at the end of their feasts. It was one of the tithes in the time of the Apostles.

'Ye pay tithe of mint, anise and cumin.'

St. Matthew, Chapter xxiii. 23.

and it is mentioned several times in the Bible.

To make Aniseed tea the seeds should be bruised before the hot water is poured over them; and the following is a good substitute for the Liqueur Anisette.

ANISE BRANDY

Infuse an ounce of the seeds in a pint of good brandy and cork well.

This is excellent for those inclined to asthma.

BROOM

Botanical name	Cytisus scoparius (Linn.)
Natural order	Leguminosae
Old names	Genista, Besam, Bisom, Browme, Green Broom
French name	Genêt
German names	Ginster, Besenkleestrauch
Italian name	Ginestra scopa
Spanish name	Hiniesta
Under the dominion of	Mars
Symbolises	Humility, neatness
Part used	Tops
Natural habitat	Europe, including Great Britain

The country names and the old names for the yellow Broom all refer to the use of its branches as a broom for sweeping. The branches are still used for garden sweeping and for some hard brooms; and in France it is called 'Genêt à balai'.

The plant is of particular interest to English people because its original name *Planta Genista* was the origin of the name of the Plantagenet kings. A sprig was worn by Geoffrey of Anjou as he rode into battle and his grandson, our Henry II, adopted it as a badge.

With a great sprig of broom which he bore as a badge in it,
He was named from the circumstances Henry Plantagenet.

(This is a quotation from the Ingoldsby legends.) The Broom is also the badge of the Forbes. It is supposed to be the 'Cytisus' of Virgil.

The flowers produce no honey, but the bees hover round it a great deal and collect the pollen.

Broom buds were originally used in England as a condiment much in the same way as we now use Capers. They were preserved in vinegar, and a dish of them was on every table at the coronation festivities of James II.

The plant has slight narcotic properties and sheep who browse on it become almost drugged.

In medicine the young tops are very much used in dropsy, especially if the heart is affected, and they are sometimes combined with Squills: but it is not a medicine for the amateur to indulge in.

The plant known as Spanish Broom, *Spartium junceum*, belongs to the same family and has much the same properties in a still more active form. Dyers Broom is also a member of the same genus, but it is chiefly used in all countries for its yellow dye. Its botanical name, *Genista tinctoria*, records its uses, as do also the French and German names.

Butcher's Broom is a totally different plant belonging to the order of the lilies. It has many of the same properties as the other Brooms, but is safer to use.

PERSICARIA
Polygonum amphibium

CANELLA

As if nature's incense pan had split,
And shed the dews i' the air.

Botanical name	Canella alba (Murray)
Natural order	Canellaceae
Other names	White Cinnamon, Wild Cinnamon, Winter's Bark Tree
French name	Cannelle blanche
German name	Weisser Zimmtbaum
Italian name	Cinnamomo salvatico
Turkish name	Yabani darçin aḡ
Part used	Bark
Natural habitat	West Indies, Florida

This very beautiful tree often grows in the West Indies to a height of fifty feet. Its leaves are somewhàt like Bay leaves, the bark is a greyish green, and the small purple flowers grow in umbels, with the fruit or berry in the centre. The inner rind is the part of the tree that is collected for its aromatic properties, and it has a smell that is a cross between Cinnamon and Cloves.

The whole tree is aromatic and the flowers, when dried and moistened again, have the scent of Musk. If the bark is burned it gives a very pleasant fragrance.

The bark is sometimes used in medicine for palsies, but its chief use is as a condiment which flavours and helps digestion.

CAPSICUM

The greedy merchants, led by lucre, run
To the parched Indies and the rising Sun;
From thence hot pepper and rich drugs they bear,
Bartering for spices their Italian ware.

Dryden

Botanical name	Capsicum minimum
Natural order	Solanaceae
Other names	Cayenne, Bird's Pepper, African Pepper, Clivers
French names	Poivre de Guinée, Piment
German name	Echte Beissbeere
Italian names	Pepe di Guinea, Pimento, Peperone
Spanish names	Pimiento, Pimiento di Guinea
Under the dominion of	Mars
Part used	Fruit ripe and dried
Natural habitat	Zanzibar. Cultivated in most tropical and sub-tropical countries

Without Cayenne Pepper we could make no good 'devils' or curries, in fact it is as necessary in the kitchen as it is on the table as a condiment. We use it with oysters, stews, eggs, and many meat and vegetable dishes.

In medicine, herbalists consider it of great value, and they add it to most of their prescriptions.

The word Cayenne is derived from a Greek word meaning 'to bite' and it is its biting power which warms and comforts and prevents chills in cold weather and hot, and in all climates. It is a local stimulant with no narcotic properties. It reduces dilated blood vessels in those addicted to alcohol; it makes a most useful gargle for a sore throat; and it greatly helps a sluggish circulation.

Cayenne was introduced into Great Britain in the middle of the sixteenth century.

CARAWAY

A capital stew with spices and sherry—
Like the Boniface mayor of St. Edmondsbury.

Botanical name	Carum Carvi (Linn.)
Natural order	Umbelliferae
French names	Carvi, Cumin des prés
German name	Kümmel
Italian name	Carvi
Spanish name	Alcaravea
Part used	Fruit
Natural habitat	Central Europe, Asia

The Caraway plant with its white umbelliferous flowers will grow almost anywhere, in any country. In England it is only cultivated on a very small scale in Essex and Norfolk, and most of the Caraway seeds that we buy come from Holland.

The plant is so useful in cooking, in salads, and in domestic medicine, that it should be in every garden. The seeds have stimulating and carminative properties, and, powdered and put into hot water, will make a pleasant digestive drink after a meal. The young roots can be used as a vegetable, the leaves are excellent in salads which they flavour deliciously, and the seeds are used in soups, stews, puddings and cakes. The liqueur called Kümmel is made from them. On the Continent Caraway seeds are put into bread and decorate the outside of loaves and rolls.

Caraway bread is sold in Jewish quarters in London. Petticoat Lane is full of stalls on Sundays where it can be bought.

In William Shakespeare's days and still earlier, a dish of Caraway seeds was an accompaniment of most meals. Roasted Apples were served with a sauce of Caraway seeds—an old custom which is still maintained at some of our colleges at Oxford and Cambridge.

I can remember a silver box containing Caraway comfits which always stood on my grandmother's dressing table, and she never had a meal without taking one after it.

The seeds have a reputation for strengthening vision, and there is a very old tradition that they are endowed with retentive properties and can prevent theft and infidelity in love. They were very much used in magical potions and love charms.

They are given to pigeons to prevent them from straying, and with success apparently. Their use was well known to the ancients, and the bread that Julius Caesar gave to his soldiers was said to be made from the roots. The Arabs call them Karawya. Pliny recommended them for a complexion that was too pale, and the seeds are sometimes used in hysterical complaints.

A poultice of Caraway seeds is a very swift and effective cure for boils in the ear. For earache or anything to do with the ear it is a safe remedy.

It will also cure a sprained ankle. Spirits of Caraway can be used in the same way as Dill water to soothe fretful children.

Every part of the Caraway plant can be eaten so it is one of the most useful herbs to cultivate in the kitchen garden.

CARAWAY BRANDY

Steep 1 ounce of Caraway seeds and 6 ounces of loaf sugar in a quart of brandy. Let this stand nine days. Then strain and bottle.

SPIRIT OF CARAWAY

Take of Caraway seeds, bruised, $\frac{1}{2}$ pound; diluted alcohol, 9 pounds.

Macerate for two days in a closed vessel; then pour on as much water as will prevent empyreuma, and draw off by distillation 9 pounds.

CARAWAY COMFITS

These are made by dipping Caraway seeds in boiling sugar taken to candy height.

Caraway comfits were believed to keep the sight.

CARDAMOM

This is a handful of cardamoms,
This is a lump of ghi:
This is millet and chillies and rice
A supper for thee and me.

Botanical name	Elettaria cardamomum
Natural order	Zingiberaceae
French names	Amome, Cardamome
German name	Cardamome
Italian names	Cardamone, Cardamomo, Amomo
Turkish name	Hemame, Kakule, Hiyl
Part used	The dried ripe seeds
Natural habitat	Southern India

The Cardamom plant is a perennial herb cultivated and found wild in the forests of Malabar and Mysore. It is a handsome plant, with leaves growing in the form of blades. The flowering stems grow near the ground and produce small yellow flowers with a purple lip. The fruit, which is the valuable part of the plant, is picked when ripe, and washed by Indian women in special water to which soap nuts are added.

The seeds are a usual ingredient of curry powders, and are added as a flavouring, and also for their carminative and stimulating properties.

CASCARILLA

The wreathing odours of a thousand trees
And the flowers faint gleaming presences
And over the cleavings and the still waters
Soft indigo and hanging stars.

J. C. Squire

Botanical name	Croton Eleuteria
Natural order	Euphorbiaceae
Country names	Sweetwood Bark, Bastard Jesuit's Bark
French name	Cascarille
German names	Aromatisch Quinquine, Kaskarillen-strauch
Italian name	Cascariglia
Spanish name	Cascarilla
Turkish name	Anbar kabuğu
Part used	Bark
Natural habitat	Bahama Islands

The Cascarilla tree never grows higher than a shrub, but it is extremely decorative on account of its metallic appearance, and its small white flowers are exceedingly fragrant and so is the bark.

The bark is sometimes mistaken for Peruvian Bark and if added to Peruvian Bark will often make that medicine agree with those who in the ordinary way cannot take it. Cascarilla bark gives a Musk-like smell if it is burnt and it is often added to tobacco to cure nervous headaches. It has slight narcotic properties and greatly aids digestion and prevents nausea.

CASSIA

The short Narcissus, and fair daffodil
Pansies to please the sight and Cassia to smell.

John Dryden

Botanical name	Cinnamomum Cassia
Natural order	Lauraceae
Country names	Chinese Cinnamon, Canton Cassia, Bastard Cinnamon
French name	Canéficier, Laurier Casse
German names	Kassia, Kassien-zimmtbaum
Italian names	Cassia, Lauro cassia
Spanish name	Casia
Part used	Dried bark
Natural habitat	China

We use Cassia today chiefly to scent pot-pourris and to flavour chocolate; but in China it is much more used as an antiseptic and as a digestive tonic, and to flavour other medicine. The bark is stronger and less delicate than real Cinnamon and the smell is not as good, but it is often sold for the real and has much the same uses and properties.

It has a history as old as any of the spices and is mentioned in the Bible many times.

It was a very usual ingredient in cosmetic recipes and perfume bags of the seventeenth and eighteenth centuries.

TO CANDY CASSIA

Take as much of the powder of brown Cassia as will lie upon two broad shillings, with what musk and ambergris you think fitting; the Cassia and perfume must be powdered together, then take ¼ pound of sugar, and boil it to a candy height; then put in your powder, and mix it well together, and pour it in pewter saucers or plates, which must be buttered very thin, and when it is cold it will slip out. The Cassia is to be bought at London: sometimes it is in powder and sometimes in a hard lump.

SWEET GALE

Myrica gale

CINNAMON

Lucent syrups tinct with Cinnamon.

John Keats

Botanical name	Cinnamomum zeylanicum
Natural order	Lauraceae
French names	Cannelle, Cinnamone
German names	Zimmtbaum, Kaneel
Italian name	Cannella
Spanish name	Canela
Part used	Bark
Natural habitat	Ceylon, Malabar, Cochin-China, Sumatra

For years the Cinnamon tree was not cultivated owing to a theory that cultivation would destroy its virtues. This idea was probably spread by the Dutch, who had a monopoly of the ancient trade.

In the eighteenth century it began to be grown in Jamaica, Brazil, Mauritius and India, where it is still cultivated.

The value of Cinnamon bark can hardly be overrated and it has behind it a history and a tradition as ancient as the countries which are its usual habitation.

The tree grows best in almost pure sand and it likes much rain and much heat. It reaches a height of twenty or thirty feet and is not unlike the Bay tree in leaves, flowers and fruit. The trunk is rough, but the bark of the branches is smooth. The leaves have a spicy taste and so have the berries, but the part collected commercially is the inner bark of the shoots, and this has the Clove-like taste and smell we are all familiar with.

St. Francis de Sales in his *Devout Life*, comparing another tree with it, says 'it refreshes and revives the heart by the sweetness it brings to those who are engaged in it, as the Cinnamon does in Arabia Felix to them who are laden therewith'.

The antiseptic and cleansing properties of Cinnamon are proverbial, and it is more and more used in prophylactic medicine against colds, chills and infections. The powder has stimulating, astringent and carminative properties, and is extremely useful in tuberculosis, because it cuts short the growth of the germ and prevents further infection.

Cinnamon powder taken in milk is a cure for dysentery. Strong Cinnamon tea taken at the beginning of mumps will reduce the violence of the complaint and prevent complications; and Cinnamon brandy is excellent to take at the beginning of a cold or at the beginning of, and during, influenza.

CINNAMON BRANDY

Bruise 3 ounces of Cinnamon bark and put it into a bottle of good French brandy. It can be used in a fortnight.

Dose: 1 or 2 teaspoonfuls with 2 tablespoonfuls of hot milk.

Cinnamon is one of the ingredients in ivory jelly, which was made from powdered ivory and given at one time to consumptives.

A decoction of Cinnamon has been known to cure Cancer and the following recipe is given by Dr. Fernie.

Make a decoction by boiling 2 pints of water with 1 pound of the bark till reduced to 25 ounces.

Pour off without straining and give in $\frac{1}{2}$ ounce doses, $\frac{1}{2}$ pint to be taken daily.

A good way to make constant use of Cinnamon is as an accompaniment to a junket.

The syrup is a good way in which to give it to children.

CINNAMON CANDY

Mix $\frac{1}{2}$ ounce of the powder with 1 pound of powdered white sugar and $\frac{1}{2}$ pint of water. Boil to a syrup and spread it on a flat greased dish and cut into slices before it gets hard.

Cinnamon mixed with honey will cure freckles if it is applied locally; and Cinnamon water makes an excellent mouth wash.

CLOVES

Mr. Trotter acquiesced in this agreeable proposal: and having deposited his book in his coat pocket, accompanied Mr. Weller to the top, where they were soon occupied in discussing an exhilarating compound, formed by mixing together in a pewter vessel, certain quantities of British Hollands and the fragrant essence of the clove.

Pickwick Papers

Botanical name	Eugenia caryophyllata
Natural order	Myrtaceae
Country name	Eugenia aromatica
French names	Clou, Giroflier
German name	Gewürznelke
Italian name	Garofano
Spanish name	Raja
Symbolises	Dignity
Part used	Fruit
Natural habitat	Molucca Islands, Southern Philippines.

This beautiful tree, which never grows to its full height out of its own country, will only grow well near water where it can absorb the moisture. This increases its natural weight and dishonest dealers often profit by this inflation. In the Molucca Islands, where the best Clove trees grow, they often reach a height of thirty feet, their bright green leaves, which are rather like Bay leaves only much bigger, standing on long foot stalks and their beautiful blue flowers (which are peach colour when in bud) make them an object of great beauty. The bark of the tree is a soft grey colour. The tree never reaches its full loveliness, because if it is allowed to flower, the cloves, which are the seeds, are spoilt for commercial use, so the buds are beaten off the tree as soon as the calyxes are red. The whole tree is exquisitely scented and exhales a perfume which is as refreshing as it is delicious. Cloves are the most stimulating of all the aromatic spices. They are cordial, warming and strengthening and they have the combined property of soothing the nerves as well as stimulating them. They are also, like all spices, powerfully antiseptic.

As a tisane for nausea, Clove tea has been recommended for centuries. For an internal colic a mixture made of Cloves and Allspice with Ginger and Cinnamon which has been infused for a few days in brandy and left in the sun, will give instant relief.

William Coles says in his *Adam in Eden*: 'The Portugal women that dwell in the East India draw from the cloves when they be green a certain liquor of distillation of a most fragrant smell which comforteth the heart and is of all cordials the most effective.'

In cooking, Cloves are the right flavouring for Apples, and an Apple pie without Cloves is not a traditional English Apple pie.

It is an old custom in England to make Clove pomanders to put amongst linen to scent it. These are Oranges or Lemons into which Cloves have been inserted so that they entirely cover the outside of the fruit.

Cloves are an ingredient of many old English recipes, especially English punches and drinks. Dickens speaks of gin and Cloves as a combination in vogue in his time, and old drinks like Bishop and Brown Betty are both made with Cloves. Carnations have the scent of Cloves and for this reason used to be called Clove Gilly-flowers.

RECIPE

For an internal colic

4 ounces of mixed Cloves and Allspice, with some crushed Ginger and Cinnamon in a quart of brandy and leave it to stand in the sun for a few days, then give as a dose 1 teaspoonful in a wine-glassful of water.

CLOVE SYRUP

Infuse 4 ounces of bruised Cloves in a pint of white wine for three days in a glass by a gentle heat, then having strained out the Cloves, add to it 1½ pounds of white sugar and boil it gently to a syrup.

CORIANDER

Sweet Chervils cottage valued weed
And Coriander's spicy seed.

Botanical name	Coriandrum sativum (Linn.)
Natural order	Umbelliferae
French name	Coriandre
German name	Koriander
Italian name	Coriandro
Spanish name	Cilantro
Symbolises	Hidden worth
Parts used	Fruit, leaves
Natural habitat	Southern Europe, Peru, Egypt, Arabia

Coriander is an Eastern condiment which was introduced into Europe by the Romans. It is so much used in the East in cooking, in curries, and in medicine that it is constantly referred to in Eastern tales like the *Arabian Nights*.

In Peru and in Egypt, Coriander seeds are put into soup. They are an ingredient of the old drink called Hippocras.

The seeds become more fragrant after they are dried, and they improve with age. Coriander seeds were used in medicine by Hippocrates and are slightly narcotic, but today they are chiefly used in Europe as a flavouring for other medicines. They have stimulating and carminative properties and improve the taste of curries. They are also used in the making of gin and the fresh leaves can be used with advantage in salads and soups.

The plant has a strong smell, the leaves are not unlike parsley though more indented, and the flowers grow in round tassels as Dill flowers do. It is sometimes found in fields near rivers in the Eastern counties of England, but it is not indigenous. The Romans introduced it to England and it has been cultivated in gardens, and is cultivated today in Essex for gin making. It is quite easy to grow.

Take of Cardamine, carpobalsamum of each half an ounce, coriander seeds prepared, nutmegs, ginger of each two ounces, cloves two drachms; bruise and infuse these two days in two gallons of the richest sweetest cider, often stirring it together, then add thereto of milk three pints, strain all through an hippocras bag, and sweeten it with a pound of sugar candy.

Edward Spencer

CUMIN

Botanical name	Cuminum cyminum (Linn.)
Natural order	Umbelliferae
Country names	Bishopsweed, Herb William, Bull-wort, Ethiopian Cumin
French name	Cumin
German name	Römischer Kümmel
Italian names	Cimino, Cumino
Spanish name	Comino
Under the dominion of	Venus
Symbolises	Cupidity
Part used	Fruit
Natural habitat	Egypt

This is another of the small umbelliferous plants like Coriander and Caraway which has been used as a spice from very early times. Cumin comes to us, as Coriander does, through Egypt from China and Arabia.

It is one of the most popular of the European grown spice shrubs and grows without any difficulty in England and even ripens its fruit as far north as Scotland.

The leaves are rather like Fennel and the flowers grow in rose-coloured and white umbels and are succeeded by small round seeds 'of a quick hot scent and taste'.

It used to grow wild round Gravesend in Nicholas Culpeper's lifetime.

The ancients said that the seeds taken internally, or smoked, produced in the face an unnatural pallor; and according to Horace they were deliberately used to acquire a pale complexion.

The same means can be taken to cure pallor. This is the homoeopathic system of like curing like.

Cumin seeds mixed with Bay-salt are given to pigeons when they are ill and they are used in veterinary preparations. Partridges also like them.

In cookery they are put into curries, and cheeses; and they can be used like ordinary pepper and ground in a mill at the table.

They greatly aid digestion and act as a mild stimulant.

DILL

Vein healing Vervain and head purging Dill.

Edmund Spenser

Botanical name	Peucedanum graveolens
Natural order	Compositae
French names	Aneth, Fenouil puant
German name	Dill
Italian name	Aneto odoroso
Spanish name	Eneldo
Under the dominion of	Mercury
Part used	Dried fruit
Natural habitat	Southern Russia and countries bordering the Mediterranean

Dill grows better in England than in other countries, and it contains such valuable mineral salts, and is so soothing to the nervous system, that it should be grown and used far more than it is. It could easily have a place in the kitchen garden, and its aromatic scent gives it a pleasant smell, which is another inducement to grow it more generally.

The name Dill is derived from a Saxon word meaning to lull. Dill water is a great nursery medicine for lulling babies to sleep. It was used in this way long before it had been analysed and discovered to contain so many of the inorganic salts.

It has slight narcotic properties and contains a considerable percentage of calcium, phosphorus and sulphur.

Dill was very well known to Dioscorides, and Pliny has written about it, and also Virgil. It has an ancient reputation as a soothing medicine, and as a condiment to help digestion. The Germans pickle their small Cucumbers with Dill and put the seeds into soups, and the French use them as a flavouring for cakes. The leaves can be used in salads, and the seeds can be made into Dill vinegar to use with salads. The old-fashioned Dill water is a capital remedy for

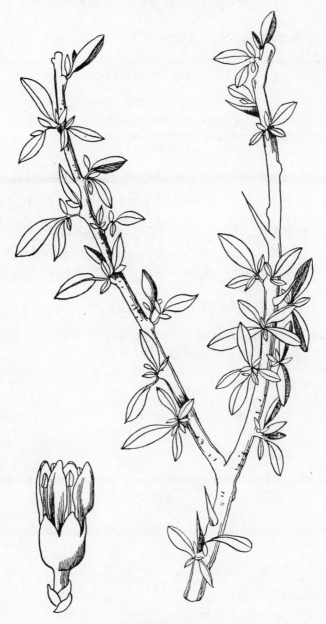

MYRRH

Commiphora myrrha

indigestion in adults as well as children and it is safe as well as effective.

In witchcraft, Dill 'hindered witches of their will'.

DILL WATER

Dill fruit   100 grammes
Water   200 millilitres
Distil 1,000 millilitres; use distilled water.

CUCUMBERS PICKLED WITH DILL

Use the young tops of the Dill plant and put a layer in the bottom of a vessel, then put in a layer of small Cucumbers and then a layer of Dill leaves and so on. Then fill up the vessel with boiled water and add for each gallon of water $\frac{1}{4}$ pound of allom and 2 ounces of salt. Cover—press down with weights.

DILL VINEGAR

Infuse an ounce of the seeds in a pint of white wine vinegar for a fortnight well stoppered, then filter and use.

DILL WATER

Dill seed, bruised, 1 pound; water sufficient to prevent an empyreuma. Draw off 1 gallon.

GALANGAL

Cool violets and orpine growing still
Embathed balm and cheerful galangal
Fresh costmarie and healthful camomile.

Edmund Spenser

Botanical name	Alpinia officinarum
Natural order	Zingiberaceae
Country names	China Root, India Root, Colic Root,
	Catarrh Root, Lesser Galangal
French name	Galanga mineur
German name	Galgantwurzel
Italian name	Galanga minore
Arabic name	Khulingan
Part used	Dried root
Natural habitat	China, Java

The root of the Galangal is a mild form of Ginger which has been known in Egypt and Arabia for at any rate a thousand years if not longer. The plant is named after the well-known Italian botanist, Prospero Alpino, who lived in the seventeenth century; it must not be confused with Galingale, *Cyperus longus,* known in France as Souchet. It is used principally in Russia to make a liqueur called Nastoika, and as a spice in Lithuania and Esthonia.

It is also sometimes used as a sedative remedy for sea sickness and as a cure for catarrh. Galangal has stimulating and carminative properties and aids digestion.

GINGER

Sinnament, Ginger, nutmeg and cloves
And that gives me my jolly red nose.

Botanical name	Zingiber officinale
Natural order	Zingiberaceae
French name	Gingembre
German name	Ingwer
Italian name	Zenzero
Spanish name	Jenjibre
Under the dominion of	Mars
Part used	Root
Natural habitat	Asia. Cultivated in West Indies, Jamaica, Africa

Ginger is described as black and white according to whether it is peeled or unpeeled. The white which is dried without being scalded is generally considered the best.

What is known as Cargo Ginger is the cheapest form of all. It is sold loose and is large lumps of the root covered with a soft sugar. It is excellent for ordinary purposes but is cruder in taste than the more expensive kinds of Ginger.

In cooking, the powdered Ginger is used; and Ginger tea is made from the powdered root.

The poet Coleridge was a great believer in Ginger tea, which he took every afternoon. He advised his wife to give it to their son Hartley.

Queen Elizabeth's famous powder in which she had so much faith, was a mixture of Ginger with Cinnamon and Aniseed, Caraway and Fennel seeds.

Ginger is one of the best stimulants that we have in domestic medicine. It is safe to use, pleasant to eat, warming and comforting to the digestion and helps a sluggish circulation.

After a chill, or to prevent one, there is nothing better than a glass of Ginger wine, or a lump of crystallised Ginger.

In cooking, Ginger is almost as indispensable as Cloves and Nutmegs. English Gingerbread is as famous as Plum cake; and the Gingerbread sellers, of whom Tilly Doll was the most famous, were the great attractions at English fairs.

In Hull there is a street called the 'Land of Green Ginger'.

The root is the part of the plant that is used and the best Ginger root comes from the West Indies. What is called Green Ginger is the root before it is dried.

Ginger has a perennial root from which the flowering stalk rises directly. The end of the stalk is scaly and from each scale grows a single white and blue flower. The plant is very easy to cultivate, requires little care and is easily propagated.

It is said to have been first transplanted from the East Indies by Francisco de Mendoza in the early part of the sixteenth century.

The wild Ginger, *Asarum Canadense*, belongs to a different family and order altogether, though it is often called Indian Ginger. It is an aromatic plant which is used in medicine for chest complaints—the oil from it was once used in perfumery.

JUNIPER

And with glass stills, and sticks of Juniper
Raise the black spright that burns not with the fire.

Bishop Hall's *Satires*

Botanical name	Juniperus communis
Natural order	Coniferae
French name	Genévrier
German name	Gemeiner Wachholder
Italian name	Ginepro
Spanish name	Enebro
Under the dominion of	The Sun
Symbolises	Protection
Parts used	Leaves, fruit
Natural habitat	North Africa, North Asia, North America, Europe

The Juniper tree is a small evergreen shrub which is quite common in chalky districts in England. Surrey, Kent, Essex and Buckinghamshire are some of the counties in which it grows.

The berries do not ripen till the second year. They are used in the making of Hollands and a French beer called Genièvre. Steeped in alcohol they make a ratafia which is excellent. The berries are extremely stimulating to the kidneys and they are constantly used in various forms as a cure for dropsy.

The aromatic scent of the tree made it popular as a strewing herb, and it exhales a pine-like odour which is extremely healthy. The berries are sometimes given to consumptive people, who take from ten to twenty at a time fasting. The berries contain a cordial oil, an alkaloid called juniperin, resins, sugar, fat, formic and acetic acids and malates.

A rob of Juniper is another favourite way of administering the plant medicinally. The Swedes make the berries into a conserve which is good with cold meat, and in Germany Sauerkraut is flavoured with them. They are also used by themselves as a spice, and a decoction of the ripe berries is drunk instead of tea amongst the Laplanders. The Juniper tree is much revered in Catholic countries because there is a tradition that when the Virgin and the infant Christ were fleeing from Herod into Egypt they took refuge behind a Juniper bush.

Elijah also was protected from the persecutions of Ahab by the Juniper tree and it has come to be a symbol of protection. 'Swete is the Juniper but sharp his bough.'

CONSERVE OF JUNIPER

Cook the berries in water till soft without breaking them, then press out the pulp and mix it with three times its weight of loaf sugar, well beaten together.

ROB OF JUNIPER

Take of the juice of Juniper berries well strained, 8 pounds. Boil it with a gentle fire to the consistence of honey, and bottle.

A rob is the juice of a fruit made so thick by the heat either of the sun or the fire that it is capable of being kept safe from putrefaction.

MUSTARD

Botanical names	Brassica alba (Linn.), Brassica nigra (Linn.)
Natural order	Cruciferae
French names	Moutarde blanche, Moutarde noire
German names	Echter Senf, Echter Kohl
Italian names	Senape, mostarda
Spanish name	Mostaza
Under the dominion of	Mars
Symbolises	Indifference
Part used	Seeds
Natural habitat	Asia Minor, North Africa, Europe

There are two kinds of Mustard in general use—the black and the white. The white is a smaller plant than the black and it is this kind that is grown with Cress to make what is called 'Mustard and Cress'.

The white Mustard is much less strong than the black; though the Romans used the black as a vegetable, and its leaves are very good in salads.

The young leaves of the white are also put into salads and were recommended by John Evelyn as 'of incomparable effect to quicken and revive the spirits, strengthening the memory, expelling heaviness'. The Mustards belong to the Cruciferous order of plants, none of which are poisonous, and all of which have antiscorbutic properties, which means that they purify the blood.

Black Mustard contains a good deal of sulphur and is very much valued in medicine, though in Mustard plasters it is usually mixed with the white to prevent it being too strong. The seeds make a stimulating bath if added to the hot water. Both kinds of Mustard make good fodder for sheep. Originally the Mustard we use as a condiment, which is made from the black Mustard, was made into balls with honey, vinegar and Cinnamon and was sold in this way. Tewkesbury was a great centre for Mustard balls. It was not until the eighteenth century that Mustard powder was invented, the inventor being a Mrs. Clements of Durham, who became famous for her powder made from black Mustard, which was called 'Durham Mustard'.

The French mix their Mustard with herbs of various kinds which give it quite a different taste, and at Dijon there still exists one of the old Mustard shops with decorative jars of Mustards of many varieties. Continental Mustard is nearly always mixed with herbs.

Both black and white Mustard originated from the wild varieties.

The field Mustard that we call Charlock, *Sinapis arvensis*, is a good substitute for ordinary Mustard; and *Brassica napus*, known popularly as Rape or Cole Seed, was used at one time as a salad herb.

Garlic Mustard, *Sisymbrium alliaria*, was so popular in the country as a salad herb and to put into sauces, that it acquired the name of Sauce Alone. This is a name, however, that country people give to several plants that are used in the same way.

Another Mustard plant, *Sisymbrium officinale*, is better known in France, and was known in the eighteenth century under the name of Yellow Julienne.

NASTURTIUM

Bright the nasturtium glows and late at eve
Light, lambent, dances o'er its sleepless bed.

Bidlake

Botanical name	Tropaeolum majus (Linn.)
Natural order	Tropaeolaceae
Country names	Indian Cress, Canary Creeper
French names	Capucine grande, Cresson d'Inde
German names	Kapuzinerkresse, Kapucinerkresse
Italian names	Nasturzio d'India, Astuzia
Spanish name	Capuchina
Under the dominion of	The Moon
Symbolises	Patriotism
Parts used	Leaves, flowers, seeds
Natural habitat	Europe, including Great Britain

The Nasturtium is said to have arisen from the blood of a Trojan warrior. Its bright-coloured flowers add gaiety and flavour to a salad, and every part of the plant is comforting and warming. The seeds make an excellent pickle.

TO PICKLE NASTURTIUM BERRIES

Take Nasturtium berries gathered as soon as the blossom is off, and put them in cold spring water and salt; change the water for three days successively. Make a pickle of white wine vinegar, mace, nutmeg, slice 6 shalots, six blades of garlic, some peppercorns, salt, and horseradish cut in pieces. Make your pickle very strong, drain your berries very dry and put them in bottles; mix your pickle well up together but you must not boil it; put it over the berries and tie them down close. *See* Watercress.

322

PATCHOULI

Pogostemon patchouli

NUTMEG

There springen herbes grate and smalle
The licoris and the setewole
And many a clove gilofre,
And note muge to put in ale
Whether it be moist or stale.

Geoffrey Chaucer

Botanical name	Myristica fragrans
Natural order	Myristicaceae
Country name	Myristica moschata
French name	Muscadier
German name	Muskatnussbaum
Italian name	Noce moscata
Spanish name	Nuez moscada
Part used	Dried kernels of the seeds
Natural habitat	Banda Islands, Malay Islands

The Nutmeg Islands are in the Indian ocean. There are twelve of them and the strength and aroma of the trees is said to be so powerful that Birds of Paradise become intoxicated with the scent.

Nutmegs taken in large quantities are narcotic, and Nutmeg tea taken last thing at night is a mild soporific which will induce sleep in the wakeful.

The silver graters our grandmothers carried on their chatelaines were to make Nutmeg tea, which they gave as much for a languid digestion as for a restless night. A whole Nutmeg was used for each cup.

The Nutmeg tree is larger than the Clove tree, which also comes from the Moluccas; and the Nutmeg has larger leaves and white bell-shaped flowers and provides us with two different kinds of spices—Nutmegs which are the kernel of the fruit, and Mace which is the thin membrane of the shell which holds the Nutmeg.

324

The tree bears no fruit till it is nine years old. After that it continues to fruit for nearly a hundred years.

Both the Nutmeg and Mace have much the same properties. The Nutmeg when cut resembles the human brain, and Robert Turner in his famous herbal of 1561 says: 'God has imprinted in the plants, herbs and flowers as it were in hierogliphics the very signature of their virtues: as the nutmeg being cut, resembles the brain.'

NUTMEG BRANDY

Grate 3 ounces of nutmeg. Put into a quart bottle and fill up with good brandy. Cork and shake every day for a fortnight—then pour off without disturbing the sediment.

3 or 4 drops will flavour $\frac{1}{2}$ pint of liquid.

To help the sleepless—10 drops in a glass of hot water or milk. The dose can be repeated after 2 hours.

PEPPERS

*It doth assuage the fits that ague make
If that you use thereof before you shake.*

Botanical name	Piper nigrum (Linn.)
Natural order	Piperaceae
French name	Poivre noir
German name	Schwarzer Pfeffer
Italian name	Pepe nero
Spanish name	Pimienta
Under the dominion of	Mars
Part used	Dried unripe fruit
Natural habitat	South India, Cochin China, East and West Indies, Malay States, Malabar, Siam

There are numerous varieties of Pepper, but both black and white come from the same tree. The white is prepared from the black by being steeped in water and decorticated, and is therefore much deteriorated. The best black Pepper comes from Malabar, but it is almost unobtainable today in England. In the Pepper trade it is said that the best Pepper for weight is Malabar, for colour Sumatra, and for strength Penang.

Of the Sumatra Pepper the Molucca is considered the best. As the value of Pepper has gone from the white, which is used in the kitchen, a mill of black Pepper is as necessary on every dining table as a salt cellar.

The Hungarian Pepper which gives its sweet flavour to so many Hungarian dishes is better known as Paprika; and the old-fashioned Grains of Paradise is a Pepper from Ethiopia known there as Kanany. Cayenne is a Capsicum and the varieties called Guinea Pepper, Cherry Pepper, and Bell Pepper are all species of Capsicums.

This is Pomet's recipe for the best mixture of pepper and spice. He wrote a history of drugs which is still a standard work.

Black Dutch Pepper	5 lbs.
Dried Cloves	1½ lbs.
Dried Nutmegs	1½ lbs.
Dried Ginger	2½ lbs.
Green Anise	¾ lb.
Coriander	¾ lb.

Powder separately and then mix.

Pepper is a stimulant and a carminative which aids digestion and helps the gastric juices to function. It makes food more interesting and gives zest to the appetite. Vegetable stimulants like Pepper assist in keeping up the temperature of the body and prevent exhaustion. Our grandmothers drank a posset of Peppercorns boiled in whey.

No poignant sauce she knew, no costly treat,
Her hunger gave a relish to her meat.
A sparing diet did her health assure;
Or sick, a pepper posset was her cure.

John Dryden

PERSICARIA

Unbidden then the borage springs,
Grey lichens creep beneath.
And graceful persicaria flings
Her rosy wreath.

Agnes Strickland

Botanical name	Polygonum amphibium
Natural order	Polygonaceae
Country name	Amphibious Persicaria
French name	Persicaire
German name	Flöhkraut
Italian name	Persicaria
Turkish name	Çoban dayaḡi
Russian name	Potschednaga trawa
Dutch name	Perserkruid
Under the dominion of	Mars
Symbolises	Restoration
Parts used	Seeds, herb
Natural habitat	Europe, including Great Britain

This plant belongs to the Buckwheat family. It is not unlike its close relations, the Bistort and the Knotgrass, and, like them, prefers to grow by water or in a damp position. As a cooling blood purifier this plant is preferred in France to Sarsaparilla.

The Biting Persicaria or Water Pepper is another species of Polygonum. The seeds are a very old substitute for Pepper.

In Australia a species known as *Polygonum cymosum* is used instead of Spinach.

All the Polygonums are powerfully astringent. In medicine, Pepper possets and Pepper plasters cure colds and fevers and act as counter irritants to painful limbs.

SAFFRON

Saffron conveys medicine to the heart, cures its palpitation, removes melancholy and uneasiness, revives the brain, renders the mind cheerful, and generates boldness.

Francis Bacon

Botanical name	Crocus sativus
Natural order	Iridaceae
French name	Safran
German name	Saffran
Italian name	Zafferano
Spanish name	Azafran
Under the dominion of	Sun and the sign Leo
Symbolises	Beware of excess
Part used	Flower pistils
Natural habitat	The Levant

Saffron is the Karcom of the Hebrews. Its praises are sung by Solomon. As a dye and a perfume it was known to the Persians, and Cleopatra used it for her complexion. The plant is a Crocus. It is said to have reached England from the East during the reign of Edward III, through a pilgrim who carried it in his staff, and this was the beginning of the cultivation of the Saffron that gave its name to the town of Saffron Walden, where it was grown. The town grew rich through Saffron and incorporated three of the flowers in its coat of arms.

It became the custom there to present the powder in a silver cup to the reigning sovereign when she visited the town. In the time of Queen Elizabeth a pound of Saffron, consisting of the pistils of forty thousand flowers, was worth five guineas.

Saffron Hill in Holborn also takes its name from the Saffron plant; but probably because it was for so long the Italian quarter, and Italians colour their risotto with this yellow powder. This use of Saffron in cooking is said to have been first mentioned by

Apicius, the earliest writer on diet. In Italy Saffron is very much cheaper than it is here and is still used today in risottos and other Italian dishes.

In the eighteenth century Saffron was made into balls in the same way that Mustard was, because this was the way it kept best, and then it was crushed and sprinkled over salads. John Evelyn includes Saffron balls as one of the necessary adjuncts to a salad in his day.

Saffron tea is an old remedy for measles, and it is put in the drinking water of canaries when they are moulting. In the form of a syrup it was given to restore an exhausted brain; and Nicholas Culpeper thought it so powerful as a heart tonic that if it were taken immediately it was likely to harm the heart instead of helping it.

One of the earliest manuals on cookery mentions a dish called Jascellum made of Saffron, grated bread, eggs and sage.

Saffron has narcotic properties, and Francis Bacon describes a sleeping draught that was made of Saffron mixed with Apples and syrup of Roses.

Saffron was used at one time in Lenten dishes, and in pastries and sweetmeats, for its restorative power and its cordial effect on the brain and heart. 'He has slept in a bag of saffron' is an old saying to describe someone who is unusually cheerful. In Ireland the sheets were dyed with Saffron to strengthen the limbs of those who slept between them; and Saffron given in wine in doses of ten or at the most twenty grains, has saved the life of consumptives.

This useful Crocus with its golden flower pistils grows wild near Derby and round Halifax, but the Saffron powder we buy comes from the Levant.

Another wild Crocus which we call Meadow Saffron has as ancient a reputation in medicine as the *Crocus sativus*. It is the *Colchicum autumnale*. Its effect on gout and rheumatic pains is often instantaneous, and for this reason it is sometimes incorporated in patent rheumatic medicines. It is, however, far from a safe medicine, and though it cures quickly, the disease is apt to recur with greater violence. The French name for Meadow Saffron is 'Mort aux chiens'.

Mythologically the Crocus arose out of the blood of a young man of that name who was killed while playing quoits with Mercury.

BUTTERWORT

Pinguicula vulgaris

The botanical name Colchicum is taken from the town of Colchis, where the enchantress Medea grew poisonous herbs and practised her black arts.

AN EXCELLENT MEDICINE FOR DRY CONVULSIVE ASTHMA

Give at bedtime 8 or 10 grains of choice Saffron, pulverised grossly in a little syrup or conserve of violets to embody it with.

CONFECTION OF SAFFRON

Macerate for 24 hours $\frac{1}{2}$ pound of coarsely powdered Saffron and the same of Zedoary, then press and strain and reduce the liquid by evaporation to $1\frac{1}{2}$ pints. Add to it 2 ounces of cinnamon, the same of nutmegs and 1 ounce of cloves, and $\frac{1}{2}$ ounce of smaller cardamom seeds. Make into a confection with 2 pounds of double refined sugar.

SWEET GALE

I love to go forth ere the dawn to inhale
The health breathing freshness that floats on the gale.

Botanical name	Myrica Gale (Linn.)
Natural order	Myricaceae
Country names	Dutch Myrtle, Bog Myrtle, Golden Withy, Bayberry, Withywind, Pimento Royal, Candleberry Myrtle
French name	Galé
German name	Gemeine Wachsstrauch
Parts used	Leaves, branches
Natural habitat	Higher latitudes of Northern Hemisphere. Great Britain, including Scotland

The Sweet Gale is one of the Myrtles. It grows in the north of England and particularly on the Scottish moors and the Irish bogs as well as in the east and south of England. Its catkins are sometimes boiled to yield wax for burning but it is not nearly as productive of wax as the true Candle Myrtle (*Myrica cerifera*), which is used for soap, candles and sealing wax.

Sweet Gale is chiefly used to flavour beer, a use to which it has been put from the earliest times. So important was it for beer-making that laws were passed to protect Sweet Gale bushes from being destroyed or damaged.

The leaves have been used as a substitute for ordinary tea and they are so sweetly scented that they are often made into sachets to scent linen and pot-pourris.

The plant is also used to dye wool and to keep away insects.

The French use the berries in soups and so do the Swedes, and all European countries make beer with it. In China the leaves are made into a tisane which is cordial and stomachic.

Sweet Gale is the badge of the Campbells.

Chapter VII

NATURAL PERFUMES

NATURAL PERFUMES

NATURAL PERFUMES

I plunge my hand among the leaves;
(An alien touch but dust perceives,
Nought else supposes)
For me those fragrant ruins raise
Clear memory of vanished days when they were roses.

Austin Dobson

To make a good pot-pourri the Rose petals must be dried when the sun is hottest, and picked when there is no moisture in the air. June Roses smell the sweetest, so this is the time to collect them and dry them. They should be spread out very thinly on wooden trays or sheets of white paper.

Any blue, yellow, red or purple flowers, with or without scent, should be collected too, to mix with the Roses later and give a note of gaiety to the pot-pourri, especially to the dry pot-pourris.

Later in the summer, at the beginning of August, the Lavender flowers and the Rosemary flowers and the Jasmine blooms must be picked and dried, and the sweet-scented green leaves like lemon Verbena and sweet-scented Geranium. When all are dried they are mixed together, the Roses greatly predominating. The spices must be carefully blended before they are added to the flowers.

In the case of the moist pot-pourris the Rose petals should not be fully dried; they should have the substance of leather, and the bay salt or ordinary salt should be sprinkled over them before anything else is added. In the dry pot-pourris no salt of any kind is used, and the Rose petals must be entirely dried.

The amount of salt required for a moist pot-pourri usually is in the proportion of five pounds to a peck of Rose petals. This is made up of equal proportions of common salt and bay salt.

Most flowers lose their scent when dried; there are a few exceptions like Lavender, Rosemary, Marjoram and Thyme, which are of a spicy nature. Woodruff becomes more fragrant when dried, and there are certain barks and leaves and seeds which only develop their scent after being dried.

It is these which form the basis of the sweetest pot-pourris.

Dried Rose leaves have a faint aroma of their own which is drawn out by spices. Carnations also, and Jasmine flowers, especially the Chinese species.

Rose petals must always predominate in any pot-pourri in which they are an ingredient, for their very presence calls up a memory of their living scent. Theophrastus says, 'The admixture of Rose perfume whether in scents or in flavours if it be well blended, is beneficent by removing the heaviness and strength of other scents.' The Greeks blended their powders and spices so carefully, Theophrastus tells us, that after mixing them they shut them up in a box for several days, then opened them and took out the spice that seemed to smell the strongest—they repeated the process until they were so blended that no one scent predominated.

The following mixture of spices makes a good moist pôt-pourri:

$\frac{1}{2}$ lb. powdered cloves
$\frac{1}{2}$ lb. powdered allspice
$\frac{1}{2}$ lb. brown sugar
2 ozs. orris root
2 ozs. powdered calamus
$\frac{1}{2}$ lb. powdered gum benjamin
$\frac{1}{2}$ pint brandy

For a dry pot-pourri this is a good combination:

Take of orris root, sweet calamus, cypress root, dried lemon peel and dried orange peel of each a pound; a peck of dried rose petals. Make all except the rose petals into a gross powder, then take coriander seeds 4 ounces, nutmegs $1\frac{1}{2}$ ounces, and cloves 1 ounce and mix with the other when powdered. Then add musk and ambergris 15 grains mixed. Then take 4 large handfuls of lavender dried and freed from the stalks, of sweet marjoram, orange petals, and young walnut leaves 1 handful each all dried. Mix together and place in it bits of cotton perfumed with essences.

338

A good pot-pourri should keep for years, if it is not left uncovered too long at a time.

It is usual in English country houses to have a family recipe for pot-pourri. These recipes which have come down the ages form a fragrant link between the past generations and the present.

GUM BENJAMIN

BENZOIN

When they make compound perfumes, they moisten the spices with fragrant wine.

Theophrastus

Botanical name	Styrax Benzoin
Natural order	Styracaceae
Country names	Gum Benzoin, Gum Benjamin, Siam Benzoin, Sumatra Benzoin
French names	Benzoin, Benjoin
German name	Benzoebaum
Italian names	Belzuino, Storace benzoino
Spanish name	Benjuí
Part used	Resin
Natural habitat	Siam, Sumatra, Java

Gum Benjamin has not a very ancient history behind it, as some of the aromatic resins have. It is first mentioned by Ibn Batuta at the beginning of the fourteenth century; he refers to it in his travels as Java Frankincense. The next record is a century later, in 1461, when a present of Benzoin was sent by the Sultan of Egypt to the Doge of Venice of that period. The gift included Gum Benjamin, sugar, sugar candy, carpets and china.

At the beginning of the sixteenth century a regular trade in Benzoin was being carried on with Venice; but it was not till 1563 that we have a good description of the industry, from Garcia de Orta. From that time it was regularly shipped to Europe; and at the beginning of the seventeenth century England was receiving regular supplies from Siam and Sumatra.

The trees which produce Gum Benjamin are of quick growth and can be produced from seed. They have very broad stems and lovely foliage, and for the first few years require no attention. Incisions are not made in the trunks till they are seven or eight years old and then they exude for about twelve years, after which time they are cut down.

The gum that has the most white tears is considered the best. It is used very largely in incense, especially in the Russian Church. It is extremely useful in cosmetics for its astringent and preservative powers, and enters into the composition of many astringent face lotions.

The Benzoin of America—a bush growing on the banks of streams and in marshy ground from Canada to Florida, belongs to the order of Laurels, and is therefore allied to the Camphor and Cinnamon trees and to the Avocado Pear. Its bark, buds and berries are all aromatic. The leaves have been used as a substitute for tea in North and South Carolina, and the powdered berries to replace Allspice as a spice. It is a shrub growing to a foot or more in height, with yellow flowers growing in umbelliferous clusters.

SWEET CALAMUS

. . . Round
Each blade of grass, each spray
Of acorus, a fragrant essence breathes
Nature's own incense shed to sanctify these wreaths.

Calder Campbell

Botanical name	Acorus Calamus (Linn.)
Natural order	Araceae
Country names	Sweet Flag, Cinnamon Sedge, Sweet Rush, Myrtle Grass, Myrtle Sedge, Sweet Myrtle, Gladdon
French name	Acore odorant
German names	Kalmus, Acoruswurz
Italian name	Acoro aromatico
Spanish name	Calamo
Under the dominion of	Saturn
Symbolises	Resignation
Part used	Root
Natural habitat	Europe, excepting Spain

To the uninitiated the stiff sword-like leaves of this Sedge have all the appearance of the Yellow Flag and are only distinguished from it by the scent and the crimped edges of the leaves. The flowering stem, which resembles the leaves except that it is longer, solider and triangular in form, is densely covered with small greenish-yellow flowers.

The plant was introduced into England from the East at the end of the sixteenth century and was grown by Gerard in his garden in Holborn. It propagates very easily and grows anywhere near water—at the edge of streams or rivers. Every part of it is sweetly scented and because of its fragrance it was in great demand for strewing churches and houses at festival times. A large trade was carried on in the Fen district where the market was sup-

GROMWELL
Lithospermum officinale

plied with Sweet Sedge grown in Norfolk and Suffolk. During the reign of Henry VII, Cardinal Wolsey was censured for his extravagance in the use of this herb, which was very expensive because of the cost of transport.

The Norfolk Sedge goes by the name of Gladdon, and the Gladdon harvest was one of the important features of life on the Broads.

The word Acorus is derived from a Greek word meaning the pupil of the eye, for which the Greeks used the plant as a medicine.

The Sweet Sedge is also used in the treatment of dyspepsia and is a good substitute for Peruvian bark. It was an ingredient in the famous Stockton Bitters. It is a stimulating tonic and an antiseptic, and, powdered, can be used to replace Cinnamon. It can be made into wine, or can be administered in the form of an infusion, or the juice can be extracted and used medicinally.

Though the plant is sometimes called Sweet Flag it is a Sedge and not an Iris, and belongs to a different order.

It must not be confused with Orris root, which is obtained from one or more of the Flags or Irises; but, in common with Orris root, its odour improves with age and drying.

In Egypt it is called Cassabel.

CANDIED SWEET CALAMUS

Take a pound of double refined sugar and boil it to candy height, then mix in as much powdered Calamus as is required. Pour into saucers or drop on to a white paper to the size required and leave to set.

CAMPHOR

Botanical name	Cinnamomum camphora
Natural order	Lauraceae
Botanical name	Dryobalanops camphora
Natural order	Dipterocarpaceae
French name	Camphrier
German name	Kampferbaum
Italian name	Lauro canfora
Spanish name	Alcanfor
Symbolises	Fragrance
Part used	Gum
Natural habitat	China, Japan, Borneo, Sumatra

The Camphor tree is one of the oldest medicinal trees known. Marco Polo described it as 'the Balsam of disease'. Camphor is produced from two different trees, the oldest being the *Laurus camphora*, a large forest tree growing wild in Japan and China, from which Camphor was distilled. The Camphor that comes from Borneo and Sumatra is the *Dryobalanops camphora* from the trunk of which Camphor is obtained.

The tree often reaches a height of ninety feet and has a circumference of six or seven feet in diameter. It does not produce Camphor until it is fifty years old, and is said to flower only every four years.

The Chinese use the Borneo Camphor for embalming their dead, and their own Camphor for medicinal purposes.

The effect of Camphor on the system is partly stimulating and partly sedative. In moderate doses it increases the heat of the body and in large doses lowers the power of circulation. It is often used to numb the peripheral and sensory nerves and is sometimes injected for this purpose, but it ends by paralysing the nerves if this is done often.

One of its great uses is to keep away moths and insects and to preserve clothes and books from destruction.

Its odour makes it very attractive and it is used in incense and burning perfumes, and drawers are lined with it.

FRANKINCENSE

And the Lord said unto Moses,
Take unto thee sweet spices, stacte and galbanum; these sweet
spices with pure frankincense: of each shall there be a like weight.

Botanical names	Boswellia thurifera, Boswellia frereana, Boswellia
Natural order	Burseraceae
Other names	Olibans, Olibanum, Megaar, Lubon Meyeti, Salai Tree
French name	Oliban
German name	Weihrauchbaum
Italian names	Olibano, Incenso
Spanish names	Olibano, Incienso
Part used	Resin
Natural habitat	Southern coast of Arabia, Eastern Africa

The traffic in Olibanum or Frankincense is of very great antiquity, and pictures discovered in the Temple of Deir el Bahri in Upper Egypt illustrate the practical working of the industry seventeen centuries before the Wise Men of the East presented their offering of Frankincense and Myrrh and other precious spices to the infant Christ at Bethlehem.

Plutarch tells us that Alexander the Great captured a valuable collection of Olibanum when he took possession of Gaza in Palestine; and from Herodotus we know that the Arabians paid in tribute a thousand talents of Olibanum yearly to Darius, king of Persia. There are various other records of tithes and offerings in the form of Frankincense in the first centuries, including the Emperor Constantine's gift to the Bishop of Rome for his church. When the Arabians traded with the Chinese in the tenth century one of the chief commodities was Olibanum, and today there is a large demand for incense all over the world.

The gum is found in the leaves and bark of several species of the Boswellia trees. It even exudes from the flowers in the form of a milky juice. It is shipped from Bardera and other ports in Somaliland to Bombay via Aden, and in much smaller quantities from Arabia.

Frankincense is the most important ingredient in all incense used for worship, but it is sometimes combined with Benzoin and Storax or with Myrrh.

The following is a typical formula:

Frankincense	10	ounces
Benzoin	5	ounces
Storax	$1\frac{1}{2}$	ounces

At one time incense consisted of four ingredients to symbolise the four elements, fire, air, earth and water. The actual formula of Moses' incense has never been divulged and was said to have been divinely revealed.

SCENTED GRASSES

*Flowers by heedless footsteps press'd
All their sweets surrender.*

Botanical name	Cymbopogon citratus
English name	Lemon Grass
Botanical name	Cymbopogon maritima
English name	Ginger Grass
Botanical names	Vetiveria Zizanoides, Andropogon muricatus
English names	Kuss-Kuss Grass, Cuss-Cuss
Indian name	Khas-khas vetivert
Natural order	Graminaceae
French name for Lemon Grass	Herbe citron
German name for Lemon Grass	Citron gras
Italian name for Lemon Grass	Erba di limone
French name for Ginger Grass	Nard
German name for Ginger Grass	Indianischer Nardus
Italian name for Ginger Grass	Spigo nardo
French name for Kuss-Kuss Grass	Costus arabique
German name for Kuss-Kuss Grass	Arabische Kostus
Parts used	Herb, oil
Natural habitat	India, East Indies, Burma, Ceylon

The Scented Grasses of India and the Tropics have been famous for their oil, from the most remote ages. The Egyptians, the Greeks and the Romans used them in their pomades for perfuming the body after bathing; and they still play an important part today in the blending of scents. The famous Cuss-Cuss grass of the East Indies is woven into mats to put amongst linen to perfume it, and the root of the same grass, known as Vetivert, is powdered and used in pot-pourris and also

349

in sachets for scenting linen. It is chiefly used in India for making Khas-khas tatties. These scented screens are a great feature of Indian bungalows. The Cuss-Cuss grass grows to a height of about six feet and it is found near lakes and rivers in the plains of India and in Burma and Ceylon. Lemon Grass has a very similar scent to the lemon Verbena plant and is used in blending perfumes.

IRISES

Thou art the iris, fair among the fairest
Who armed with golden rod
And winged with the celestial azure bearest
The message of some God.

Botanical names	Iris germanica, Iris pallida, Iris Florentina
Natural order	Iridaceae
Other names	Blue Flower de luce, White Flower de luce, Florentine Iris
French names	Flambe, Iris bleu, Iris de Flora
German names	Deutsche Lisch, Blaue Iris, Florentinische Iris
Italian names	Iride germanico, Iride salvatico, Iride Fiorentino
Symbolises	A message
Part used	Root
Natural habitat	Eastern Mediterranean

These are the three Irises which give us Orris root, and in the day of Gerard they were all cultivated in England.

The *Iris Germanica* is sometimes called Blue Flower de luce; the flowers are deep blue with a yellow beard and the petals are veined with purple. It smells rather like Orange blossom and goes by the name of German Iris.

The *Iris pallida* is also sweet-scented and the flowers are pale blue.

The *Iris Florentina*, called in old books White Flower de luce, has large white flowers with a yellow beard and the petals are slightly tinged with lavender.

Orris root comes principally from Tuscany and in the spring these Irises make lovely patches of colour in the landscape between Florence and Sienna.

The powdered root itself is put into a most attractive bronze wrapping and sold at the Farmacia of Santa Maria Novella in Florence.

Orris root has a very ancient history. It was known to Theophrastus and described by him. There are various references to it in the Bible, and right down the ages it has figured in the wardrobe accounts of kings. In the reign of Edward IV it was mixed with Anise, and in the reign of Queen Elizabeth it was used by cloth manufacturers to scent what was then described as 'swete cloth'.

It has the great advantage of acting as a fixative of other perfumes, so in a pot-pourri it preserves the scent of the other ingredients and also adds its own.

A BURNING PERFUME

Take ¼ pound of damask roses, beat up the petals, and then add an ounce of orris root powdered and steeped in rose water. Beat well together and add 5 grains of musk and 2 ounces of powdered gum benjamin. Add a little powdered sugar and make up into round cakes and lay them on white paper to dry. Set them in a sunny window to dry for a few days. Make them in June.

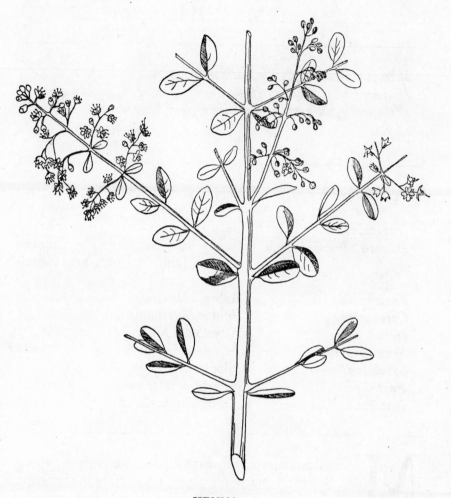

HENNA

Lawsonia alba

MYRRH

Within my garden plot, lo, I am present now.
I gathered have the myrrh and spice that in abundance grow;
With honey, milk and wine I have refresh'd me here.

Michael Drayton

Botanical names	Balsamodendron myrrha, Commiphora myrrha
Natural order	Burseraceae
Eastern names	Karan, Bola, Bal, Mirra Balsamodendron, Didthin, Bowl, Vola Heera-Bol
French name	Arbre à Myrrhe
German name	Echter Myrrhenbaum
Italian name	Albero del Mirra
Spanish name	Arbol de Mirra
Symbolises	Gladness
Part used	The gum in the stems
Natural habitat	Arabia, Somaliland

Myrrh is associated with Frankincense in early Egyptian and Semitic literature because it was combined with it, as it is today, in making incense; the proportion of Myrrh to Frankincense being approximately half, or less, to the amount of Frankincense. The formulas vary, but they are based more or less on the formula that Moses fixed for the Jewish ceremonial rites.

Myrrh was also an ingredient of the famous Egyptian Kyphi, which was prepared, according to Plutarch, by a magical formula, and was used in incense and also in medicine, as well as for fumigation.

Theophrastus speaks of two kinds of Myrrh, the solid and the liquid, but so far the liquid has not been identified. A hundred and fifty pounds of it was, according to the chroniclers of the times, presented to St. Silvester in Rome early in the fourth century as a present from one of the Egyptian towns.

Whatever it was it probably came from Arabia, and not from Somaliland, as so much of it does today; though we do know that the Myrrh of the ancients did not always come from Arabia, and that some of it came from the African coast.

The word 'myrrh' is derived from an Arabic word 'mur' meaning bitter.

In the Anglo-Saxon leech books of the eleventh century, Myrrh combined with Frankincense, or Olibanum as it was usually called, was recommended in medicine; and the mysterious Welsh physician of Myddrai prescribed it in the same way in the thirteenth century.

The Myrrh that comes from Somaliland is brought every year to the great fair held at Bardera in the winter months, and there it is bought by the Indian merchants and shipped to Bombay.

Apart from its aroma the gum is powerfully antiseptic and makes one of the best mouth washes and tooth powders that we have. It is astringent as well as healing and it has tonic and stimulating properties. For spongy and unhealthy gums it can hardly be equalled. The gum is partially soluble in water as well as in alcohol.

The best Myrrh today is known commercially as Turkey Myrrh. Its Eastern name is Karan. The plant grows in low bushes and rarely exceeds a height of ten feet. The gum exudes naturally from the bark without incisions being made.

MYRTLE

Ours is a garden green and fair
And bright with flowers in June
And spicy shrubs waft odours there
To the high harvest moon.

Botanical name	Myrtus communis
Natural order	Myrtaceae
French name	Myrte
German name	Echte Myrte
Italian name	Mirto
Spanish name	Mirto
Under the dominion of	Venus
Symbolises	Love
Part used	Leaves
Natural habitat	Europe

The Myrtle was originally the emblem of Mars but became dedicated to Aphrodite after she took refuge from the Satyrs in a wood of Myrtles. In Venus' crown, Myrtles were blended with Vervain.

The Romans wore wreaths composed chiefly of Myrtles blended with other flowers, and these became such a fine art that the name of the best chaplet maker, Glycena, has been preserved in history. The market where the wreaths were made was called the Myrtle market.

The Greeks used Myrtle for strewing graves and mixed it with Bleeding Amaranthus.

It has been used symbolically in many different ways; but as it was owned by Venus it is not surprising to find it used as a love token. In Tuscany, lovers give each other a spray of Myrtle, which they must produce when they meet each other again or the engagement is broken; and in Germany the Myrtle is the correct bridal wreath. It stands for the protection of virgins, and symbolises purity and fertility. The loveliest virgin in Athenian lore was turned into a Myrtle tree to protect her from persecution.

In Somersetshire a flowering Myrtle is a symbol of good fortune.

The leaves have a very distinct aroma of their own, and Myrtle water distilled from them is exceedingly pleasing. It was said to be used by Venus as an intimate toilet water.

The plant is powerfully antiseptic owing to the myrtol it contains, and it also has astringent properties. In medicine the leaves were used for their stimulating effect on the mucous membranes, and for the chest pains and dry coughs of consumptive people.

The leaves make a pleasant addition to pot-pourri; branches of Myrtle were used for strewing in the days when floors were scented with sweet-smelling herbs and furniture was scoured with its antiseptic juices.

See Sweet Gale.

OPOPANAX

Botanical names	Pastinacea opopanax (Linn.), Opopanax Chironium, Ferula opopanax
Natural order	Umbelliferae
Other names	Opopanax, All Heal
French names	Opopanax, Panais sauvage
German name	Gummipastinak
Italian name	Opopanaco
Part used	Resin
Natural habitat	Persia

The scent we know as Opopanax is an antispasmodic gum resin said to be produced by the juice of the *Pastinacea opopanax*. It has the same advantage as Patchouli in fixing the scent of other perfumes. The plant is allied to Lovage, Dill, Anise and other sweet-smelling Umbelliferous plants. Other authorities give as the source of the gum the roots of the *Opopanax Chironium*, from which plant the ancient gum was probably derived and shipped to Europe from Persia.

PATCHOULI

An amber scent of odorous perfume
Her harbinger.

John Milton

Botanical name	Pogostemon patchouli
Natural order	Labiatae
Country name	Pucha-pat
French name	Patchouli
German name	Patchoulypflanze
Italian names	Pacciuli, Patchouli
Turkish name	Tefarik
Part used	Herb
Natural habitat	Paraguay, East and West Indies

Patchouli is usually connected in the English mind with something strong-smelling and cheap. This is probably because the oil which is distilled from this very aromatic plant is used so often as a basis for cheap perfumes and to scent cheap soaps.

Actually it should be employed as a fixative of other perfumes, and, with the exception of Opopanax and Tonquin Beans, is one of the few vegetable fixatives that we have.

In India people become accustomed to the scent because the leaves are used so much in sachets, to scent drawers and to pack with shawls. The leaves when well matured improve very much, and so does the oil when it is kept. The leaves are a useful addition to pot-pourris if used in small quantities, because they preserve the scent of the other ingredients.

In India Patchouli leaves have a useful reputation in medicine. The Indians regard them as prophylactic against disease, and use them in nervous diseases.

The plant grows to a height of about two and a half feet, has purplish white flowers which grow in spikes, and egg-shaped aromatic leaves which give out a strong scent when bruised.

359

SANDALWOOD

Quinquireme of Nineveh, from distant Ophir,
Rowing home to haven in sunny Palestine,
With a cargo of ivory,
And apes and peacocks,
Sandalwood, cedarwood, and sweet, white wine.

John Masefield

Botanical name	Santalum album (Linn.)
Natural order	Santalaceae
Sanskrit name	Chaudana
French name	Santal blanc
German name	Weisser Sandelbaum
Italian name	Sandalo bianco
Spanish name	Sandalia
Parts used	Wood, oil
Natural habitat	India

Sandalwood is mentioned in such early Sanskrit literature as the Ramayana and Mahabharata. It has been used in the embalming of Cingalese princes since the ninth century, and in India is almost exclusively reserved for funeral rites and to burn as incense in the Temples.

The tree is quite a small one and is a native of the mountainous parts of the Indian peninsula. The best wood grows on dry rocky land; if the soil is too rich the tree produces no heart wood and is therefore of little value for perfume. In the Salernian school three kinds of Sandalwood were recognised—the white, yellow and red; and in those days oil of Sandal was regarded as an important medicine.

Today the wood is made into boxes and burning blocks, and the oil is used in the heavy Eastern type of perfumes.

STORAX

Sabean odours from the spicy shore
Of Araby the Blest.

John Milton

Botanical name	Liquidambar orientalis
Natural order	Hamamelidaceae
Other names	Liquid Storax, Liquidambar, Balsam Styracis
French names	Storax, Liquidambar, Styraciflue
German names	Storax, Mexicanischer Amberbaum
Italian names	Storace, Liquidambar
Spanish name	Estoraque
Part used	Gum from the bark and branches
Natural habitat	Asia Minor

Two distinct substances under the name of Storax have been known since the sixth century. One is the resin of the *Styrax officinalis*, a solid resin which was used by Dioscorides and is almost unobtainable now, and the liquid Storax with a consistency of honey from the *Liquidambar orientalis*. The liquid Storax is the one that is sold today. It is known in the East as Rose Malloes and the process of collecting it is carried on by the Yuruks, a wandering tribe of Turcomans who work in the forests in the extreme south-western parts of Asia Minor.

The outer bark of the trees is thrown away and the inner part is boiled in sea water until the resin separates from it. Its smell at first is almost unpleasant; but after it is kept a considerable time it acquires a sweet balsamic odour, and as an ingredient in incense and pot-pourri is much in demand.

The earliest reference to Liquidambar is in the writings of two Greek physicians of the sixth and seventh centuries, called Aetius and Paulus Aequinela, who used it in medicine as Dioscorides had done.

TONQUIN BEAN

Now the composition and preparation of perfumes aim entirely, one may say, at making the odours last.

Theophrastus

Botanical name	Dipteryx odorata (Linn.)
Natural order	Leguminosae
Country names	Tonka Beans, Coumarouna odorata, Rumara
Part used	Seeds
Natural habitat	Brazil, British Guiana

Tonquin Beans have a strong scent of Coumarin and belong to the same type of odour as new-mown Hay, Cowslip, Clover and Woodruff.

They are a very usual ingredient of pot-pourris and sachet powders because they act in the same way as musk and amber in fixing the perfume of the flowers and leaves. In medicine the Tonquin Bean is used as a heart tonic, but it has narcotic properties and must be used only under direction.

Chapter VIII

COSMETIC HERBS

COSMETIC HERBS

Chapter VIII

COSMETIC HERBS

Herbs are the best cosmetics as well as the safest. From the earliest times herbs have been used to increase woman's beauty; but knowledge of this kind is always guarded by its possessors as a potential, if not an actual, source of income, and if not a source of income at anyrate a source of power.

I have chosen for this chapter the herbs that, on the whole, are more usefully employed as cosmetics than in any other way; the Avocado Pear tree, the Witch Hazel tree and the Elder tree are exceptions. The fruit of the Avocado is extremely nourishing as food; and both the Witch Hazel and the Elder tree are vulneraries of a high order. Lady's Mantle is also an old wound herb. Other cosmetic herbs are Lilies of all kinds, Roses, Marshmallow, Silverweed, Queens' Delight, etc.

Mineral cosmetics can never equal the beauty creams and lotions made from the plants described in this chapter.

I begin by speaking of the Avocado Pear tree, because it is now known that the oil obtained from this tree has the power to penetrate through the dermis and epidermis to the corymb and so is able to bring nourishment to the glands. It also contains a combination of vitamins that is rare. Vitamin D, the sun-ray vitamin, is one of them and its value in nourishing the skin is undeniable. We all know the benefit that invalids derive from sunshine; and on any skin that has become lifeless and drab through debilitating illness this oil has a most recuperative power.

The Avocado beauty lotions have to be most carefully made to prevent the loss of these vitamins, which are destroyed by cooking.

The oil of the Almond tree, which must also be cold expressed to retain its properties, is a great preserver of beauty, and has the least acid reaction of any oil. In Eastern countries, where the skin becomes parched more quickly than in the West, this oil has been known from the earliest times as the greatest protection against the ravages of hot climates and drying winds. The Almonds themselves, as well as the oil, are used for whitening the skin, especially the hands. Next in order of importance comes the Elder tree, because every part of it, the bark, leaves, flowers and berries, has a soothing and beautifying effect on the skin. From time immemorial women, and particularly English women, have concocted lotions, creams and ointments from Elder flowers and Elder berries for softening the skin, for removing sunburn and blemishes and freckles, and for their emollient properties generally. Elder-flower water, with its very distinctive scent, takes the place of Rose-water to cleanse the face and to prevent sunburn as well as to cure it.

Fumitory is another plant used for freckles, and the twigs of the Common Ivy boiled in butter is a sunburn cream. Witch Hazel is more astringent than the Elder tree. The water distilled from it tones up relaxed muscles, allays inflammation of the veins and reduces them when they are too pronounced. Like the Elder, it is an old 'wound' herb; but it is so much used as a tonic for the eyes and the skin that it may be ranked first as a cosmetic.

The use of Lupins goes back to the time of ancient Greece and Rome. The Roman women made the powdered roots into a paste for their faces; and flour of Lupins was a necessary ingredient in nearly every beauty recipe of the seventeenth and eighteenth centuries. Henna takes us back to Egypt. Egyptian women paint their toe nails as well as their finger nails with it, and women of all nationalities recognise that as a hair dye it is unsurpassed. Indeed it is the only safe way of dyeing the hair a light colour, and, skilfully blended, it produces lovely shades of gold, red and auburn.

The Strawberry plant has slimming properties. The juice whitens the skin and removes tartar from the teeth; and the red and green Osiers make an excellent tooth paste to whiten the teeth and prevent decay.

Jaborandi stimulates the growth of hair and so does Southernwood, called in the country Lad's Love because it helps young men to grow a beard. Lady's Mantle, though used in England chiefly as a wound herb, is much more valued by the Arabs as a restorative of beauty under the name of Alkemelyeh; the pow-

JABORANDI

Pilocarpus jaborandi

dered root of Lords and Ladies is the famous Cypress powder which Parisians used to whiten their skin. In England its use was confined to starching the frills of court exquisites, and Cypress powder in Victorian days was used as a face powder only by women of doubtful character.

Two old-fashioned herbs, Butterwort and Gromwell, have cosmetic uses. Butterwort dyes the hair a golden yellow and Gromwell, as Culpeper calls it, was made into a rouge to colour the cheeks.

The distilled water of Burning Bush is an old-fashioned tonic water for the skin; and all parts of the Burdock, its leaves, seeds, and roots, are wonderful blood purifiers and not only sooth and clear a bad skin, but feed the tissues and improve its condition generally.

All these are the greatest aids to beauty, but none of them surpass nature's own cosmetic, the early morning dew, which is for the early risers only.

AVOCADO PEAR

Alleys of blossomed fruit trees girt a cool
White marble screen about a bathing pool,
The Palace rose beyond among its trees,
Splay-fronded figs and dates and cypresses.

John Masefield

Botanical name	Persea gratissima (Gaertn.)
Other names	Alligator Pear, Persea Americana
Natural order	Lauraceae
French names	Avocatier, Persée
German name	Avocatobaum
Italian name	Pero avvocato
Turkish name	Perse aḡ
Parts used	Fruit, oil
Natural habitat	West Indies

The Avocado Pear is the only edible member of its large family. The fruit is highly nutritious not only because of its oil but also on account of its vitamins. It contains vitamins A, D, and E, and also a large proportion of phosphorus, sulphur and chlorine. In America, Avocado Pears are either eaten as a hors d'œuvre with a cold mayonnaise or mousseline sauce or as a salad with oil and vinegar.

One of the great modern uses of the Avocado Pear tree is for its oil, which, used as a cosmetic, has a greater power of penetration than other vegetable oils. It is, therefore, employed by itself and in combination with other oils as a conveyor of vitamins and nourishment to the glands that lie behind the skin.

It is particularly useful for skin that has become lifeless owing to general debility or to lack of vitality as the result of long or serious illness.

Avocado oil contains a combination of vitamins that is rare and this coupled with its penetrative faculty makes it a great acquisition to modern beauty creams and lotions. Great care has to be exercised not to destroy the vitamins, which cooking renders negligible, and to overcome its naturally rather offensive odour.

The use of the Avocado Pear economically and as food is essentially a modern habit and there are therefore no traditional recipes —at any rate no European ones.

BROOMRAPE

Which has no root and cannot grow or prosper but by that same tree it clings about.

Botanical name	Orobanche major
Natural order	Orobanchaceae
Other name	Herbe Leonina
French name	Orobanche
German name	Erbsenwürger
Italian name	Orobanche
Dutch name	Leeuvenstaart
Under the dominion of	Mars
Part used	Juice
Natural habitat	Europe, including Great Britain

The Broomrape is a parasite on the Broom and springs up from the roots of the Broom with stalks about two feet high and leaves and flowers of a reddish-yellow colour. It has the peculiar appearance that is common to all parasites, and every part of it is more or less one colour and has the effect of a faded plant. The flowers grow in long thick spikes and the stem is often as thick as a walking stick and clammy to the touch. The juice is an old remedy for removing freckles from the face and also for clearing the skin of all disfigurements.

BURDOCK

In the nook the large burdock grows near the great willow,
In the flood, round the moorcock dashes under the billow.
To the old mill, farewell, to the rock, pens and waters,
To the miller himself, and his three bonny daughters.

John Clare

Botanical name	Arctium lappa, Lappa major
Natural order	Compositae
Country names	Happy Major, Beggar's Buttons, Love Leaves, Cockle Buttons, Thorny Burr, Fox's Clote
French name	Bardane
German name	Klette
Italian names	Lappola, Bardana
Spanish name	Bardana
Under the dominion of	Venus
Symbolises	Importunity
Parts used	Herb, seeds, root
Natural habitat	Europe, including Great Britain

In the seventeenth century the common name for the Burdock was Happy Major, in the Middle Ages it was called Bandona and the French and the Spaniards still call it Bardane and Bardana. The plant gets its botanical name from a Celtic word meaning 'hand', because it catches at everything it comes in contact with. The flower is rather like a thistle and the whole plant is rough-looking. It grows by the road side and in ditches and fields and is very familiar on account of its burs which stick to anything with a rough surface.

It is impossible to exaggerate the usefulness of every part of this plant, both as food and medicine. The young stems stripped of their rind make a most excellent vegetable, or used raw can be eaten with oil and vinegar, or candied make an excellent sweetmeat. They should be picked before the plant actually comes into flower.

As a purifier of the blood nothing can surpass it and it is so wholesome that it can be taken by anyone and taken indefinitely.

CANDIED BURDOCK STEMS

Take the best refined sugar, break it into lumps and dip it piece by piece in water, then put them into a silver saucepan and melt over the fire. Let it boil till it draws in hairs, then put in the burdock stems and place them on a sieve afterwards to dry near the fire.

BUTTERWORT

Refreshed with heat, the ladies sought around
For virtuous herbs, which gathered from the ground
They squeezed the juice, and cooling ointments made,
Which on their sunburnt cheeks and their chap'd skins they laid:

John Dryden

Botanical name	Pinguicula vulgaris
Natural order	Lentibulariaceae
Country names	Yorkshire Sanicle, Butter Plant, Steep Grass
French names	Grassette, Pinguicule
German names	Fettkraut, Butterkraut
Italian names	Pinguicola, Erba da taglio
Spanish name	Grasilla
Part used	Leaves
Natural habitat	Europe, including Great Britain

The Butterwort is a plant that has been used in dairies for centuries to coagulate milk.

It is called by the Laplanders Tait Grass and they mix it with reindeers' milk and make it into a drink called Tacotmioelk —a kind of Yoghourt.

The plant has an old reputation as a hair dye. The leaves are used in the same way as henna and dye the hair a bright golden yellow.

SYRUP OF BUTTERWORT

Macerate 2 pounds of the leaves in 5 pints of boiling distilled water for 24 hours. Strain the liquor after pressing the leaves and add enough double-refined sugar to make into a syrup.

CUCKOOPINT

Oft under trees we nestled in a ring,
Culling our Lords and Ladies. Oh ye hours!
I never see the broad leaved Arum spring,
Stained with spot of jet—I never see
Those dear delights which April still does bring
But memory's tongue repeats it all to me.

John Clare

Botanical name	Arum maculatum
Natural order	Araceae
Country names	Lords and Ladies, Starchwort Arum, Parson and Clerk, Wake Robin, Friar's Cowl, Ramp, Quaker
French names	Bonnet de grand prêtre, Pied de veau, Pain de Lièvre, Le Gonet, Chou poivre
German names	Aronswurz, Fleckenzehrwurz
Italian names	Aro comune, Giglio d'oro
Under the dominion of	Mars
Symbolises	Ardour
Part used	Root
Natural habitat	Europe, including Great Britain

The Cuckoopint is the only English species of the order of Arums, which contains a large number of ornamental tropical and riverside plants.

It is familiar to nearly everyone in the autumn by its green sheaf full of crimson berries, and is found in almost every bank and ditch. In the spring the plant is equally familiar, with its green arrow-shaped leaves stained with purple marks. It has tuberous roots, like the potato, which have been used as starch right down the ages. In England it went by the name of Portland Arrowroot and Portland Sago.

During the reign of Queen Elizabeth, starched ruffles became so exaggerated that a bill was passed through Parliament to prevent them being more than a yard deep—if they exceeded this measurement they were cut down at the city gate by the man in charge.

The yellow ruffles of the notorious Mrs. Turner were also starched with Portland powder and as she appeared in court at the trial of Sir Thomas Overbury wearing them, and was afterwards hanged in them, they ceased for a time to be so popular.

The Parisian Cypress powder which created such a sensation for its dazzling whiteness when used on the face was also made from Arum roots, and in Italy the plant is made into a cosmetic to remove freckles.

The juice of the plant has also been turned into soap.

In the days of wars and sieges, when food ran short, Arum roots were made into bread, and Julius Caesar's army was said to have lived on it under the name of Chara, which is the Roman name for Arum powder.

According to Aristotle, bears that were starved in his days recovered by eating the roots, and thrushes and pheasants still thrive on it.

ELDER

With purple fruit when elder branches bend,
And their bright hues the hips and cornels bind
Ere yet chill hoar-frost comes, or sleety rain,
Sow with choice wheat the neatly furrow'd plain.

Botanical name	Sambucus nigra (Linn.)
Natural order	Caprifoliaceae
Country names	Pipe Tree, Bore Tree, Bour Tree,
	(Old English) Hylder Eldrum
French name	Sureau
German name	Holunder
Italian names	Sambreo, Sambuco nero
Spanish name	Sauco
Russian name	Busine
Under the dominion of	Venus
Symbolises	Zealousness
Parts used	Bark, leaves, flowers, berries
Natural habitat	Europe, including Great Britain

There is an old tradition about the Elder tree that it must never be burnt nor even cut down without the permission of Hylde-Moer, the Elder tree mother, and country people in England today will certainly never bring it into the house to be burnt and dislike even rooting it up. Originally it was planted near houses to prevent the evil work of witches, and buildings of any age in England have nearly always got an Elder tree close to them, as for instance, the one just outside Westminster Abbey. Judas is said to have hanged himself on an Elder tree.

The wood is very hard and makes good musical instruments, especially pipes and flutes. Pipe tree is one of its old country names.

The Italian pipes they call Sampogne in Italy are made from Elder wood.

The healing virtues of the tree are proverbial and every part of it, from the bark to the berries, has a soothing and healing effect on the skin. William Cole says: 'There is hardly a disease from the head to the foot but it cures.'

The flowers and the berries have been used in cosmetic lotions for centuries to cure sunburn, to remove freckles, to soften, to whiten, to cleanse, and to remove wrinkles.

ELDER ROB

Take of ripe elderberries 5 parts
Take of sugar 1 part

Boil with a gentle heat to the consistence of thick sugar. Dose: $1\frac{1}{2}$ ounces to 2 ounces. Can be used to get rid of a chill or for a gargle.

ELDER VINEGAR

Take of dried elder flowers 1 part
Take of vinegar 12 parts

Macerate for 12 days, clarify with milk and filter.

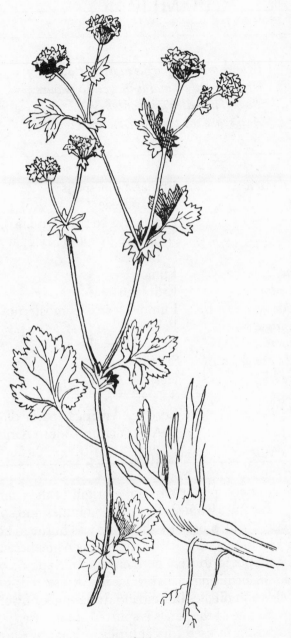

LADY'S MANTLE

Alchemilla vulgaris

FUMITORY

Whose red and purple mottled flowers
Are cropped by maids in weeding hours
To boil in water milk or whey
And scare the tan from Summer's cheek.

Botanical name	Fumaria officinalis
Natural order	Fumariaceae
Country names	Fumitory, Nidor, Kaphnos, Earth Smoke, Vapour, Beggary, Wax Dolls
French name	Fumeterre
German name	Erdrauch
Italian names	Fummo terro, Fumosterno officinale
Spanish name	Palomilla
Dutch name	Duivelskervel
Under the dominion of	Saturn
Parts used	Herb, seeds
Symbolises	Spleen
Natural habitat	Europe, America, parts of Asia, Australia, and South Africa

There are two opinions as to the origin of the name 'Fumitory'. It comes from *fumus*, meaning fumes, and some think it was so called because the plant was burnt to keep away evil spirits, and others, that it was given this name because it was traditionally supposed to have been created by vapours out of the earth. It is a self-fertilising plant setting its own seed. It grows like a weed in fields and ditches in England. It has pink flowers topped with purple and one of the petals is spurred at the base.

The plant has been used for centuries in magical rites; in Germany it is called the 'Thunderer's Plant'. Its country names either refer to smoke or to its use as a cosmetic. It is called Wax Dolls in Kent.

It has a great reputation as a cure for freckles and as a skin tonic. It purifies the blood and tones up the liver, and used internally or externally, or both, greatly improves a bad skin.

It is sometimes taken in the form of a syrup or the syrup is mixed with syrup of Roses or syrup of Peach flowers. Dioscorides recommended it as a depilatory to use after more drastic treatment had been given in the first instance.

GROMWELL

The herb belongs to dame Venus, and therefore if Mars cause the cholic or stone, as usually he doth if in Virgo, this is your cure.

Nicholas Culpeper

Botanical name	Lithospermum officinale
Natural order	Boraginaceae
Country name	Gromel
French names	Herbe aux perles, Grémil
German name	Steinsame
Italian names	Lacrime dei campi, Miglio cattivo
Spanish name	Lithosperme
Dutch name	Steenzaad
Under the dominion of	Venus
Parts used	Seeds, leaves, root
Natural habitat	Europe, including England

In Nicholas Culpeper's time there were three different species of Gromwells used in herbal medicine—one was the Lithospermum Heavenly Blue of our modern rock gardens—and the other two were known as the Smaller Gromel and the Garden Gromel. The Gromels are characterised by seed-like pearls which are very noticeable on the branches in the winter when the leaves have fallen from them. The plants have the appearance of being hung with pearls, the seeds turning from their summer green to the grey colouring of pearls. The flowers are sometimes white and sometimes yellow. The most ornamental of all the Gromels is that known as the Gromwell, *Mertensia maritima*, which is found in the Hebrides and the west of Ireland. It also grows on the Welsh coast and is sometimes called Sea-side Mertensie.

The purple flowers, which grow in handsome racemes, have fleshy-looking corollas dotted with small yellow spots; and the leaves, which taste of oysters, are covered with a whitish green powder. The seeds of the Gromwells are an old cure for dissolving stone in the kidney.

In Sweden a rouge is made from the roots of the Corn Gromwell, *L. arvense*. This plant is sometimes called Bastard Alkanet to distinguish it from the true Alkanet which also belongs to the Borage family. The true Alkanet was known to the ancient races and used by them to dye wool purple.

Today it is cultivated in the South of Europe and used as a colouring for rouge and other cosmetics. Its botanical name is *Anchusa trichoris*. The French call it La Bugloss; the Germans, Ochsenziemer; the Italians, Ancusa; and the Dutch, Ossentong.

HENNA

Thus some bring leaves of henna to imbue
The finger ends of a bright roseate hue,
So bright that in the mirror's depth they seem
Like tips of coral branches in the stream.

Moore

Botanical name	Lawsonia alba (Linn.)
Natural order	Lythraceae
Country names	Lawsonia mermis, Egyptian Privet, Smooth Lawsonia, Jamaica Mignonette
French name	Henné
German name	Hennastrauch
Italian names	Alcanna, Cipro
Turkish name	Kena aḡ
Arabian names	Al Henne, Al Khanna, Mehudi
Parts used	Flowers, root, leaves
Natural habitat	Egypt, India, Levant, Syria, Persia, Kurdistan

The Henna tree is a shrub so laden with heavily scented white and yellow flowers that its perfume can be smelt a long way off. Every part of the tree is used by Eastern women to increase or restore their beauty. The powdered leaves make the best hair dye that is known and give the auburn colour that is so admired. Sudanese women make it into a paste with catechu, cover their heads with it and leave it on all night. A paint is made from the fruit to dye their nails red, infusions of the leaves are taken internally to give them a good complexion, and oil is made from the plant to keep their limbs supple. Finally, the flowers are distilled into a reducing perfume, which they use.

IVY

I hang no Ivy out to sell my wine.
                                    Braithwaite

Botanical name	Hedera helix (Linn.)
Natural order	Araliaceae
French name	Lierre
German names	Sten, Gemeiner Epheu
Italian names	Ellera, Edera
Spanish name	Hiedra
Under the dominion of	Saturn
Symbolises	Fidelity
Parts used	Leaves, berries
Natural habitat	Europe, North and Central Asia

The Ivy is dedicated to Bacchus and is said to have grown in great profusion in his birthplace, Nyssa, which is why the tree was used as a wineshop advertisement in the same way that public houses today hang their signs outside.

The plant is more safely used as a cosmetic than for internal use, though an infusion of the berries is said to be a remedy for rheumatism and dropsy.

The young leaves make a good and reliable ointment for sunburn. The Ivy leaves and twigs are boiled in oil or hog's lard, and then removed, and the oil when cold is used as a pomade.

Ivy outside a house has the reputation of making the walls damp, but this is quite a fallacy—what it does do is to destroy whatever it covers by clinging to it too tenaciously.

JABORANDI

Jaborandi has a selective action for the skin.

Ellingwood

Botanical name	Pilocarpus jaborandi
Natural order	Rulaceae
Portuguese names	Arruda do mato, Arruda brave jua-nandi
Part used	Dried leaves
Natural habitat	Brazil

Jaborandi is one of the most powerful hair tonics because it excites secretions and opens the pores of the skin. It is a remedy for baldness, but it must be used with great care, and it is not wise for the amateur to experiment with it.

LADY'S MANTLE

It is proper for all those wounds that have inflammations.

Botanical name	Alchemilla vulgaris (Linn.)
Natural order	Rosaceae
Country names	Bear's Foot, Lion's Foot, Nine Hooks
French names	Pied de lion, Alchémille
German names	Frauenmantel, Sinau
Italian names	Alchemilla comune, Piè di lione
Spanish name	Alquimila
Swedish name	Maria Kapa
Dutch name	Leeuvenvoet
Under the dominion of	Venus
Parts used	Herb, root
Natural habitat	Europe, including Great Britain

The Alchemillas take their name from Alchemy because of their reputation of producing wonderful cures. Only three of the family grow in Great Britain, the Lady's Mantle, the Parsley Piert and the Field Lady's Mantle, *Alchemilla arvensis*, but they are also found in the Himalayas and as far north as the Arctic regions. The plant is used by herbalists to cure wounds, especially when inflammation is present.

The Arabs call it Alkemelyeh, and the women use it to restore their beauty when they have lost their looks through age or ill health.

The plant has a stem so weak that it never holds itself erect and divides at the top into two or three branches with yellowish-green heads from which whitish flowers come. The flowers are followed by yellow seeds not unlike poppy seeds. The root is long and black and has many strings and fibres.

It grows in pastures in Kent and Hertfordshire and other parts of England, flowers in May and June and always remains green.

LUPINS

That intermixture of delicious hues
Along so rash a surface, all at once,
In one impression, by connecting force
Of their own beauty imaged in the beach.

William Wordsworth

Botanical name	Lupinus albus
Natural order	Leguminosae
Country name	White Lupin
French name	Lupin sauvage
German name	Blaue Lupine
Italian name	Lupino salvatico
Turkish name	Yabani turmus
Under the dominion of	Mars, in the sign of Aries
Parts used	Herb, seeds
Natural habitat	The Levant. Cultivated in Europe

Lupins probably came originally from Egypt. Theophrastus, Pliny and other writers refer to them as an article of food and we know that the Romans cultivated them and used them in medicine as well as in making bread.

In the beauty books of the seventeenth and eighteenth centuries powdered Lupins are a common ingredient in what would be called today face packs.

The powder was mixed with Lemon juice or with the gall of a goat or with both. It was applied to the face to cleanse it and remove blemishes, and Culpeper said it was used to remove the marks of smallpox, which was in those days so prevalent.

The white Lupin is probably the species from which all the brilliantly coloured varieties of today have evolved, but in some parts of England the blue appears to grow wild.

Economically the Lupin has been put to various uses. Fibre has

OSIER

Cornus sericea

been made from it for weaving, soap for washing the hands, oil for cooking and flour for bread.

In medicine the seeds have anthelmintic properties, and the roots discutient and digestive powers.

The great value of the Lupin is that it will grow in light sandy soil and that it improves the soil by absorbing nitrogen.

It does not grow well in a rich soil.

OSIERS OR DOGWOOD

Content with food, which nature freely bred,
On wildings and on strawberries they fed;
Cornels and bramble berries gave the rest,
And falling acorns furnished out a feast.

John Dryden

Botanical names	(Red Osier) Cornus sericea (Linn.), (Green Osier) Cornus circinata (Linn.)
Natural order	Cornaceae
Country names	Silky Cornel, Female Dogwood, Swamp Dogwood
French name	Cornouille
German name	Welde
Italian name	Vinco
Spanish name	Mimbrera
Symbolises	Frankness
Parts used	Root bark, bark
Natural habitat	Florida to Mississippi

The bark of the Osiers, or Cornels, as they are sometimes called, is used in their own country as a substitute for Peruvian bark in fevers. They also make stimulating tonics and have been prescribed for jaundice and liver complaints.

The powdered bark of the Red Osier makes an excellent tooth powder. It makes the teeth white and preserves the gums.

The Red Osier is a shrub that grows in damp woods. It has silky branches, almost purple in colour, whitish yellow flowers and blue berries. It is said to increase the temperature of the body.

QUINCE

                                      William Shakespeare

Botanical name	Pyrus Cydonia (Linn.)
Natural order	Rosaceae
Other names	(Old English) Melicotone
French name	Cognassier
German names	Echte Quitte
Italian name	Cotogno
Spanish name	Membrillo
Under the dominion of	Venus
Symbolises	Temptation
Parts used	Seeds, fruit
Natural habitat	Persia and Crete

The Golden Apple of the Hesperides, the Apple with which Eve tempted Adam, and the Apple which Paris awarded to Venus on Mount Olympus are all identified with the fruit of the Quince tree. The Romans regarded the Quince tree as sacred and they made it the bridal dish at the wedding feast before the consummation of a marriage. Shakespeare makes a reference to this when Lady Capulet orders 'quince in the pastry' for the marriage feast of Romeo and Juliet.

The fruit of the Quince is of a golden colour, it is shaped rather like a Pear and contains five cells, each of which holds twelve seeds. It was very much prized at one time and Quince trees were as much cultivated as Apples. They are very slow in bearing fruit and the trees are an ugly shape, but once they begin to bear they require no attention. The jam that was made from Quinces was called marmalade, a word which at that time only referred to Quinces and was invented for Quinces.

The old English name of the fruit was Coyne, and the marmalade was eaten as much for its cordial property as for pleasure. It was also said to strengthen the digestion.

The seeds are used for dysentery and in gargles and eye lotions, but their chief use today is in cosmetics. A mucilage of the seeds makes the best hair fixative, and their astringent properties make them useful in lotions to give firmness to the flesh and a good contour to the face.

RHATANY

In all places, then, and in all seasons,
Flowers expand their light and soul like wings,
Teaching us by most persuasive reasons
How akin they are to human things.

Botanical name	Krameria triandra
Natural order	Polygalaceae
Country names	Peruvian Rhatany, Red Rhatany, Puma-cuchu
Spanish names	Raiz para los dientes, Mapato
Part used	Dried root
Natural habitat	Peru

The botanical name of the Rhatany plant is derived from a Hungarian doctor called Kramer, who discovered its uses.

It is a low shrub with ornamental red flowers and thrives best in sand. The Portuguese make an infusion of the root in brandy to give a roughness to some of their Port wines.

The root is powerfully astringent, and mixed with Orris root and charcoal makes a most useful tooth paste for spongy gums. It tightens up loose teeth and can be used with perfect safety.

SOAPWORT

Med'cine is mine, what herbs and simples grow
In fields and forests, all their powers I know
And am the Great Physician called below.

John Dryden

Botanical name	Saponaria officinalis
Natural order	Caryophyllaceae
Country names	Fuller's Herb, Bruisewort, Bouncing Bet, Wild Sweet William, Sweet Betty, Latherwort, Hedge Pink
French names	Savonnière, Saponaire
German name	Seifenkraut
Italian name	Saponaria
Spanish name	Jabonero
Dutch name	Zeepkruid
Parts used	Root, leaves
Natural habitat	Central and Southern Europe

It is open to doubt whether this plant or the Gipsophila is the Struthinin of the ancients which was used by them instead of soap. Most of the plants belonging to the order of Caryophyllaceae contain a soapy principle. The pink does, also the scarlet Lychnis and the Nottingham Catch Fly, but the plant that actually goes by the name of Soapwort (the *Saponaria officinalis*) is the one that is chiefly used economically to take the place of soap. The herb contains a mucilaginous juice that will lather in hot water and is used in shampoos to wash the hair.

The plant will grow in England but this is not its natural habitat. It is a perennial and grows to about four feet in height, has bright pink flowers, and blooms from July till September.

The *Gypsophila struthinin*, as it has been classified by Linnaeus, also grows in Europe and the United States of America. In Calabria it is used for washing clothes. It is also a perennial herbaceous plant but only grows to about two feet in height.

The Soap Nut tree from which Indian women obtain the nuts they wash their hair with is the *Saponaria trifoliatus*. The French call it Savonnier; the Germans, Seifenbaum; and the Italians, Saponaria.

SOLOMON'S SEAL

Yet, labouring well his little spot of ground
Some scattering pot herbs here and there he found,
Which cultivated with his daily care,
And bruised with vervain, were his frugal fare,
Sometimes white lilies did their leaves afford,
With wholesome poppy flowers, to mend his lonely board.

John Dryden

Botanical name	Polygonatum officinale (All.)
Other names	Convallaria polygonatum, Polygonatum vulgare (Desf.)
Natural order	Liliaceae
Country names	Lily of the Mountain, Sealwort, St. Mary's Seal, Ladder to Heaven, Many Knees, Jacob's Ladder, Lady's Seal, Whitewort
French names	Sceau de Salomon, Échelle de Notre Dame, Salle de Notre Dame
German name	Weisswurz
Italian name	Sigillo di Salamone
Spanish name	Sello de Salomon
Under the dominion of	Saturn
Part used	Root
Natural habitat	Northern Europe, Siberia

Solomon's Seal is a woodland plant, which makes it extremely useful for shady parts of the garden. It will grow under trees and in poor soil; and is extremely decorative with its lovely white lily-like flowers running down the stalk like bells with a green background of leaves. They are not only useful in the garden but make one of the best decorations for the house because of their height, and they are lovely arranged in vases.

The root of the plant when cut transversely bears what appear to be hieroglyphics and has given rise to the theory that it was sealed by Solomon, who is said to have been conversant with the virtues of all plants.

It has an old reputation as a wound herb, and is supposed to knit bones together in the same way as Comfrey. Its name of Seal may have been derived from its medicinal virtues in sealing wounds.

The plant belongs to the Lily family and contains Convallarin in common with Lily of the Valley, which it somewhat resembles, only on a much larger scale.

The young shoots can be cooked and eaten like Asparagus, and the roots after maceration in water make a nutritious food. A decoction of the root in wine was given to anyone with broken bones and drunk daily till they had healed, and the root was also applied externally in the form of a poultice.

A distilled water of the plant makes an excellent cosmetic lotion to remove freckles and to clear the skin from blemishes; and has been used in this way by women since the time of Galen, who prescribed it as a cosmetic.

SOUTHERNWOOD
LAD'S LOVE

Where thrift and lavender and lad's love bloom,
There fed by food they tower to rankest size,
Around the dwelling docks and wormwood rise.
Here the strong willow strikes her shiny root,
Here the dull nightshade hangs her deadly fruit.

Botanical name	Artemisia Abrotanum (Linn.)
Natural order	Compositae
Country names	Lad's Love, Boy's Love, Old Man, Appleringie
French names	Garde robe, Aurone
German names	Stabwurz, Abberaute
Italian names	Abrotino, Cidronella
Spanish name	Artemisa
Under the dominion of	Mercury
Symbolises	Jest, bantering
Part used	Herb
Natural habitat	Southern Europe

Southernwood is allied to Wormwood and means Southern Wormwood. It has a very pleasant aromatic lemon scent and has been famous for centuries as a hair grower. One of its most popular names, Lad's Love, originated from the use young men made of it to help them to grow a beard in order to appear older than they really were. The herb was made into stimulating hair pomades which had a great sale.

Southernwood also has an old reputation as a wound herb.

It is eaten raw in salads in Italy and cooked as a vegetable. It makes a pleasant tisane and can be drunk for its stimulating tonic effect.

It is closely related to Tarragon and Mugwort, two other Artemisias.

STRAWBERRY

The strawberry grows underneath the Nettle,
And wholesome berries thrive and ripen best
Neighbour'd by fruit of lesser quality.

William Shakespeare

Botanical name	Fragaria vesca (Linn.)
Natural order	Rosaceae
French name	Fraisier
German name	Erdbeere
Italian name	Fragola
Spanish name	Fresa
Under the dominion of	Venus
Symbolises	Foresight
Parts used	Leaves, fruit, stalks, roots
Natural habitat	Northern Hemisphere, excluding the Tropics

'Doubtless God Almighty could have made a better berry but he never did.'

Most people would agree that Dr. Boteler's remark has summed up for them what they feel about Strawberries. It is universally acknowledged that the Strawberry is the most delicious of all fruits.

The garden variety is descended from the wild Strawberry of the woods, which is found even in England in sheltered places in the south. In France the wild fruit is collected and brought to Paris and in the early Autumn wild Strawberries and Crème d'Isigny can be had in all good Paris restaurants for the asking.

Strawberries, wild or cultivated, have such good use medicinally, that the old theory that they disagree with gouty subjects is entirely a fallacy caused by the fact that when they are eaten they stir up acidity in order to cure it.

A tea is made from Strawberry stalks as it is from Cherry stalks and can be taken as a vulnerary; an infusion of the leaves acts as a tonic to the kidneys.

The juice of Strawberries, either wild or cultivated, but preferably the wild, removes tartar from the teeth and is so good for preserving the teeth and getting rid of discoloration that it is prescribed in homoeopathic medicine for those purposes. The root makes an excellent dentifrice.

The Strawberry has other cosmetic uses as well. It reduces superfluous flesh locally and is made into lotions and creams to whiten the skin, to remove freckles, and to preserve a good contour. The Strawberry is so wholesome that even if it is left to perish it does not ferment while it is decaying.

Strawberries are the most accommodating of fruit, they will grow as far north as Lapland and they even provide an important ingredient for the Christmas pudding of the Arctic region, which, known as Kappatialmas, consists, according to Dr. Fernie, of Strawberries mixed with reindeers' milk and dried into the form of a sausage.

The Strawberry is dedicated to the Virgin Mary.

WITCH HAZEL

The wreathing odours of a thousand trees.
And the flowers faint gleaming presences,
And over the clearings and the still waters
Soft indigo and hanging stars.

J. C. Squire

Botanical name	Hamamelis virginiana (Linn.)
Natural order	Hamamelidaceae
Country names	Spotted Alder, Winter Bloom, Snapping Hazelnut
French name	Hamamélide
German name	Virginischer Zauberstrauch
Italian names	Amamelide, Trilopo
Turkish name	Guvercin ağ
Symbolises	A spell
Parts used	Bark, leaves
Natural habitat	Eastern United States and Canada

The Witch Hazel tree, through its bark and its leaves, supplies us with one of the most useful and pleasant healing, astringent waters that is known. It subdues inflammations, acts as a tonic to the skin, tightens up loose tissue and removes the red veins that sometimes disfigure what would otherwise be a beautiful face.

Witch Hazel extract has a peculiar action on the muscular fibre of the veins, without influencing the circulation, and is therefore extremely useful in curing unsightly and prominent veins on the legs as well as on the face.

It has a most soothing effect on the eyes and is so safe that it can be used, diluted with Rose water or Elder-flower water, either to bathe the eyes or to make fomentations and eye pads, which can be kept on all night.

For centuries the tree was shrouded in mystery because it was used by water diviners and others with special powers, whose gifts until comparatively lately were thought to be the work of the devil.

The Witch Hazel is a shrub which grows in damp woods in America and Canada. It has the peculiarity of not opening its yellow flowers till its leaves fall off. Its virtues have long been known to the American Indians.

INDEX OF BOTANICAL NAMES

407

INDEX OF ENGLISH NAMES

INDEX OF COUNTRY NAMES

414

418

INDEX OF FRENCH NAMES

INDEX OF ITALIAN NAMES

INDEX OF GERMAN NAMES